IN SEARCH OF
ABSOLUTE TRUTH

IN SEARCH OF
ABSOLUTE TRUTH

RIG VEDA VOLUME 1

RAMESH MALHOTRA

IN SEARCH OF ABSOLUTE TRUTH
RIG VEDA VOLUME 1

iUniverse books may be ordered through booksellers or by contacting:

iUniverse
1663 Liberty Drive
Bloomington, IN 47403
www.iuniverse.com
844-349-9409

Because of the dynamic nature of the Internet, any web addresses or links contained in this book may have changed since publication and may no longer be valid. The views expressed in this work are solely those of the author and do not necessarily reflect the views of the publisher, and the publisher hereby disclaims any responsibility for them.

The views expressed in this work are solely those of the author and do not necessarily reflect the views of the publisher, and the publisher hereby disclaims any responsibility for them.

Any people depicted in stock imagery provided by Getty Images are models, and such images are being used for illustrative purposes only. Certain stock imagery © Getty Images.

ISBN: 978-1-5320-8665-6 (sc)
ISBN: 978-1-5320-8663-2 (hc)
ISBN: 978-1-5320-8664-9 (e)

Library of Congress Control Number: 2020925193

Print information available on the last page.

iUniverse rev. date: 05/24/2023

All the proceeds from the sale of this and other books are dedicated to funding the construction of an elementary school in the Himalayas to bring higher knowledge as a service to the local community.

Our universe is regulated by esoteric powers that influence every creation without prejudice: unmanifested or manifested, embodied or disembodied, evil or not evil. The quest to know and unveil the secrets of such powers has been going on for centuries and will go on for many more to come.

CONTENTS

PREFACE

For centuries, science and technology have attempted to explain what humanity could not understand. They have achieved nothing more than a means to an end. Science even today elects to ignore, disregard, or conveniently forget that certain bodies of knowledge predate even humanity.

Finding something forgotten or lost is not an invention or discovery, and just because something is not yet confirmed or proven does not mean it does not exist. Pythagoras and others discovered that the earth was round, not flat. Similarly, gravitation, magnetism, and electromagnetic waves have prevailed before scientists identified such concepts. The existence of DNA now being defined in truth dated from before it was called a discovery. No question that science and technology are helping humanity to transit from unknowns to knowns.

As an educated scientist and businessman, I am very interested in unveiling the secrets of nature known to ancient spiritual scholars. In 2013, I published Spiritual Wisdom based on holy scripture, Bhagavad Gita. Over the past seven years, I have been working to unveil truths buried in the Vedas. These Vedas were composed by spiritual scholars over many years before the second millennium BCE, extending into the Late Bronze Age. The revelations described in such scriptures are based on vibrations and oscillations of sounds used to unveil absolute truth. They were first translated into Sanskrit and later into many languages. They served as invaluable tools in studying comparative etymology and learning ancient wisdom, principles of physical evolution, and spiritual involution even before different disciplines of science were developed.

Through my investigation and research, which is based on personal devotion, I have uncovered many aspects relating to the genesis of the dynamic universe, the creation of the planetary system, and further, its relationship to all creation and especially to humanity, which has prevailed for a long time on earth and will further take many more investigations to unveil absolute truth.

I discovered that finding knowledge buried in holy scripture is like climbing a mountain. Your judgment and perception are constantly refined as you get higher and higher in understanding the Vedas. You come to know the absolute truth only when you reach the peak and look around and see there are many hills that make the mountain peak the absolute truth.

SYNOPSIS

The dynamic universe consists of different horizons, each distinct in nature and with a specific function. They are all connected and serve one universe. The most significant part of the dynamic universe is that at the top, there is a heavenly region. It is all illuminated; all matter has been transformed into energy. This illumination lights up all parts of the dynamic universe.

Right below the heavenly region is the celestial region. In this region, selected chunks fully manifested as a ground float as if in magma. Their movements are limited depending on their positions in the region, but they remain unidentifiable. The supreme, godly powers of causation establish their domicile in this region to regulate all the activities.

The region below the celestial region is supported by a highly tumultuous, volatile environment that produces unpredictable, undefined bodies. They constantly change their shape. In this region, the supreme powers of causation operate independently. They create a wide range of splendours, only a few of which can be seen—the sun, the moon, and the stars. They generate external illumination along with their orbital rotation. They even give birth to other forces such as gravitation, magnetism, and radioactivity.

Within the esoteric region, manifested physical bodies appear, serving as the cosmic bodies such as our planetary system. These cosmic bodies are illuminated with light provided from the heavenly. These cosmic bodies can be physically identified based on their surface below the surface, which lives in total darkness comprising melted matter—magma.

The manifested, semi-manifested, and unmanifested bodies, all moving, are called terrestrial bodies. They are regulated by the supreme powers of causation, forming fourteen invisible spheres. Each of these spheres is influenced by physical and spiritual powers. They represent the material worlds, including the underworld, where there is no light.

Each sphere encompasses individual sovereignty, which with mythical powers of causation, creates imperishable and perishable bodies. Since creation, they have prevailed and will continue to prevail, as they are the ones that are regulated by the immortal, universal soul, which regulates the cycles of life and death.

The material world and underworld are constantly subjected to powers of attraction and aversion, thus generating positive and negative forces and creating living creatures with noble or evil souls prevailing on the surface. The region hidden below the surface provides opportunities to create unmanifested and unregulated living things.

Each activity performed by any living creature leaves memories that cause living things to be subjected to physical discomfort and mental depression.

The goal of all living beings is to free themselves from the shackles of these memories and attain inner peace and tranquillity. They peacefully accept the cycles of life and death.

The goal of living beings is to perform moral, righteous, and compassionate acts and lose individual identities after death to merge with the immortal universal soul and attain the freedom to go beyond the cycles of life and death.

In the first volume of In Search of Absolute Truth, I examine the information included within the first five chapters of the Rig Veda, and the others will be presented in the second volume.

PART 1
ELEMENTAL PROGRESSION

The ultimate creator resides outside the universe. It consists of two parts: the undifferentiated and the differentiated. The undifferentiated is dormant and has a nonbaryonic nature. The differentiation consists of three strata: the heavenly stratum consisting of interstellar energy; the lower stratum, earth, representing the interstellar mass; and the middle stratum filled with esoteric powers. Through mental powers, daily sacrifice, personal hardship, and devotion, ancient spiritual scholars attained eternal wisdom. They identified fourteen invisible spheres of influence regulating the dynamic universe. Seven are identified to represent the top part of the esoteric region connecting with the heavenly region (Svarga). The other seven are identified as the underworld, which connects with the earthly region (Prithvi). The top seven are exposed to light, while the lower seven are not. The upper seven make the differentiated into a vibrant, dynamic universe, unlike the undifferentiated universe. The space between Svarga and Prithvi constitutes the esoteric powers. It forms different zones (Lokas). These higher zones are called Yahrtis. In descending order, they include absolute truth (Satya Loka), eternal truth (Brahma Loka), spiritual truth (Tapas Loka), manifested truth (Janas Loka), natural truth (Mahas Loka), cerebral truth (Bhuvas Loka), and rudimentary truth (Bhu Loka). Unmanifested and manifested bodies reside in the higher spheres where they are regulated by the godly

1

power. Below the lowest part of the higher world (Bhu Loka), there are seven worlds (Lokas) within which prevail unregulated bodies (Patala). This consist of spheres, which, in descending order, include illusion (Atala Loka), ghosts and goblins (Vitala Loka), demons and dragons (Sutala Loka), the voracious (Rasātala Loka), the home of evil powers (Talātala Loka), the hooded serpent (Mahātala Loka), and hell (Naraka Loka). The different realms of unregulated bodies are ruled by demonic powers. These fourteen zones (Lokas) constitute the manifested world, including the material world. They are created and controlled by the powers established by the creator to be regulated by the primordial supreme powers of causation regulating the newly created worlds. All the regulated embodiments in the upper spheres are constantly fighting against the unmanifested, unregulated embodiment residing in the underworld. The living beings with noble souls generate positive forces, and they continually fight negative forces generated from the evil souls prevailing in the darkness or underworld. This makes it difficult to bring equilibrium because of the battle each fight to overpower the other.

CHAPTER 1
IMPERCEPTIBLE DOMINION

Brilliant Illumination

The imperceptible dominion encompasses various supreme powers of causation that are invisible and prevails beyond comprehension. According to Rig Veda, the genesis started with a ferocious fire serving as the godhead, Agni. Through transferring cosmic mass into cosmic energy, it generated illumination that, in turn, established the highest stratum and generated the supreme powers of causation.

According to Rig Veda, Book 1, Hymn I, the fire was identified as the heavenly priest (Hotar), created to regulate the upper stratum filled with illumination. The ferocious fire manifested to serve as an envoy (Agiras), who, with a sapient mind, was granted powers and blessings needed to displace ignorance with awareness, thus turning night into day. The envoy became the radiant ruler serving the dynamic universe. It prevailed as the illuminated immense ruler (Surya) residing in the heavenly region. Instead of being the immense ruler, it established the eternal laws (Varuna) to guard all creation. To regulate the associated solar flares, it created heavenly power (Rudras), which, with vibrations, generates waves (Vayu) that sound like wind. They are used to create hymns to communicate and spread illumination beyond the heavenly region.

According to Rig Veda, Book 1, Hymn II, with libations, the waves (Vayu) shed mythical juice (Soma) that yearns to seek friendship and love. The eternal love (Mitra) brought ecstasy and created a union among supreme powers of causation (Varuna-Mitra). This invoked the first free-flowing primordial force as fluid (Shakti), which, like fuel, creates the eternal flame. This fame, through rituals and rites, enhances to give birth to a union of a godhead (Angi-Indra), who jointly serves as the foe-destroying power. This union is supported by the heavenly illuminated body (Surya). The first union (Angi-Indra) came to serve as the chiefs of the manifested dynamic universe. They are supported by two nimble hands serving as the twin demigods (Aśvins) like the two flying horses. They bring rich sacrificial food that transforms prevailing physical energy into invisible spiritual energy. Both transform common manifested courses to turn wondrous common horses into stallions and female animals into milk-bearing animals.

According to Rig Veda, Book 1, Hymn III, the praiseworthy twin demigods (Aśvins) provide heroes with mighty physical and spiritual powers. They generate thoughts and cultivate quests, all expressed through songs and libations. With physical and spiritual power, they manifest to create the wonder-workers (Nāsatyas). They cover the marvellous pasture and, through a purification process, create the pathway like bright flames, all filled with libations that come to manifest with a red colour (plasma) running among the holy embodiments such as singers. They can offer worship with their hands and sing prayers. They come to support heavenly powers. This full support comes from the godly power serving as one.

They protect, reward, and cherish the illuminated heavenly region with mythical juice that empowers the divine will to worship and perform work. They milk animals to support godly powers (Satakartu). The bearers of godly power (Satakartu) change their shapes and appear as guileless or fearless serpents (Rig Veda, Book 1, Hymn IV). They are offered worship along with pleasant songs to invoke the goddess

4

(Sarasvatī) of water. The goddess unlocks cosmic vapours and incites the desire to cultivate and water like mighty floods. Their inner light brightens all and makes them virtuous.

The godly powers become ecstatic when they drink the mythical juice. Once they become accustomed to such ecstasy, they acquire eternal wisdom and become benevolent. They pray and sing spiritual songs. Ultimately, they become assimilated and move from one place to another, serving as devotees of the godly powers. They become better than others and perform godly, wondrous deeds as blessed souls. They dwell as a godhead and become holy souls. They offer sacrifices with grace. With blessed wings, they fly to overpower evil forces.

After drinking Soma (Rig Veda, Book 1, Hymn V), their holy souls become strengthened to serve as warriors and help their friends gain knowledge. They pour the mythical juice to honour the godhead (Indra). They sing songs, worship, and serve the holy souls as companions. They pour forth mythical juice to please Indra and help others attain the richest treasures. They, as twin demigods, acquire the physical strength needed to fight. They make sure no enemies can challenge them. With songs, the worshippers enjoy the spiritual experience, especially when the mythical juice is mingled with curd. Once they have acquired strength and pre-eminence, they become lovers. They quickly drink the mythical juice to bring out bliss. This turns their holy souls into spiritual teachers. As spiritual teachers, they provide guidance and bring in thousandfold nutrients that fill stomachs. They make sure no power can hurt them; they stand around the carriage, ready to be yoked. The spiritual teachers pray to save the bright, ruddy steeds from being slaughtered.

They move in the sky with shining light, and like bold chiefs, they bring forth light to serve the spiritual teachers (Rig Veda, Book 1, Hymn VI). When they appear as unborn babes, they assume sacrificial names to serve the tempest of gods. They even break down the mountains to look for any souls hiding in caves. Once they find any, they worship them as mighty ones and serve as divinities and deities. This makes them fearless, joyous, and shining, innocent hosts. The mighty ones come rushing down from heaven to hear loud crying coming from the wanderers' place, where they are singing songs of praise as seekers. They yearn for help, sitting right below the illuminated heavenly region. As worshipping singers, they establish themselves with high praise and with glorified choirs, they honour the godhead, which appears in the region below the celestial region to serve the underlying regions created by the rising of the heavenly body (Surya).

Serving as a mighty divinity, it yokes farther away from the heavenly region. According to Rig Veda, Book 1, Hymn VII. Agni and Indra come down in their golden carriage armed with thunderbolts. They see afar into the frays where other godly powers like them need help. The appalling thousands left behind as spoils fight demons coming out of darkness, the underworld.

To face this mighty battle, Indra invokes friends who are being attacked by evil monsters and are becoming insecure. Indra, a forever powerful, armed wonder, appears with a thunderbolt. It comes riding in the cloud to support heroes. They move down from the heavenly level to relieve stress. They drive through with herds as their mighty irresistible ruler. Indra regulates all creation and comes to dwell in the newly created celestial region just below the heavenly region. Indra and Agni offer a feast that brings delight to victory. They provide the mythical juice, which as eternal wealth, repels their foes in battle. With thunderbolts, Indra, along with the heroes, brings the immortal weapon that acts as the missile-darting force used to conquer the embattled foes.

Indra extends its powers in the wide region that is all covered by heaven (Rig Veda, Book 1, Hymn VIII). They offer eternal love to all creation (Mitra), serving them like loving sons. This helps the heroes fight using holy thoughts as weapons instead of physical weapons to generate invisible spiritual power provided by the mythical juice. Even the heroes from the heavenly stratum bring cosmic vapours to the celestial region that swells to bring mighty powers coming with free-flowing water filling the ocean. With great vigour, the worshippers spread like branches on a tree. With praise, they bring lovely gifts such as vegetables and fruit.

They provide strength to protect each other by pouring forth the juice. This activates courage in, all supported by mighty powers (Rig Veda, Book 1, Hymn IX). Indra offers them unlimited power to organize themselves by creating different categories to control all things. They praise and honour the godhead (Agni-Indra) by serving as their guardian. They sing songs, offer drinks, and worship and receive bounty, including manifested cattle and horses provided by Indra, the lord of wealth.

The mighty powers become organized into different categories, serving as heroes. They make sure the work is being accomplished according to the creator's desire. They observe all tasks that are being performed by heroes (Rig Veda, Book 1, Hymn X). They fill the open space with cosmic vapours and set boundaries based on mythical juice that prompts heavenly praise and song. Along with Indra, the heroes understand the quest and accept the challenge to drink the mythical juice, which transforms seekers into worshippers who attain higher powers. Those who succeed prosper with strength and make personal sacrifices through sharing friendships. Along with the juice, they attain great pleasure, riches, and might that lead to freedom.

The sacrifices bring extended life and eternal wisdom. They meet with Indra to receive heavenly power to live and serve as learned sages (Satakratus). All reside in the illuminated heaven far away from the dark underworld and earth. Indra brings thunder and lightning to provide them wealth and protection. They transform cosmic vapours to create an abundance of water, which comes into the celestial region creating crying sounds. Learned sages serve as prophets (Kuśika) for a given period. They attain prolonged lives along with gifts to worship. As prophets, the Śatakratu come to fill the expanding region between heaven and earth.

These prophets, along with the holy, righteous warriors, serve the region with lordly strength and friendship. Without fear, they become glorified conquerors who provide immortal support and sustenance. With wisdom, as a youth, they crush evil powers and destroy evil dwellings. They serve as sustainers who kill evil power hiding in the mountains. This allows the learned sages serving as prophets to behold mighty deeds. They, with songs of praise, come to glorify Indra. They bring precious gifts even more than in the thousands, serving the holy prophet (Śatakratu) abundantly. As manifested, bright bodies (Rig Veda, Book 1, Hymn XI), they appear in the space, filling the celestial region with illuminated bodies such as the sun, moon, and stars. They appear strong as they pour the mythical juice along with singing songs of praise to make them strong evil slayers.

The prophets (Śatakratu), satisfied with mythical juice, join with the eternal laws (Varul)a) and come to serve as the immortal, universal soul of God (Paramatma). Serving as guardians, they fill the craving for manifested bodies created from the union of eternal love and the eternal laws (Indra-Varul)a). They spread with bounteous strength among thousands. Their unions with merit create devotees who are provided with powers to bring glory. These manifestations attain and retain heaps of eternal wealth. They share with others as coming vibrations that generate inner wealth expressed in songs and prayers. This helps them build shelters for their protection and serve spiritually rich disease healers (Kakṣīvāns) and spiritual teachers (Auśija) who come to serve with praise and offer eulogies.

According to Rig Veda, Book 1, Hymn XII, the lord of the house (Agni) invokes all oblations to fill much-beloved godly powers. They serve as its herald and strew the sacred grass. This willingly wakes up godly powers to come on the sacred grass. Radiant Agni pours holy oil to burn up the evil forces. Inflamed with ferocious fire, it gives birth to wise, young envoys (Angrisas) who bear ladles in their mouths. With praise and sacrifice, they manifest to serve as ever true sages. They drive away grief and provide a strong defence. They offer the sacred gift as a favour that purifies any oblation offered as the godly powers. Lauded by their newest song of praise, they bring opulence to heroes and food for their offspring. This brings with its effulgent, eternal flame to invoke, among others, the godly powers that, with pleasure, come along with loud sounds.

Cosmic Bodies

According to Rig Veda, Book 1, Hymn XIII, well-kindled Agni brings along godly powers to offer holy gifts with worship that serve as the purifier of the son of the sage (Narasama), contributing sweetness to the taste. This creates embodied cosmic souls that sprinkle wisdom as they manifest as wise, cosmic bodies (Manus). They come to serve as priests. They sit on the sacred grass dripping with immortal power, and they throw open the doors to welcome the divine will. They come with unfailing assistance offering rites to bring the morning light (dawn) and the evening light (dusk).

To celebrate their arrival, the three goddesses (Iḷā, Sarasvatī, and Mahī) make their sacrifices. Each brings delight as they sit on the grass. They call on the creative force (Tvaṣṭar) to be borne as the wearer of many and serve in many forms the powers of the divine will. They, as the sovereign of the wood, their renowned godly powers come with oblations to offer the ultimate last sacrifice (Svāhā) by honouring the mighty powers serving as divinities and deities. They bring the godhead Agni with mythical juice (Soma) to serve the divine messengers (Kaṇvas) of the godhead Indra.

According to Rig Veda, Book 1, Hymn XIV, they, with songs of worship, resurrect the ancient, supreme powers of causation (Agni, Indra, Vāyu, Bṛhaspati, Mitra, Pūṣan, Bhaga, and Aditya). They bring along demigods serving as the cosmic host (Marut) to pour forth the mythical juice (Soma). That gladdens and eventually exhilarates with the concentrate by adding drops of Meath already in the cup. Even sons of Kanvas, who adore having grass to sit on, bring offerings prepared with swift steeds to bring Soma to serve the godly power. All adored as the strengtheners of the eternal laws, they unite with dames and drink the mythical juice with essence (Meath) and, through their tongues, offer solemn sacrifice.

The sunlight brings wisdom along with Soma; this invokes the priest to bring all godly powers to come with full awaking at dawn. With all the godly powers and fully supported by the trinity (Indra, Vāyu, and Mitra), they, with splendorous drink, are ordained to bless the first manifested cosmic body (Manus), who comes to serve, offering each rite while sitting with Agni. They offer bliss as a sacrifice to harness the blood cells (Red Mares) to create the manifested embodiment. Godly powers awaken such among all the cosmic body as representing the first cosmic body (Manus)

During special seasons (Rtu), the cheering drops of Soma appear and sink deep within the embodiment (Rig Veda, Book 1, Hymn XV). Once settled, they create a purified drink that provides the opportunity to join with sanctified juice and is offered as precious gifts from Indra to the cosmic host (Maruts). Serving both males and females is accepted as a recurrent sacrifice that brings wealth. Like Agni, with godly powers, they appear at places where they could settle down.

The mythical juice provides a godly bounty (Brāhmana). This, as a divine bond of friendship (Mitra-Varuna), serves as a mighty power that none deceives. Soma serves the wealth giver by offering the rite along with sacrifice to praise the godly powers. Those who drink such seasonal (Rtu) juice become wealth-givers offering Soma as they depart for the fourth time. Serving as wealth-givers, they are honoured with bountiful gifts. The demigods (Aśvins) drink the mythical juice with eternal potency that brings along bright eternal flames. They make sacrifices to become pious souls.

The bay steeds are strong and bright like the sun's rays (Rig Veda, Book 1, Hymn XVI) when they drink the Soma. They come along in the morning, signing praise songs to Indra's carriage. This easily increases their might and welcomes him with hymns that reach Indra's heart. Soma makes Indra serve as the Vrtra-slayer. They, with delight, remove evil powers and, with wishes and desires, serve as holy thoughts and sing with praise to the holy prophets (Śatakratu).

According to Rig Veda, Book 1, Hymn XVII, the union of the imperial lords (Indra-Varuṇa) while serving the guardians helps individuals control their cravings. They show like every singer as ready relief sings with devotion to call on. With eternal wisdom, their embodiments come nearest to the imperial lords. They share their powers to become benevolent, give bounteous strength, and become among the thousands as the praise givers with powers that merit the highest laud.

They provide protection and gain great stores of wealth. The imperial lords (Indra-Varul)a) provide wealth in many forms to keep it victorious and, through songs, help creations win and provide shelters from where they offer joint eulogies to dignify individual souls.

Serving as spiritually rich healers, they learn to generate liquid sugar, which generates drops of nectar (Amrita) using their glands. This provides additional protection from the union (Indra-Varul)a), so the glands continue to provide the nectar (Amrita). This allows perishable bodies to become imperishable and allows individual spirits (Atma) to accept the immortal, universal soul (Paramatma).

The embodiments of those who offer personal sacrifices as gifts (Daksina) are saved from distress, and they become the imperishable deity of prayer (Brahmanaspati), which passes through assemblies of wondrous godly powers. They draw near the deity to learn and share with the eternal wisdom (Rig Veda, Book 1, Hymn XVIII). This stirs up thoughts of prosperity; in one voice, they offer prayers as the fierce, imperishable deity of prayer (Brahmanaspati), who incarnates in the form of a lion-man (Narasimha), to protect devotees from evil.

The devotees who make sacrifices (Rig Veda, Book 1, Hymn XIX) with Soma plants and milk attain mental powers with blessed eternal flames. They are recognized as the hosts of the cosmic region (Maruts). They, as demigods, produce dreadful sounds that make even the mighty ones serve the higher heavenly illuminated, which become overwhelmed. Such terrible sounds with mighty forces devour all foes. They sit far away from the luminous, celestial region; they come down to protect themselves by establishing a sky vault that serves as their shield. The activities of the Maruts encircle with cosmic vapours and move along with them and reach down to the deep oceans prevailing in the terrestrial region. They, with their bright beams, spread over the oceans and bring eternal wisdom as the early draughts of the mythical juice.

The Maruts further pour out cosmic vapours to create free-moving material bodies that hold the individual living spirits (Atma) and represent the unembedded universal souls (Paramatma). The free-moving living spirit (Atma) produces vibrations and hymns to fill the cosmic region. They produce eternal powers that lavishly invoke unique sounds. These sounds bring forth the immortal life force (Prana), representing the five winds (Vayus) that bring the cosmic water to fall from heaven onto earth.

Within the terrestrial region, Prana comes to manifest and fill the terrestrial region with bodies. Indra provides manifested bodies with the mind and heart needed to generate spiritual thoughts. Agni shows them how to harness the life force (Prana), serving as five winds (Vayus). The life force through the wind permeates the manifested body as breath, which supports the voice. The twin demigods (Aśvins) use the life force to create different voices that are used to pull the horses, and the male voice (Nāsatyas) is used to pull the carriage. After making sacrifices and drinking water and the mythical juice, the voice is transformed into female animals that produce milk.

Similar independently moving celestial bodies (comets, asteroids, and meteors) bring the mythical juice (Rig Veda, Book 1, Hymn XX) and fill the terrestrial region. This is all supported by honest and effectual powers of vibrations that transformed young cosmic bodies (Ṛbhus), which come to support the cosmic host (Maruts). They bring Soma used as the grit by the cosmic host (Maruts) to manifest itself into seven noble powers (Septarishis). These powers appear as the manifested physical embodiments, all regulated by noble souls (Āditya). They come to serve as kings and rule the manifested mortal and unmanifested immortal embodiments.

To further expand the capabilities of the seven noble powers, the cosmic host (Maruts) joins with noble souls (Āditya) to create an innovative soul (Tvaṣṭar). Using such creative powers, Tvaṣṭar transforms from one life force, serving as one sacrificial ladle to carve out two and more sacrificial ladles. The Āditya use such libation ladles to manifest into twenty-one spiritual ruling powers. They perform their pious acts to win more and to serve like seven heavenly priests (Septarishis). Twenty-one spiritual ruling powers offer eulogies three times a day to the seven supreme powers of causation, where each prayer is assigned to govern the expanding region.

Serving as the chiefs (Maruts; Rig Veda, Book 1, Hymn XXI), they offer the mythical juice to Agni-Indra. They agree to help each other create sacred hymns and libations to invite the supreme powers of eternal love (Mitra) to come and support them. They expand the union to form the trinity (Indra, Agni, and Mitra) to crush fiends and demolish evil and any unproductive souls such as childless mothers. The trinity watches over the expanding terrestrial region and offers their bliss to prevailing vital powers.

Next, they invite the Aśvins to serve as the best charioteers for the union of godheads (Indra-Agni) coming from heaven and passing through the celestial and cosmic regions to serve the newly established ground (Prithvi) above the expanding terrestrial region. In a carriage, they bring the mythical juice for all to drink and become fully awakened.

According to Rig Veda, Book 1, Hymn XXII, the Aśvins welcome the rising sun, and they appear in the evening ahead of the rising moon. They bring drops of honey for pleasantness, and they sacrifice by sprinkling the mythical juice. The protectors serving as the noble powers go far from their homes. With praise and support, the Aśvins bring along the goddess (Savitar), who knows all the holy ways to bring water and support all the offspring that generate wondrous wealth. Savitar looks on among all manifestations that are cultivating friendship, and by being seated among all, they enjoy the good and beautiful eternal fire provided by Agni. They willingly share the mythical juice with the creative souls (Tvaṣṭar), who can provide manifested embodiments with limbs or wings needed to perform their duties as well as provide great protection.

The youthful godly powers (Hotrā, Bhāratī, and Varūtrī) along with their spouse goddesses (IndrāI)ī, VaruI)ānī, and Agnāyī) enter the mid-air region to offer personal contributions (DhiṣaI)ā) and serve as mighty pairs residing in mid-air. They offer sacrifice, provide nourishment, and find a place where, with singing sacred songs, they can explore the richness that flowing water brings. They create the stratum in the esoteric region, where grass grows widespread, thus creating a thornless ground (Prithvi). With dwelling within shelters, they grow and create the godly-gracious place (Gandharan) where the guardian godly powers (Vishnu) come to reside. None can deceive in such a sacred place, which is three levels above the terrestrial region. At this place, they provide a sublime domicile filled with prayers and serve to illuminate the seven upper worlds (Lokas) that prevail above the ground (Prithvi).

Within these upper worlds (Lokas), the Vāyu, as the imminent wind along with Indra, establish a union (Indra-Vāyu). They serve heavenly powers and use the mythical juice to invoke the cosmic demigods (Maruts). The singers worship and learn to invoke and expand with other manifested bodies through expanding swift minds and a thousand eyes. They experience noble thoughts and serve as the renowned sanctified souls.

With godly might, they drink the mythical juice to uphold the law. They join with the shining light and provide the union (Mitra-Varuna), which serves as the guards of eternal love (Mitra). They defend them and provide spiritual knowledge. They become exceedingly rich and powerful, strengthening the union (Indra-Maruts). They fill up with the mythical fluid and agree to support all the troops and distribute gifts to noble souls (Adityas).

They join with solar divinities (Pusan) and form the union (Adityas-Pusan). Thus, they secure safe paths for mortals and immortals by providing them with a mythical vision provided by Agni. Serving as solar divinities, Agni brings the eternal flame and leads them to prevail in the manifested material world.

Solar divinities (Pusan) protect them from bandits and wild beasts that travel in the same direction as the noble powers (Adityas). They protect individual manifestations from being exploited by the dishonourable. They serve as guides for worshippers and devotees seeking rich pastures where they are supported by Indra, who conquers evil powers (Vṛtra) by striking down, and the demigods (Maruts) make sure no wicked master can overpower them.

In this new world of solar divinities (Pusan), they come along with the dual demigods (Aśvins) and multiple demigods (Maruts), which support the divine powers. The universal soul (Paramatma), jointly with the immortal spirit (Atma), regulates perishable embodiments by providing the juice regulated to the newly created ground (Prithvi).

Celestial divinities, along with mighty cosmic deities, come to serve as the guardians and serve with the heavenly father (Surya) and earthly mother (Aditi). Through their offspring, they conquer and rule the dynamic universe. With thundering voices, they bring victory along with their offspring appearing as the supreme powers of causation. They are all born laughing, generating lightning, and graciously guarding everyone everywhere.

The solar divinities (Pusans) bring bright, illuminating power designated to protect places where many-coloured embryos grow on sacred grass and establish a different place for resting. In each place, they look for hidden primordial energy (Shakti), which, like the coiled mythological serpents that sit in the cave, remains concealed on the grass from where it appears in many hues.

The Pusans find male oxen and six holy cows to serve as godly powers that plough hard ground into the soil, thus unveiling any buried eternal powers and making the ground fertile. The godly female is worshipped as the sisters of priestly ministrants who, like the heavenly mothers, convert water into milk enriched by the mythical juice. These immortal solar divinities (Pusans) gather under the heavenly body (Surya) and earthly mother (Aditi). They serve other goddesses' female animals, which see no sweetness in the purified waters. The immortal solar divinities help them discover the sweetness in the milk and learn to produce with the fluid that serves as a healing balm. They all quickly come to find that such fluid is like medicine that keeps them from harm even when they are exposed to the heat and the light of the sun.

Splendours

According to Rig Veda, Book 1, Hymn XXIII, the purified water removes sin and evil from manifested bodies. Such blessed water comes from Agni and penetrates the manifested physical body and transforms it into splendour. The blessed splendour through the eternal flame even travels through offspring to lengthen their lives. Such splendour is honoured by the godly powers as they come to experience the living spirit (Atma), which transfers individual embodiments into seers who are honoured as noble souls (Rsis). This even inspires poets to recite hymns that, with intense meditation, make them realize the eternal knowledge in hymns, like the hidden powers in the water.

According to Rig Veda, Book 1, Hymn XXIV, the seven noble souls (Septarishis) acquire an eternal flame after attaining eternal knowledge. It is provided by Agni to expand individual physical embodiments to comprehend the supreme powers of causation that manifest among auspicious bodies (Rsis). They, as the children of the godly mother (Aditi), come to experience the existence of the perishable living spirit (Atma) that manifests and is supported by the imperishable universal soul (Paramatma). The individual embodiments, mortal and immortal, acquire the ability to think, learn, and restore knowledge provided by the heavenly father (Surya) and are supported to expand through the offspring of the earthly mother (Aditi). This all remains hidden until it is unveiled by the mighty divine will (Devavani), which regulates each manifestation.

The divine will itself is supported by the father (Surya), which brings the godly power (Savitar) to provide precious things to each manifestation, which remain secret until it is unveiled, which continually shares wisdom with others. The godly power (Savitar) is highly praised, especially when approached by those who must help one who has fallen ill or has been misplaced by his own hand or another's and can no longer be freed from all forms of hatred.

The patron (Bhaga) of high dominion known by other noble souls becomes free to help the individual living spirits fly like birds and meet the unmanifested universal soul. The spirit on the ground can merge with purified waters and flow forever over hills and become an integral part of minerals, rocks, plants, trees, and other living things. In the baseless region with the eternal laws, spirits can stay erect like branches of a tree and develop deep roots that make them steady. The eternal laws and the sun's rays make a path for spirits to travel and not stray from.

Whenever the spirit departs from the embodiment, it joins the heavenly bodies such as constellations to remain strong. Every such union with prayers asks for oblations from the eternal laws to make sure they stay with them and spirit is not taken away from them. While serving night and day, the ruler of the holy law tells the manifestations to go through with faith and believe in their heart, so the spirits remain bound to the embodiment like a tail to a dog. It is only with faith that a bond (Śunaḥśepa) is developed with the mortal material world governed by eternal laws that can be released. While serving as the sovereign, the spirits remain tied to the universal soul that delivers the spirit in such a manner that all parts are supplicated through the ruling of the noble power (Āditya) that never deceives, loosens the bonds, and binds spirits to the noble power.

By offering sacrifices to the noble powers (Adityas), it pushes the sinning evil powers (Asura). The spirits never lose the bonds (Śunaḥśepa) with the mother (Aditi), who recites the eternal laws regulated day after day and supported by the sinless godly powers. They protect manifestations from being destroyed by wrath or anger.

When every manifestation or embodiment learns to bind its heart to the hymns and the eternal laws, everyone gains mercy and strength in their bonds with the spirits like horses to their charioteer. Spirits receive support from the eternal laws, like birds building nests in the air.

According to Rig Veda, Book 1, Hymn XXV, the spirits receive support from the eternal laws that lets them serve as the lords of mighty warriors who never fail their faithful worshippers. From the godhead hero, the spirit learns the path to fly and serve as sovereigns over the sea. Through comprehending the prevailing powers and serving manifested splendours on land and water, they learn the holy law through spirits and the monthly moons. They even comprehend through progeny the principle of re-embodiment like the later birth of moons.

Knowing their mighty godly powers (Rig Veda, Book 1, Hymn XXVI), they all, above the pathway of the wind (Vayu), keep leading to the place where the eternal laws dwells. From there, they serve the spirits as godhead heroes who attain eternal wisdom to serve among all manifestations and make them come down to enforce the eternal laws. They perceive various wondrous things, including what has been and what needs to be done. The noble souls with eternal wisdom establish paths for the manifestations' love for prolonging lives.

The eternal laws finds the spies and enemies hiding in a shining robe. Wearing golden armour, they appear threatening to the manifested godly power. Like birds, godhead heroes find the evil powers whose minds are bent wrong and tyrannize the godly powers. Without any personal sacrifice, they offer incomplete glory that yearns to see the ultimate ruling power. Such manifestations with holy thoughts end up moving onward like animals moving to different pastures.

Once such embodiments are enlightened, they speak with eternal wisdom, drink milk like the mythical juice, and give birth to many manifestations serving like priests. They enjoy what is dear to them, and they can observe godly powers as they move above the earth, accepting prayers and divine songs. Godhead heroes hear the eternal laws calling out from spirits with grace, and they hear the cries from the eternal laws that fills their longing.

While serving as the kings of terrestrial bodies, the godly powers (Aditya) help the eternal laws and others. They release spirits from the heavenly bond and then untie the celestial and cosmic bonds and let spirits loosen their terrestrial bonds. They join the godly power (Aditya), which wears robes with honour and blesses devotees and the eternal flame.

Godly powers with blessed words establish worship and develop their relationship with their choice of spirit; like father and son, they serve as worthy friends (Rig Veda, Book 1, Hymn XXVII). By understanding the powers of the ancient trinity, they serve as the foe destroyers like the ancient herald sitting on sacred grass as godly powers gladly offer rites with songs that hearken fellowship. In a never-ending course, the mighty divinities of the celestial region and deities regulating the cosmic region offer sacrifice and serve the devotees or priests. Offering gifts, they serve as the heads of households and use the eternal flame to adore and grant priests much wealth. With prayer, priests support the eternal flame, which as a mortal manifestation offers eulogies to the universal soul. With such offerings, they find great pleasure in making their sacrifices and are established as universal souls and immortal, unmanifested bodies.

Appearing as sons of strength (Rig Veda, Book 1, Hymn XXVII) through speech and worship, they bring domesticated, long-tailed animals that are glorified by sacred rites like the imperial lord. With far-striding heavenly bodies, they support all forms of life and bring great contentment to all. The unmanifested bodies serving as the imminent ones, the sons of strength (Rudras), appear with Agni and provide the eternal flame and protect living noble souls. They sing the newest songs of praise to the mighty powers in the celestial and cosmic regions as well as the terrestrial region. The universal soul receives splendid gifts and joins with the sons of strength, who regulate the winds, create waves, enhance the air, and make rivers flow with their eternal strength.

God, appearing as the universal soul, protects spirits fighting righteous and moral wars. It even urges them to peacefully end the quarrel by making them understand that all mortal manifestations will be vanquished and that the spirits cannot be destroyed even by the glorious power. Spirits dwell in mortal bodies that endure like warriors that pass through fights with the power of hymns and win the spoils.

As absolute truth, the son of strength, the imminent one (Rudras), serves as the lord of the universe who regulates the solar wind coming from the heavenly body and creates the roaring windstorms that are praised as the mightiest of the mighty, which manifest as the primordial power (Shakti) that can handle any form of horror.

The primordial power (Shakti) operates like a grinder in the terrestrial realm (Rig Veda, Book 1, Hymn XXVIII). It constantly rises from a point and drops down to a point designed to hold the mythical juice. It is a shield monitored by godly powers to make sure that the juice from the primordial power (Shakti) is properly guided and revered to serve the lord of the universe (Rudras) in finding noble souls ready with accomplished eternal truth to gain absolute truth. Like a drum, the primordial power (Shakti) sends forth loud, clear sounds as a signal to manifested bodies, which with their mouths open, receive the mythical juice, and invoke the primordial power's (Shakti) strength and sacrificial power. Like the Aśvins eating herbs, it produces a sweet drink with fermented residue that can be extracted and filtered through an ox hide to produce the mythical fluid. When it is taken with faith, it generates passion and turns physical strength into eternal strength. Until the inner spirit (Atma) is blessed, it remains hopeless. The primordial power causes them to perform great, influential deeds. Once they are blessed with the sweet mythical juice, they attain awareness through their blessed inner spirits and attain powers.

According to Rig Veda, Book 1, Hymn XXIX, the juice destroys the depreciatory nature and makes one attain new power. Each slaying reviler destroys those who in secret injure others and, by seeking strength from the mythical juice, fulfils evil desires. With the support of multiple godly powers and the mythical juice (Rig Veda, Book 1, Hymn XXX), worshippers become as pure as the mythical juice and experience a joyous rapture that generates in the belly the pious force and goes into a depth to accommodate it like a vast ocean. Within the embodiment, it frees the imprisoned spirits to move freely among the enlightened souls. Such embodiments learn to build soulmates through sharing hymns of praise and experiencing joy. Like the enlightened souls with pious power, using their hundred powers, they help those fighting the righteous wars.

In every need, in every fray, they call each other their friends or soulmates and jointly become the mightiest of all. They hear from those who bring successes of a thousand kinds and reinforce mighty strength among the enlightened souls. Like the ancient heroes, they go home to pray with their parents, and, with singing praise, they attain precious gifts brought from their ultimate loving as friends and serve as Indra, which comes thunder-armed, drinks the juice, and serves each individual desire along with a splendid feast.

All who are pleased with grace and praises, such as pious souls (Śatakratu) along with the creative power (Tvaṣṭar), support the divine will (Devavani). They are like horses bringing a carload of gold. Making their deeds even wondrous, the twins (Aśvins) appear with enduring wealth to support all domesticated animals. They serve mortal and immortal embodiments and perform wondrous deeds while travelling in waters.

Through revolving dual manifestation as a pair placed in front, the multiple godly powers serve (Rig Veda, Book 1, Hymn XXXI) in an enjoyable manner appearing in the morning, accompanied by the sun. Serving as the daughters of the sun, they appear like rain clouds that gain strength to serve mortal manifestations. The sun sends great bliss among other riches to those serving as saviours. Even though it takes some time for them to accommodate themselves to the prevailing environments, they become perishable but never give up their immortal nature. They appear among terrestrial regions as morning light and evening light.

Using the power of absolute truth, they serve as the divine will to two heavenly forces, Agni and Indra. They spread the holy law and eternal wisdom and reveal mythological entities appearing as perishable beings such as pious powers, the female (Mātariśvan), and ferocious powers as the male (Vivasvān). Both are internally empowered with the eight great elements of nature (Aṣṭa-Vasu); the first five represent the basic, perishable physical elements (Vasus) of causation—fire, earth, water, air, and ether. They balance three as imperishable spiritual elements and bring brilliant powers—the sun, the moon, and the stars. As Aṣṭa-Vasu, they manage the thirty-three mighty powers of causation regulated by the primordial powers (Shakti). They manifest and regulate the imperishable powers of the universal soul and serve magnified mortal embodiments that serve as the mortal parents.

With the direct light generated by ferocious fire, Agni regulates its first moving planetary bodies, the sun with direct light and the moon, which reflects the sun's light, and stars with self-generated light. Shakti created the sun to house the imperishable spirit that serves as the house lord (Nahuṣa), from which are born all living things destined to serve the revered father. Appearing enriched patrons (Iḷā), they acquire eternal flames and become pious guards that, like four-eyed living creatures, guard all embryos and create various embodied kingdoms.

Filled with eternal strength, like lizards, they learn to stand on two legs to protect themselves. These living creatures, with their hearts and affection with prayers, come from embodied, impious souls. They find security through loudly praising holy souls, and they gain support from what fulfils their individual desires. Like their enriched patrons (Iḷā), they learn to care for the wise and those with weak hearts; they offer worship just like simple persons. As priests, they offer folklore to receive rewards and food. For showing such kindness, they acquire eternal wisdom and bestow favours on others.

Those who have committed sins and have drifted from their obligatory responsibilities (Karma) to friends and family do not care for the pious and prayerful. They, as uninspired, are not pardoned immediately; they have to serve like their ancestors' mortal manifested beings (Manus) and are subject to death like the Puranic king (Yayāti), who received support from Agni.

Messengers

The primordial, noble, and divine power (Shakti) in its true form (Rig Veda, Book 1, Hymn XXXII) manifests to kill the evil dragon by appearing as perishable messengers (Maghavan) of Indra who spews out evil powers and dragons. Indra cleaves the mountains to expose those evil powers holding the cosmic vapours hostage. The messengers receive support from the creative power (Tvaṣṭar) to create channels that turn water into torrents before they descend into the oceans.

Using their creative power, they turn into impetuous bulls and serve all manifestations in the esoteric region. These messengers slay the firstborn dragon and kill any other evil power. With their mighty powers, they overpower other evil enchanters. By producing morning light, they uncover any evil power and disclose any demon in the esoteric region; no foe can remain standing in such light or sustain itself against such noble power. Evil powers creep into the ground and become difficult to be challenged. They watch Indra slay the evil powers (Vṛtras). They come to protect noble souls by cutting the evil powers into pieces and making them flee with their severed limbs into flowing waters. Indra pursues them relentlessly and guards marine creatures (Ahi). The evil powers look for caves for protection, but Indra smites them with thunderbolts, gives them the mythical juice, and turns them loose to fill up the mythical seven rivers.

While the dragon is still battling for nothing, Indra comes with lightning, thunder, hailstorms, and mist to make it submit to the messengers. They gain victory over the dragon, and then they appear as hawks that fly over nine and ninety rivers to get to the manifested ground. Knowing many manifested creatures could be tame and domesticated, they first take on the appearance of animals with horns so they can care for and guide mortal embodiments. With pleasure, they come with astonishing booty.

According to Rig Veda, Book 1, Hymn XXXIII, through bringing a falcon as the wealth giver, Indra brings sanctuary. All accompanied with the fairest hymns, which offer praise and support, help the messengers fight the righteous battles rather than flee from the evil powers. They gather to survive as savages (Dasyu), which have no respect for laws or rites.

The messengers escape their destruction as they elect to assist worshippers. Indra appears from the sky to blow away godless slayers. Indra lets them join with the fierce bay steeds serving Indra and fighting with the army of the blameless ancient fathers (Navagvas). They fight the evil powers until they are scattered.

The evil powers are sent to the extreme limits, at the horizon, where there is no light or sun. The leader of the evil powers covers the material wealth and, with a veil (Maya), makes such things real like gold and jewels, but they are not what they seem to be. They are scorched by the heavenly fire (Agni) to expose their true character concealed that hides the areas controlled by the evil powers. The evil powers run from areas controlled by Indra as a spiritual reality. The evil powers separate those who do not worship from those who do as soon as they see evil powers having been blown away. The evil powers are not subdued by their charms; instead, they attract those who bestow material wealth.

Having nature as an ally of power brings along eight elements of nature (Asta-Vasu), which create streams to regulate the terrestrial region. Indra, with its fierce weapons, attacks enemies and destroys their castles. Indra establishes the holy sages (Kutsa), which conquer the evil powers and their sons, who guard Asura. The messengers let horses raise dust to the heavens to draw the powers that make that steer (Śvitrā) stand up again any conqueror. In the middle region, evil powers go to the house of Tugra, which creates myths to combat noble powers until their treasure is exhausted.

During the journey, they serve as the demigods (Aśvins) and wonder-workers (Nāsatyas) and establish and maintain sustainability through three pillars of strength (Rig Veda, Book 1, Hymn XXXIV). These three pillars form a place to worship and gain strength from the imperishable universal soul. The first worship is offered with the rising sun, the second worship is offered at noon, and the third worship is offered with the setting sun or the rising moon. These worships are offered with the mythical juice and personal sacrifice to bring godly powers to banish deprivation. This worship provides sustenance during the day. They serve righteous folk and provide aid to those who deserve it. They bring happiness to others and share their food. They bring abundant wealth to the assembly, honour godly powers, and originate good thoughts. They bring prosperity with heavenly medicines accompanied by water to grant fame being held in individual bodies as well as in oceans, lakes, and underground storage areas.

All this strengthens newly created embodiments. All manifested creations receive protection from the pillars of prayers, which, like the lords of splendour, come from far away, all filled with carriages. They accompany the thirty-three godly powers supported by vital air or breath (Vayu) that supports manifested bodies. The trinity, the lords of splendour, and the demigods (Nāsatyas) come to establish the seven streams or rivers that serve as the mothers where all manifestations are properly served.

The lords of splendour come from their vault right below the celestial region as the thirty-three godly powers come with demigods to serve the mid-air region, which is filled with free-moving cosmic bodies (Rig Veda, Book 1, Hymn XXXVI). They even go to lower regions and cover the manifested terrestrial bodies. The sacred gift of the mythical juice comes to invoke the goddess of water (Savitar). As dew comes before the morning light, all are accompanied by the sun, which produces various colours accompanied by a fuel-like oil that ignites eternal wisdom, wipes out sin, and lengthens lives among manifestations, thus warding off enemies.

The trinity brings prosperity to noble offspring that represents two extremes—pure and impure, the feminine as pious power and the masculine as ferocious power. This comes with the robust powers of attraction and aversion that appear as the universal soul (Paramatma), which travels in all the regions. With unpredictability, they give birth to golden powers that appear in the sky symbolized by the morning and evening light. Both appear with their golden chariots, bringing treasures to avert misfortune and sickness. Like godly doctors, as demigods, they present kindness (Nakula) and helpfulness (Sahadeva), which, when united, create the third insightfulness (Budha). They serve as the three pillars of the lord of splendour, creating the sun, the moon, and the stars that regulate the dual powers, the cycles of life and death, and, in the underworld, as the powers of death (Yama).

Birth is established by the universal soul through placing immortal spirits in perishable astral bodies that are then placed in mortal manifested bodies. Perishable bodies appear as gentle leaders serving like noble powers (Aditya) that transform into deep-quivering evil power (Asura) once they go below the ground to join the underworld, the terrestrial region.

Solar rays wander to the ground (Prithvi) and establish points of brightness to serve all beings, including in the three desert regions and seven regions with running water. With worship, the golden-eyed goddess (Savitar) brings mortals and immortals their choice of treasures, which they can use to worship as their godly powers. Sunlight moves between the earthly region and heaven and serves as a shield that drives away sickness. It helps demigods to transform the wicked power (Asura) into a kind power and, as a noble soul, it drives off evil powers such as Rākṣasas and Yātudhānas. In the mid-air region, the golden-eyed goddess uses ancient pathways to serve manifested bodies.

To supplicate and win strength (Rig Veda, Book 1, Hymn XXXVI), holy hymns communicate with the mighty ruling ones, serving as the lords of many families. The mighty ones are worshipped as godly powers. The selected messengers are chosen by the mighty eternal flames (Agni) to offer the omniscient power needed to reach the sky in splendour. They enkindle the ancient godly powers of the trinity to appear in the form of a new trinity (Varuṇa, Mitra, and Aryaman). They offer juice to a priest that brings wealth to the worshippers. Those serving as the messengers of Agni come to serve as the lord of the house. They establish an eternal flame in the embodiment. Like messengers, they bring together godly powers that offer sacred gifts to auspicious youth that make them gracious and heroic.

The devout youth, through worship with sacrificial gifts, draw near to the illumination, which kindles fire among others and overpowers enemies. They smite evil and live in the newly manifested world between earth and heaven. The sun comes as an invoked steed that snorts and represents the animal kingdom.

Agni watches the sacred food offered by the priest ordained by the godly power to manifest as the first ancient descendant (Medhyātithi) to prevail in the mid-region, appearing as the first cosmic body (Manus), which serves among manifested bodies representing the epithet of wealth (Vṛṣan and Upastuta). They appear with the shepherd (KaI)va), who welcomes the material wealth with the offering of rites, singing, and praise to extol Agni, which brings eternal flame from the heavenly region. Making their acquired divine wealth, they develop a kinship with ancient descendants (Manus), which, as cosmic bodies, help establish the kingdoms that, as descendants, serve the king.

With strength, they preside over all and serve Savitar, which bestows strength by calling to the priests who preside over the sacrifice and offer unguents to preserve their embodiments from soreness. With the eternal flames in their bodies, they destroy all ravenous demons. They rise on two legs to help them walk with their manifested embodiments. They offer worship to all living things prevailing in the mid-region who are offered by the godly powers. With the eternal flame, they preserve themselves from the fiend and save themselves from malicious wrongs.

The youth with light like a club smite evil on the right and left, knowing that during the night, no one can plot against or allow any foe to prevail. The shepherd (KaI)va) helps their reverent friends, Medhyātithi and Upastuta. The manifested cosmic soul (Manus) calls on noble male souls (Ugradeva, Yadu, and Turvaśa) to join with female souls (Navavāstva, Bṛhadratha, and Turvīti). They jointly subdue the foe through the establishment of the inner flame that awakens all the tribes, and then, with divine laws, they set them free. With the eternal flame, embodied souls attain reverence and serve as shepherds (KaI)va). Even those evil powers blessed with eternal flame by Agni with full splendour and might through fear do not approach embodied noble souls; instead, they use their power to consume all other demons, sorcerers, and fiends.

The shepherd observes a sporting band of brilliant, unassailable youth in chariots and appearing as luminous bodies (Rig Veda, Book 1, Hymn XXXVII) and bearing weapons and ornaments as if they had been born to travel. The shepherds sing godly hymns to honour these as the cosmic host (Maruts), who serve as fierce demigods that rule like bulls among the cows. They strengthen the consuming rain with the mythical juice. Serving as the cosmic host, they become the mightiest heroes, shakers of the whole mid-air region as well as earth and heaven.

These embodied souls filled with anger and wrath drop down to race on the newly created ground (Prithvi) in the esoteric region. They cause mountains to yield and make embodied souls tremble in terror. The strength and vigour they acquired from their mothers increase. They face rain as if they were offspring of the host (Maruts), coming as embryos to manifest and create embodied souls.

Sons of KaI)va serve as shepherds offering worship to swift steeds. With the sons of Kanva serving as their offspring, as shepherds, they serve them as their servants just as they serve demigods and pray to live for a long time. They worship the demigods as sons of the godly powers, and they prepare the sacred grass to receive their mighty powers. This convinces the Maruts to stay and serve the esoteric region. As the sons of the mother (Pṛśni), they serve like demigods, and, from birth, they learn to sing the praises of all immortal embodiments and learn not to loath like a wild beast in a pasture, and thus, avoid going on the path of death (Yama).

The cosmic host (Maruts), serving as a demigod, becomes the fierce sons of the primordial force (Shakti) that moves with windless rain covering the desert places and urges the divine will not to bring destructive epidemics. They conquer all evil powers; they lie low like cows, and when faced with the lightning, they, like mothers, follow their young. They make sure they do not get lost in the water. Overwhelmed with the exposure, the demigods, as the cosmic host, spread rain clouds and generate sounds that shake earthly habitations. They make haste along streams like horses pulling carriages.

They invite with song and prayer; the divine will be fashioned like a godly force to come along with Agni to ask the lord of eternal love (Mitra) to join them in singing hymns to form rain clouds (Rig Veda, Book 1, Hymn XXXVIII). With its eternal flame, Agni casts on the cosmic host (Maruts) to decide who goes forth and to whom they shake and give eternal wisdom, so they can determine who should receive weapons to drive away foes. They look over the selected who serve as glorious warriors using mortal and righteous strength to overthrow every heavy thing. The selected ones come to serve as heroes of demigods (Maruts) and go through the forests and fissures.

Others hold back the evil powers coming from the underworld or terrestrial region; they are all supported by an omniscient force (Rudras), which, through individual strength, holds the bond that makes mountains sway like trees in the wind (Rig Veda, Book 1, Hymn XXXIX). Through the demigods' omniscient force (Rudras), they drive all creatures to drink the juice like the godly powers; this keeps their physical embodiments yoked like chariots that appear with the life force appearing as the spotted red deer.

All serving their leaders and ready to draw to the ground, they listen to all creatures who are sorely terrified. The ancient heavenly powers (Rudras) quickly know mortal manifested bodies' desires to succeed. They quickly send shepherds (Kaṇvas) to help those who can face monstrous foes. They bring demigods to protect mortal embodiments subjected to being torn apart and to bring success to those who are wise and worshipful. Those are guarded perfectly by the shepherds who in the past supported the demigods (Maruts) and provided them with lightning to see the bounteous ones (Maruts) as earth-shakers fight like darts against the poet's wrathful enemy. The manifested praying souls receive a special gift from Indra, the swift legendary power that comes as the sons of strength who can stand up along with the Maruts regulating the mid-air region.

According to Rig Veda, Book 1, Hymn XL, Indra, worshipped to win the spoils of battle with ancient traditional mythological power of eternal love, obtains wealth like good steeds they serve as mighty heroes with power, and they manifest as sons of strength, which draws the goddesses, the daughters of the sun (Sūnṛtā). They are

31

given rites to manifest as mortal powers that are given rites to serve the male heroes (Brahmaṇaspati). Each hero is provided with a fivefold gift to serve his embodiments as the holy soul bestowed as noble gifts. They help others win fame and sacred food that makes their conquest easy. Indra directly speaks to them through forming a new trinity representing the eternal laws with eternal love and eternal souls (Varuṇa, Mitra, and Aryaman).

The heroes praise godly powers with the solemn hymn as they set their dwelling place. They, like holy synods, recite godly hymns that bring felicity and graciously invite the godly powers to come and guide them to serve as ancient immortal souls. These holy souls help them become pious and sit on sacred grass covering the terrestrial region. They fill the assembly with precious things and amplify mighty lords serving as the kings. They slay those who challenge their secured dwelling place, but no one can subdue the holy souls who go unchecked and wield thunderbolts.

The new trinity protecting the divine will appears wise and is never injured (Rig Veda, Book 1, Hymn XLI); it forever prospers and is enriched. Kings with godly powers drive troubles off and lead their people to safety. The noble souls make it easy by establishing thornless pathways for them so they can seek the law and learn not to anger. While making sacrifices, they avoid negative thoughts and follow the direct path. Ever unsubdued, these noble souls gain wealth and, with every precious thing, learn to have children. The trinity prepares them with glorious laws that help them become pious. They make sure they become lovers who speak no ill words.

Holy Rights

Godly powers come as the solar divinities (Pū5an) come to remove obstructions set by evil underworld powers. They drive off wicked wolves that wait to injure godly powers. The holy souls serving as prophets stay away from the paths evil powers take. They trample the firebrands, the wicked ones, and other foes appearing to be wise wonder-workers, from whom they receive aid while the ancient sires remain far away. Serving as lords of all prosperity, they make those riches easy to be won; they lead by making their paths pleasant to tread. Solar divinities (Pū5an) lead them to rich meadows and send them on their way before the early heat to seek mighty wealth.

Being strong, wise, and dear prophets (Rig Veda, Book 1, Hymn XLIII), they ask the heavenly father and mother to grant them grace to prevail like enhanced beings. Using the powers of eternal love, law, and soul, they bring forth progeny based on remembering godly powers to regulate the manifested esoteric region. With heavenly power, as prophets, they sing hymns that bring along balmy medicines, and they pray for health and strength. Shining in the sun, they bring to light the best among all godly powers. The light of the moon grants health to them so they can generate the juice and produce progeny. The glory among hundreds of embodied souls creates mighty chiefs who protect others. The chiefs know the strength of eternal love; they produce offspring with immortal souls whom they help attain the highest place in the holy law. The immortal Agni with its messengers (Jatavedas) appears with eternal flames as if they were firebirds that bring many-hued gifts, including the dawn (Rig Veda, Book 1, Hymn XLIV).

The demigods perform an act of eternal love reflected in the dawn that grants heroic strength to generate lofty celebrity. Appearing among many, they bring eternal love (Mitra), which joins with the smoke banner Agni, and with the rays of heavenly light (Surya), they spread with sacrificial holy rites. Noblest among the most youthful, they offer rich worship to the dawn and bring through the messengers (Jatavedas) the gifts of immortal powers that the godly powers serve to embodied souls.

With Agni as the source, they serve as glorified and deathless nourishers to manifested bodies. They, as the bearers of power, seek sacred food, and they offer the best sacrifices with praise among the youthful, godly powers that worship good things. Through their honeyed tongues, they grant lengthened days and honour the holy soul, which all possessors selected as priests with godly powers.

They all speed in the morning and appear as twin demigods serving the goddesses U5has and Savitar at night, along with the lord of prosperity (Bhaga). They, as patrons skilled in rites, pour the mythical juice and invoke the eternal flame with oblations to the envoy (KaI)vas). As the messengers of Agni, they serve the godly powers with sacrifice to the morning light (dawn), and they enjoy the mythical juice. Soon after, with the eternal flame, they become visible as friends of all the embodied spirits. Like ancient living beings (Manus), they sacrifice as powerful high priests and invoke, among others, the eternal wisdom needed to serve the godly powers and, with love, serve the minister. They perform their mission by bringing the nearest godly friend, Agni, with eternal flames. They come with eternal love (Mitra) along with the holy priests serving as the Aryaman, who all are trained with ears to hear at bedtime the offering of rites to the holy spirit.

Seated on the sacred grass (Aryaman) with strengthened the eternal laws, Aryaman meet the cosmic host (Maruts), the bountiful giver who heard praise coming from tongued creatures. They are blessed with the universal soul and eternal laws as twins in morning and evening light (U5has) to be demigods who have already taken the mythical juice.

Covering the surrounding areas and regulated by the ancient primordial forces (Rudras), they worship such powers before they support immortal, manifested noble powers (Ādityas). They bless all manifested embodiments (Manus). Those who understand godly powers and follow the divine will whisper among worshippers in loving songs the three-and-thirty godly powers of causation regulating creation.

The messengers with immortal powers perform great acts (Rig Veda, Book 1, Hymn XLV) that hearken the rulers as they provide to the ancient trinity (Atri, Virūpa, and Aṅgiras). The power of the divine will serve such messengers and their offspring, who are skilled in praise and appear with the universal soul as noble souls (Aryaman). They call on Agni to bring the flame to the noble souls so they can support the ruler (Priyamedha) with proper rites. They invoke the divine will by offering bountiful eternal flames as a reward with which they offer purified holy emollients.

Sons of shepherds (KaI)va) become the loved ones serving with the source of fame from the godhead (Agni); this helps them make wondrous homes. The sons of shepherds (KaI)va) become bearers of gifts. They help find wealth and become famous for their ability to hear songs of worship of the herald, minister to the holy priest, and serve the singer worshippers who help transform the mythical juice into mystic drops (Amrita) that bring the sacred light needed to support the mortal worshipper. As good and bounteous sons of strength (Rudras), they bring inner illumination, and by controlling their breathing, they form haloes around material bodies.

Bounteous sons of strength come in the morning and serve all as hosts of heaven by offering the juice with a joint invocation as in the past as the celestial host (Rudras) expresses their offering, which all bounteous godly powers share (Rig Veda, Book 1, Hymn XLVI). The dear daughters of the heavenly power (Surya) appear with the earliest light on the ground, which the demigod (Aśvin) extols with praise to serve the offspring growing on the ground or in the water.

With their mighty power, the demigods discover the riches of each creation and find eternal wealth that could be used to focus, concentrate, or meditate. Demigods serve the giant coursers with the eternal flame, and deep thoughts cover all the regions. Using their embodiments like carriages, they fly like winged steeds. Demigods appear as liberal lovers of the flood; they serve like lords of the house or as vigilant chiefs offering oblations.

The demigods think of words as they drink the mythical juice and turn into Nāsatyas; with their strength and inner light, they pass through the darkness. They serve as a ship surrounded by calm water and produce hymns heard on the shore (Rig Veda, Book 1, Hymn XLVII). They harness their embodiments to the universe and flood the shore, waiting for the mythical juice to be accompanied by hymns. Sanctified souls (Ka,)vas) receive eternal wealth from heaven and acquire embodiments in different forms. With the heavenly power (Surya), they appear like branches that light up and look like gold. They travel the path of sacrifice to heaven. The singer waits for the demigods to provide the mythical juice and meet with auspicious males (Vivasvān), who praise the cosmic embodiment (Manus). The demigods, along with dawn, follow their way with brightness like beams approved with the solemn rites. Twin demigods grant protection to embodied Manus that none can interrupt.

The demigods protect those who strengthen the law (Rig Veda, Book 1, Hymn XLVII), and with sweetness, they shed the mythical fluid to those who offer oblations. The demigods offer sacrifice with prayers. They send sanctified souls (Ka,)vas) to listen graciously and then call for help to strengthen the law offering the drink of the sweetest juice the demigods use to help sanctified shepherds (Ka,)va) with their offspring to strive to heaven. The demigods help them serve the lords of splendour by providing the juice that strengthens the holy law. The mighty ones serve treasure to tribes (Sudās) coming from heaven or the sea.

The demigods come with sunbeams and let coursers sacrifice while the chiefs sitting on the sacred grass bestow food on those who act and give rights. The demigods (Nāsatyas), with their bodies bedecked with canopies to protect them from the sun, bring wealth to the worshippers and provide the mythical juice. With songs of praise, they come down with sanctified Ka,)vas to well-loved houses, where they drink the juice with the demigods. With daughters of the sky manifest as the goddess (U5as), they come as the morning light (Rig Veda, Book 1, Hymn XLVIII) and, with great glory, fill it with riches that attract the bounteous ones, the cosmic hosts (Maruts). They bring bounty to all the steeds and other animals that seek the light.

With the powers of U5as, the Maruts drive forth with the goddess and create a flood of thoughts, all fixed on seeking glory and serving like the chiefs of the Ka,)vas race. Ka,)vas sing and serve as the glorified princes and are invited by U5as. They come with liberal thoughts like a good matriarch who carefully tends to everything, including animals and birds. The morning light yokes steeds on a hundred chariots. Such auspicious dawn allows embodied souls to advance briefly, serving as living creatures who, with mighty light, attain excellence.

The daughter of the sky, U5as, shines on enemies knowing they cannot take away opulence. Each living creature is controlled by the lady of the light. U5as hear as they bring wondrous wealth to win and gain strength. The wonderful, embodied souls become pious, and with praise, they come with the singing priests. From the heavenly firmament, Uṣas brings all hidden godly powers in all forms to drink the juice and uses mighty powers to protect all living beings. Uṣas brings auspicious rays that can be observed in the material world and bring great wealth. Like the mighty powers, they support embodied, perishable, noble souls, provide them protection, and graciously answer any requests. Uṣas even opens the twin doors of heaven to bring inner illumination to those fighting evil foes and provides them with food and wealth. The power of the goddess provides riches to those who indulge in material wealth.

According to Rig Veda, Book 1, Hymn XLIX, Uṣas lets red steeds in the house and pours the mythical juice that allows embodiments to attain inner illumination. Moving with the power of the goddess serving as the daughter of the sky, they aid embodied souls with noble distinction. The bright goddess supports all quadrupeds and bipeds and stirs up the birds to spread into all heaven.

Radiant Bodies

Surya creates a plasma that appears as the sun that fills the constellations that, like thieves, take away the sunbeams (Rig Veda, Book 1, Hymn L) while the heavenly body (Surya) sees all illuminated with rays in the manifested world. With ferocious fire, Agni produces eternal flames as beautiful art that illuminates all by establishing radiant bodies. Serving as the heavenly body, it beholds all creation with its light and looks on the godhead of law, providing brilliant enforcing powers to the divine will that monitors all busy races and encompasses immortal, manifested, universal souls and immortal living things. The godhead of law passes through the esoteric region, where during the day, it brings direct beams coming from the sun as the divine will watch all creation. The heavenly body (Surya), through its supreme powers of causation, harnesses the planets that travel with the wind (Vayu), producing radiant hair.

With pure and bright lights, the planets are yoked like seven daughters accompanied by individual postures. They serve as the dream team that looks at the darkness from above; from a loftier position, they appear as gods. These heavenly bodies ascend to the heavenly region and remove heart diseases by taking yellow hues and creating colourful birds like parrots and starlings. These birds take yellow hues from dying trees and transfer them to green trees. These heavenly bodies give birth to noble spirits (Āditya) that rise by turning all foes into the hands of heavenly bodies instead of sending them to become a foe's prey. Heavenly bodies generate vibrations in the form of happy songs that become hymns to invoke Indra. To manifest, it first appears like an uncastrated male sheep worthy of praise that fills the region like a wide body of water.

With gracious deeds (Rig Veda, Book 1, Hymn LI), it sings praises for the betterment of all embodied souls (Ṛbhus) who yearn for strength from Indra and serve all creation in the esoteric region. These embodied spirits rush with ecstasy, all urging victory with glad shouts. They bring out noble souls (Śatakratu), disclose their ancient Agni heritage, and spread abroad as messengers (Aṅgirases) with manifested embodiments that look like animals coming out of a hundred doors. They perform ritual prayers (Arti) to invoke the eternal flame, Agni, which removes inner darkness and appears as icons (sages) that remove ignorance through awakening.

Traditionally, they present themselves as life, as flowers supported by moisture, and they become vibrant flames in fire-generating vibrations that fill the ether. They eliminate anger in purified minds and transform knowledge into intelligence, thus offering the power to attain moral and righteous judgment. All creation represents a family of noble souls (Saptarishis), which in their invisible forms (Vimada) bestow food, wealth, and sacrifice by performing audacious dances.

With such powers, the noble souls open the prisoned waters and seize the trapped treasure. To accomplish this, Indra slays the mighty dragon (Vṛtra). The elevated heavenly power (Surya) sees Indra and, with its might, blows away the monster's enchanting powers that prevail in the esoteric region. The noble souls with heroes' hearts rule the kingdom (Pipru), where they break down the forts of the evil powers. Even the evil leader (Dasyus), who believed in ruling with evil power, is smitten by Indra's power. Once they are smitten, Indra, as the leader, appears with the magical and wily Śuṣṇa to kill other both evil powers, Kutsa and Śambara.

Those evil powers that survive become converted worshippers (Atithigvait) of Indra. Even in the mighty chain of mountains (Arbuda), they walk (Rig Veda, Book 1, Hymn LII) through old waste material and strike the dead, evil power before it is born. With a hero's heart, they gather with their bounteous spirits to enjoy the mythical juice knowing the thunderbolt lies in their hands, which they can use to shred their foes.

With their strength and the distinguished punisher of the lawless (Āryas), they dare the ruler of the evil power, and they all join on strewn grass. They serve and sacrifice with strength, encouraging others to perform deeds with delight at festivals. Distinguished as the punishers of lawlessness, they become embodied, virtuous, and devout souls who help those who lack strength. Sages gather the glorified but devastated souls and invite them to come and help like the great one (Uśanā), who would reach heaven. With their mighty powers, they split its mighty greatness from mighty strength, and as separated power, they cover the heavenly and earthly regions.

As heroes with steeds all carried away with fame, they race through the air filled with vibrations and movement (Vāta). As heroes, they rejoice as singers (Kāvya) or as people with mighty powers (Uśanā). On their steeds, they cover more territory and destroy any evil forts.

By drinking the mystical juice, they receive mystic powers in the mighty fray (Śāryāta) and bring strong delight to embodied souls. This pleases Indra and the heroes, who rise in the sky. The ancient, all-skilled, mythical juice presser (Kakṣīvān) brings a wise child (Vṛcayā) to his mother (Vrsanśva), who sings hymns and tells of his deeds and discusses higher knowledge (Mena) while feasting.

Indra provides a firm doorpost and defines it as the place of sanctuary, where noble souls need to serve the divine will. The sanctified power among the worshippers pleases the supreme ruler (Ram), who, with its sanctified power, praises the self-resplendent, shining Pajras. The mighty one serves as the divine keeper. Ram comes out from the heavenly light that brings hundreds of noble souls forth with hymns to seek Indra on a carriage pulled by a strong steed to come to their aid. Firm as a mountain, Ram sustains them with divine power as the evil slayer enjoys the mythical juice. They flow by slaying the clouds at all times, remaining hidden in the clouds that support the divine will. They spread like light and appear with strength and wisdom. Ram can rapture them at any time, and with the divine will, they fill embodiments with noble thoughts.

They serve as the most liberal givers Ram serves with the heavenly juice on the sacred grass. All nobly natured, they fill a large area with the divine power they use to smite evil powers. The glorified, supreme ruler in wild joy stands and, with invincible power, joins them while staying in the rain. It helps them speed up swift streams running down a slope filled with libations and armed with thunder with vats filled with the mythical juice. They appear with the divine powers, ready to cleave the evil fences (Vala). In the mid-air region, they serve as rain obstructers. Any time they cast down divine powers like thunder, they become hard to restrain. With hymns, they magnify their divine power and reach the fast-flowing streams to fill the lake.

Using the creative powers (Tvaṣṭar), they support all such activities and give more force to those already filled with appropriate strength so they can forge thunderbolts and overpower any might. They battle evil power to free the waters so they can serve living things. Their praises reach heaven. The cosmic host (Maruts) helps those noble souls who fight faithful wars.

The heavenly dragon roars at the terror brought by Indra's thunderbolt. With the wild joy of mythical juice, they strike the mighty head of the evil tyrant and serve the region below the celestial region between earth and heaven. On the earthly region, Indra, with its powers extending forth tenfold, allows embodied souls to dwell and conquer through the famed might of godhead (Indra) messenger (Maghavan), who is ready to refine with vast, heavenly, majestic power. Bold at heart and with their might, they go beyond the limits of the heavenly region and serve in the mid-air, esoteric, and terrestrial regions. They embrace the flood on the ground and the sky as their counterpart. With the mighty heroes, they fill the great region with absolute truth. There is none other like them. Being bound with the waters, they sing praises as they encounter in mid-air the cosmic host (Maruts) regulated by divine powers, including various deities.

The givers of food to living beings (Rig Veda, Book 1, Hymn liii) were deities that guarded cosmic embodied souls (Manus). They served embodied immortal spirits that never disappointed friends or any other embodied souls. They were never asked to share, sing songs of praise, acquire wisdom, or seek riches. They did not perform any mighty deeds, and they were never asked to spread eternal wisdom, comprehend the divine will, or share such treasure.

Once they gather to establish themselves as the conquerors who brought success and hope in the highest eternal wisdom and absolute truth, they sing songs. All were well pleased to bring mythical juice along with eternal flames that took away any deficiency through the awakening of spirits in the embodiments. They were scattered like embryos or seeds, and they mixed eternal wisdom with the mythical fluid provided by the ruler, and they, as living, mortal embodiments, gave up hate and supported a union of auspicious embodiments (Vivasavn). They are further provided with all plenteous wealth, food, and strength along with an eternal flame so they can attain inner glory. Auspicious embodiments even built providence for female powers (Mātariśvan) to serve as goddesses who produce milk.

The strength-inspiring libations provided by the mythical juice make them glad heroes with the desire to fight and win the war against evil. The heroes slew ten thousand evil powers and went on from fight to fight, destroying castles after castles. Indra became their friend and made their foes bow to them; noble souls cannot be slain by even guileful demons (Namuci) or be struck down with death by the tree-like Karañja or by any malicious force (Parṇaya).

They allow very glorious powers (Atithigva) to go forth and destroy hundreds of forts (Vangrida). With their chariots and Indra, they overthrew the forty embodied kings along with 60,990 followers. They fight to protect the successor (Suśravas) and Tūrvayāṇa, all aided by Indra. The successor finds young, mighty kings (Kutsa, Atithigva, and Āyu) to protect the godly powers and forever be prosperous friends. They extol their long, joyful lives, enjoying through favour stored along with heroes.

With a fierce shout (Rig Veda, Book 1, Hymn LIV), the messengers (Maghavan) comprehend the power, strength, and the limits of auspicious embodiments (Vivasavns) that none could have, and they urge them not to experience such distressful challenges. The messengers (Maghavan), with a roar, shake up the woods and rivers and make embodied living beings run in fear. Messengers with the powers and might of Indra sing hymns of praise and invite Indra to come with divine powers and appear as daring, heavenly bulls and, with exceeding strength, serve as the master of the cosmic supreme powers of causation (Sakra) as heavenly bodies that prevail in the esoteric region. They deliver heavenly judgment on evil powers and sing to the sky father (Dyaus), which has a bold strength. By being bestowed by Sakra, they can resolve with a song any unyielding mind.

With independent sway, high glory, and strength, they draw on two bay steeds, a bull—the sun—and a carriage—the moon. They ride with daring power that is generated in the lofty heaven and smote the evil powers and with the mythical juice fight all evil enchanters. With a roaring sound that fills the woods, they put down the evil powers (Śuṣna) and keep them confined.

With the help of Indra and the ruling noble powers (Śatakratu), including its supporters (Narya, Turvaśa, Yadu, and Vayya's son Turvīti), they settle the final battle among the ruling powers. With Śatakratu pulling carriages that break down the nine and ninety barriers and with the heroic lord king of the mighty folk (Śatakratu), they offer free oblations that promote the eternal laws. They give bounteous gifts all welcome as the hymns of praise with heavenly waters coming down to create abundant streams. They bring to the chief matchless wisdom and mythical drink to perform noble activities and increase the lordly power. These abundant powers, the noble solar powers, hold the astral bodies in one hand and the mythical fluid in the other. They use both to develop fixed minds and satisfy their longing. They keep the vault in darkness until it is ready to flow out of the hollow, where it is concealed from evil powers (Vṛtras).

Indra hides in clouds and smites those who obstruct the free flow of water coming down. With bliss, Indra gives increasing glory and conquers embodied souls, which can persevere like wealthy patrons and serve as princes who support noble offspring. The greatness of Indra spreads through a wide space neither heaven nor earth could match. Awful and mighty Indra appears with the thunderbolt in the form of a bull with the ability to absorb unlimited rivers or make them expand. Like a bull, it drinks the mythical juice and makes rivers enforce divine will that makes warriors come like ancient powers and be praised for their might.

Indra can sway in all kinds of great, manifested, embodied souls (Rig Veda, Book 1, Hymn LV); it could come down with fame from the mountain. Foremost among the godly powers is the heroic might it sets in the forefront to perform each gruelling deed as the strong one that shows forth fair in the woods and is praised by its worshippers as so friendly that even in its auspicious form through their voices, it sends forth seeking the desired messenger (Maghavan). Yet such warriors stir up battles among the great embodied souls they hurl down as the resplendent one to bring faith with a bolt that can bring death or glory and pleasure. Through Indra, it increases strength on the ground they use to destroy the darkness by bringing the light of heaven.

They even go among the dwellings and shine forth wisdom to worshippers along with the mythical drink from floods. They let their hearts incline toward the bay and, with praise to Indra, serve as skilled charioteers who draw back their reins and hold back the rapid sunbeams coming through the sky, and it never leaves them astray. As famed messengers, they never fail to bear treasure and unvanquished might. They abide by their powers surrounded by ministering priests.

Messengers with embodiments' full libations rise like a horse ready to meet the mare (Rig Veda, Book 1, Hymn LVI). While staying in their golden car yoked with bay horses, they move swiftly, drinking the mythical juice and performing great deeds. They provide guidance and songs of praise, which allows them to flow like those in flood seeking company. Like an ecclesiastical governing body, they attain might as they go up a hill from where they ascend with speed coming from their loved ones. They shine in battle like snow-covered mountains. Made of iron, such messengers are fierce and strong and shatter the bonds of the evil and wily Śuṣṇa.

With the strength they receive from Indra, they become stronger and support worshippers who attend to dawn and await the sun. With unflinching might, they stir up dust storms and achieve success. They fix firmly in the esoteric region. Indra, with rapturous joy, and they smite the evil power blocking water and bringing floods. They hold up the heaven and settle on the ground. From their enchanted base, they supply the mythical juice and free the waters from the stony fences of evil.

Indra-Agni, through their avatars, appear like their desired offspring created as females (Saramā) to bear children male and female and thus serve as godly mothers who create the godly father (Rig Veda, Book 1, Hymn lxii). Both males and females serve as perishable bodies (B1rhaspati) that serve as the council to the union (Indra-Agni) in many manifested forms.

They wander in the mountain clefts looking for mortal embodiments that are hiding from evil powers. The perishable embodiments as heroes find mortal embodiments and shout and roar. The perishable bodies, along with the seven singers, represent the major constellation (Navagvas) with nine stars. In advanced demigod form, they appear to represent the support of the heavenly godheads. They charge the mountain with the support of other imperishable godly powers that, as the trinity (Daśagvas, Indra, and Śakra), bring thunder to charge evil powers in the cosmic region.

They admire the perishable embodied souls (B1rhaspati) that bring dawn to dispel the darkness using the sun's rays. Spreading out morning light on high ridges, the sun's rays are fixed in the regions they are placed right below the highest heavenly powers (Surya, Rudra, Sarasvati, Soma,

and Samsara). They manifest as the fairest marvels that perform worthy deeds and accept the five great elements of nature, which form rivers and oceans. With part of the old, ancient pair (Saramā), unwearied, winning, with lauding hymns and united, they become a life force (Bhaga), the father among both marvels floating around as planetary bodies between the earthly and heavenly regions.

Fresh born as young females and males, they travel as in ancient times around heaven and earth. With their dark limbs at night and illuminated limbs during the day, they maintain a perfect friendship. They appear fresh in colour and produce fresh milk. They always travel on old, connected paths where they can rest and preserve the immortal statutes. As sisters, they perform holy works and wait on the proud lord serving as wives and matrons. With ancient thoughts, they seek wealth, and with adoration and new lauds, they speed like the mighty powers of Indra and Agni.

Yearning as wives, they cleave to their husbands and sing hymns to the most potent lord along with the strong gods of riches. With the splendid art of the heavenly Indra, they serve the lord of mighty power. They appear as the mighty family (Gotama), which performs Dharma by offering prayers. They become immortal powers that possess the universal soul and serve as leaders yoked to the tawny coursers as immortal spirits enriched with prayer.

Holy Ones

With the aid of godlike power (Rig Veda, Book 1, Hymn lxiii), the divine will implore mortal embodiments to serve as Indra does and battle evil powers. Even Indra appears among the famous solar race as a mortal body that comes with thunderbolts to destroy castles and free the seven mortal tribes, which were servants (Sudās). These tribes live on grass like animals and render service to the noble tribe (Bharatas) serving the king of Pūru. They gain material wealth and move around like blessed souls. Indra makes sure all the divine creations, such as the Sudās, get food and water. These mortal embodiments pray to the shining bay horses— the sun, moon, and stars—in the cosmic region filled with spiritual energy and manifesting as mortal noble souls (Gotamas).

The noble souls (Gotamas), as mortal embodiments, are blessed with eternal wisdom and as manifested living kings (Purukutsa) gifted by the heavenly powers (Rudras). According to Rig Veda, Book 1, Hymn LXIV, they, as the young, divine power manifested as demigods, serve like the cosmic host (Maruts) with minds filled with wisdom. Their skilful hands perform rites offered with holy water and from that spring forth from the terrestrial host (Nodhas), which appears as the heavenly bull along with earthly cows. The heavenly divinity (Rudras), as the creator of the divine will (Devavan), removes all stains to appear on the ground serving as the terrestrial host. With divine riches and inner illumination, they serve as enlightened souls (Gotamas) that understand the heavenly power (Rudras), which serves as the ultimate source of purification. They bring shining ultraviolet rays of light that hide behind clouds. These rays scatter like raindrops to kill evil slayers. Therefore, the demon power never grows old when the heavenly divinity (Rudras) continuously uses its mighty powers to polish the shine covering the rugged mountains.

They keep the demon power from becoming the strongest power and create quivering between earth and heaven. Like the cosmic host (Maruts), the heavenly divinity (Rudras), as young demigods, show their breasts covered by beautiful gold chains and their shoulders covered with spears that can pound to pieces any evil power (Rakshas). Knowing well they were born as young demigods, they come to serve celestial hosts (Aswins), the cosmic host (Maruts), and terrestrial hosts (Nodhas). They all come ready as a heavenly body to serve mortal embodiments. They gain strength by joining with the wind (Vayu) and spreading their powers like restless shakers, which drain the udders of the sky by sending water mixed with mythical juice (Soma).

The cosmic host, along with the young terrestrial hosts, drinks the juice in solemn rites. They bring forth the mythical juice with thundering rain and turn steeds into strong horses. They spring like flying stallions and acquire mighty, wondrous power that is marvellously bright and strong. They glide among bright-red and other eternal flames, and they assume physical strength and mental power. They appear like wild elephants that eat up forests and come as mighty roaring lions, and they even appear as spotted deer. They serve as the matured cosmic host (Maruts) and young terrestrial hosts (Nodhas), and they stir up eternal wisdom to bring high knowledge to the holy priests, who bring the mighty coiled power of the immortal spirit (Atma) running like the serpents' wrath.

Young terrestrial hosts (Nodhas) accompanied by serpents' fury, mighty, immortal spirits march supported by the physical strength of heroes. They are greeted by the cosmic host (Maruts), which serves as the protector of nature (Prakriti), standing with light, so the young terrestrial hosts (Nodhas) become visible like a lighthouse before they arrive to serve the earthly and heavenly regions. Seated on their chariots like lords of all riches, the terrestrial hosts (Nodhas) with their homes of wealth as their dwellings are endowed with vigour before they come with loud voices.

Appearing as heroes with infinite armed power, they increase their powers as they drive forth with rain from clouds. With prayer and worship, they make manifested mortal embodiments become active and join the terrestrial host (Nodhas), who has served the manifested world (Prithvi). They, like the strong band of the cosmic host (Maruts), smite evil with an impulsive force.

Terrestrial hosts (Nodhas) with steeds gain treasure and prosper. In battle, like the cosmic host (Maruts), they support the worshipper's glorious strength, and with their invincible, brilliant power, they bring wealth and make them praiseworthy. They as the terrestrial host increase with prayer as the hosts of the terrestrial region.

Serving as hosts (Rig Veda, Book 1, Hymn lxv) of the terrestrial region, the holy ones serve as avatars (Gotamas) representing heavenly power (Vishnu). They support the mortal tribes of the seven noble souls (Septarishis), while the youngest terrestrial host (Nodhas) investigates dark caves for living spirits hiding from evil powers. With godly worship and power, they claim them and have them serve as holy ones. With a holy law, they protect them among other growing, newborn, noble souls. All filled with grateful food in a wholesome stream, they urge the steed to run swiftly in rushing holy rivers. They eat vegetation and bring riches in the flood. They pass through the forest as urged by the winds and spread new growth of grass on earth. They breathe through their wisest minds, and during the midmorning, they wake like holy sages. They drink the mythical juice, spring forth from the eternal laws, and become young, shining, mighty, manifested, mortal, living beings appearing like the ancestral Manus.

With the sun's glance (Rig Veda, Book 1, Hymn lxvi), as the new holy ones, they breathe life with a wealth of varied sorts. Like ancestral sons, they arrive like domesticated birds or milk-bearing animals walking to yield their treasure. They safely travel in the terrestrial region. Seeing a pleasant home, they fill it with ripened corn to feed the conqueror. With lauding, they vouchsafe their uncontrolled, eternal flames and make their dwellings shine forth like the prophets' dwellings. They fight evil forces, and like the ancestral cosmic embodiment (Manus), they serve as the master of the present and the future. They lead them to a path to attain the kindled godly powers by appearing in the evening like cows going home at night. They expand their eternal flames and rise to reach fair places in heaven, serving as rays coming to guide mortal embodiments.

With eternal flame, they find friends among mortal embodiments (Rig Veda, Book 1, Hymn lxvii). They bring gracious blessings like priests and inner peace to create stable and engrossed mental powers. As bearers, they generate thoughts filled with noble charisma. It brings all-mighty powers into the hands of mortal embodiments that have been squatting in a void and could not be reached because of the fear of facing evil godly powers.

The embodiments, through prayers within their hearts, unveil the friendly godly powers that, like the unborn, know all about who holds up the broad earth and who, with effective utterances, fixes the sky above. Through the eternal powers of Agni, they guard every spot and serve like milk-bearing animals with love. They regulate the life force and can go from one embodiment to another.

Once they unveil absolute truth, they understand all about the imperishable astral bodies in physical embodiments. They appreciate the holy law that releases the immortal astral body from its perishable embodiment by offering rites as ancient truth exposed by the great hidden wealth.

Those who commingle or do not comprehend the holy law remain restless and ascend to the sky (Rig Veda, Book 1, Hymn LXVII) without unveiling the truth or living in the darkness and not knowing the truth, regardless of whether they stand or move. They do not know the foremost greatness of godly powers that appear among all others in multiple godly forms. To all manifestations and embodiments, they bring joy through the divine will; when it moves in, it turns dry wood into a living tree. When it moves out, it turns the same tree into dry wood.

With the divine will, it is born again to support the perishable power. All created forms truly share the same godhead, which is imperishable. They represent the strength of the law; they request that all works be performed by the law and that all are quickened by the law. Those who bring oblations to the eternal laws vouchsafe are all seated next to the earthly priest so they can understand Manus's posterity and enjoy all treasures, which represent the lord. The lives of those who yearn for children are prolonged. They eagerly hear the divine word that fulfils their wish as sons obey their fathers' commands. All fathers and offspring are blessed with food, wealth, and unbarred doors.

The lovers of the morning light follow with heavenly light, which brings along their progeny to be born again (Rig Veda, Book 1, Hymn LXIX). With might that encompasses everything about their fathers' gods, their sons, Agni, serve as their sages. With their humble souls, no one can separate the sweet taste of food from the source of the food or the cow's udder from the milk. These creations all give bliss to other creations while they sit graciously in the mid-region to be born again in the dwelling of a lovely son, all pleased like strong steeds that bear folk.

Whenever heroes call on Agni, godlike power comes through the holy law, and none can break it. They gain full support, and they are granted an audience they serve as chieftains. They boast with peers, join the heroes, and drive disgrace away. Like the morning twilight, the love spreads like light. They unbar the doors and ascend to heaven. The manifested individual embodiments attain virtuous natures, which in spiritual terms is defined as devoutness. In a religious context, it means a recognition of spirit in relation to the universal soul, and through subsequent submissions, it attains liberation that allows spirits to merge with the universal soul in the form of abstemiousness in which neither has pride or self-deprecation.

With its pious nature and with prayers, the heroes as sages with their embodiments win food and support. The embodiments are guided through their pious nature regardless of race. This pious nature (Rig Veda, Book 1, Hymn LXX) allows spirits to prevail within as embryos of all things. Such a pious nature prevails even in rocks, and it resides in individual dwelling places.

The power of Agni through the eternal flame cares for all mortal embodiments and helps them attain the lord's riches to serve mortal embodiments, which are readily invoked through sacred songs. Protecting the mortal embodiments carefully, it processes thoughts and guides each to continue to serve immortal godly powers, regardless of race, as mortal, manifested, noble souls. Mortal embodiments even serve unlike through morning light during the evening light, and it helps those who are born in the eternal laws and makes them all strong. They regulate those who serve as heralds and those who use their inner illumination to perform the holy work in the eternal laws effectually.

The virtuous nature even sets intrinsic values for each embodiment belonging to the kingdom of rocks, flora, and fauna. The virtuous nature serves godly powers, which among noble souls and in many other forms serves in sundry spots. The virtuous nature even helps part the aged father's eternal wealth like a brave archer; they divide like one skilled in the art and fierce avengers loving the loved ones. They even help the cow low in the morning, and after darkness, they see red beams that, with praise, burst from the sires and set their firm fortress.

They are welcome by the ancient immortal powers of Agni, which sends the envoy (Aṅgirases) with imperishable powers coming home to welcome the roaring mountains. The messengers (Rig Veda, Book 1, Hymn LXXI) establish different races to become most active in offering sweet food. Each race strengthens with the immortal godly powers serving as the universal soul and supporting individual spirits. As the messengers, they establish residences to stir up manifested bodies among different races. Sitting in every house, they create a bright and noble force (Bhṛgu) that has established companionship and serves as a greater sovereign. They pour the juice to serve the father in heaven, who freed the noble powers from entanglements with the manifested material world.

They pitch as splendour the godly powers to serve as their offspring and invoke the eternal flame in individual dwellings. They bring along as a companion for worship the loveliest daily eternal love (Mitra), which further increases their mighty power. This makes their existence manifest as mortal embodiments that see the divine treasures. This brings to the mortal embodiments sacrificial viands accompanied by the eternal fire from heaven.

This descends with limpid moisture that increases the quest among creations to fill the embodied, immortal individual spirits supported by the universal soul. With eternal flame, it brings the inner life force (Prana) that fills with inner light and provides support to the youthful blameless hosts, the mortal embodiments. With noble thoughts, they journey towards the lord of riches (Surya).

The union of heavenly rulers (Varuṇa-Mitra) with the fair twin demigods (Aśvins) protects the glands of the mortal embodiments responsible for producing the precious nectar (Amrita) just as the mythical juice (Soma) is produced from udders. The imperishable power never breaks the ancestral link they endow the sages with; it brings deep knowledge buried in clouds. The eternal wisdom protects the embodiments from evil powers.

By the many gifts brought by the humble higher powers, each embodiment is transformed to serve as the wise ordained embodiment (Rig Veda, Book 1, Hymn LXXII). The heavenly Agni, as the lord of treasures, forever grants the immortal bounties to those embodiments, who, after not finding the creator, become devotees and follow others' tracks where they think the ultimate power prevails until they seek the highest heavenly home.

Heavenly Agni is worshipped by the holy names with holy oil. Dignified by being born noble, they are revealed through the heavenly powers (Rudras), so, as devotees, they are known as the holy ones. They prevail between earth and heaven and are transformed by the heavenly Agni to go a distance with judicious standing and serve in the loftiest station as part of the mortal band. As one-minded, mortal embodiments, they approach with their spouses and offer worship. As holy living beings, they discover heavenly Agni, all-encompassing within the thrice-seven mystic things.

Agni comes to serve the individual devotees by providing powers to produce nectar (Amrita), which preserves the individual life to serve as a guard. Among all other kingdoms of plants and animals, the one-minded mortal embodiments know all about nature and their activities, like the immortal Agni, which keeps sending food for their existence. Those who are skilled and know the paths to the divine will serve as envoys who are never exhausted. Serving as bearers of the law and eternal wisdom, they pass through the seven heavenly rivers and comprehend the path of truth (Saramā).

Through such abilities, they can differentiate all forms of riches with their firm and imperishable embodiments. They serve and support all that is created, including mortal embodiments. As learned scholars, like messengers (Aṅgirases), they approach all noble operations that lead to immortal life and support the spacious place of the godly mother (Aditi). The heavenly power appears like a gift of beauteous glory; thus, they can stand with the immortal gods. They even flow like rivers set in motion by the immortal Agni coming down and representing red steeds.

The red steeds bring patrimonial riches, including food and instruction for the wise man (Rig Veda, Book 1, Hymn LXXIII). All loving mortal embodiments prosper as guests serving as priests though serving as servants. They rightly guide mortal embodiments with true-minded godly power (Savitar), which protects them with vigour. The truth becomes glorified and appears to many as a splendid gift of breath, which gives joy and helps others win grace from the godly power (Savitar).

With sacrifice, they set forth the worshippers to move where the people gather and preserve their households, singing a hymn to a hymn (Rig Veda, Book 1, Hymn LXXIV). These hymns can be heard from afar, where the eternal flame survives among those killed by an evil power and those who, in every fight, win wealth. The envoys of Agni, through its messengers (Angiras), bring gifts of love to strengthen with sacrifice those born to serve as imminent ones, the sons of strength who bring happiness to all. While sitting on sacred grass and offering blessings to the godly powers, they bring with praise a gift offered by the fair-shining embassy. It is heard as the uninjured go forth on steeds. Fair-shining Agni, as the offeror, steps forward with splendid strength to bring heroic godly powers which offer gifts.

Accepting hymns, the godly powers bring delightful food poured as offerings in the mouth of the wisest messenger (Mātariśvan) representing Indra (Rig Veda, Book 1, Hymn LXXV). They come to support the best dependable messengers of Aṅgiras representing Agni. They come with precious prayer and serve as the kin that becomes the king and appears as mortal embodiments supported by the divine will.

The mighty godly friends (Mitra-Varuṇa) sacrifice to the heavenly Agni, which establishes the eternal flame among individuals. Their hymns please the mortal embodiments and receive the greatest blessings (Rig Veda, Book 1, Hymn LXXVI). They gain powers over those who had offered sacrifices with their mental powers; they even bring oblations to sit down and welcome the heavenly priest (Hotar), the leader who has never been deceived while serving with love and worship. They win favour from the godly powers serving heaven and earth. They offer sacrifices to ward off curses and burn the evil powers (Rākṣasas). They bring sunlight and moonlight and the mythical juice. They gladly help the godly powers become bounteous givers while appearing like the ancestral cosmic body (Manus). They invoke their children and have them be granted godly powers. They perform their task of being cleansers and presenters; they awaken living beings and bestow their material wealth on them.

CHAPTER 2
LEGENDARY DOMINION

With priestly oblations, they force cosmic embodiments (Manus), which worship the godly powers, thereby transforming cosmic embodiments to serve as the truthful invokers and as priests who bring the joy-bestowing ladle. The relationship between the eternal mind and the external world gives birth to consciousness. It frequently implies the relationship between the physical mind and nature, which generates thought to comprehend the fundamental aspects of the physical world and its surroundings. Such consciousness is simple and predominantly possessed by mortal embodiments, even animals.

After acquiring consciousness, the mortal embodiments have a great difficulty comprehending how the heavenly, legendary powers regulate the universe. Once they acquire subliminal powers, which exist and operate below the threshold of consciousness, they employ insufficiently intense stimuli that produce a discrete sensation, often intense, and enough to influence individual mental processes and behaviour. They come to understand individual thought processes that regulate ancient, imperishable powers provided by Agni through its messengers (Aṅgirases). They provide knowledge to mortal embodiments in alternate ways so they can know about the godly powers prevailing in the heavenly region. They set the morning beams from the sun as the beginning of the day. Before parting, they perform fruitful service as part of the longing for eternal faith.

On the ground, they build places where they dwell around messengers as kings surrounded by faithful friends following the godly power. Like heroes, they sit in positions of safety and appear blameless near their godsent enkindle.

Agni brings others to enkindle other dwellings with riches. The worshippers gain food and long life, which through the divine richness of the goddess (Savitar) brings oblations even in battle to free them from foes. They even take the treasure from their foes to be given to the divine power of the gods. They share such glory with Varuna, who regulates the heavenly law and offers favour from a distance. Rocks flow all night into the river and fill it by dawn with different colours. With mortal worship, such rocks come from the mid-air region and follow like shadows spreading over the whole world. Agni helps conquer steeds with steeds, men with men, and heroes with heroes. The lords of wealth transmit to fathers and princes a hundred winters filled with hymns of praise.

As the ordained, they serve with pleasant hearts and spirits and use the mighty power to hold the steeds of riches with godsent gifts of glory.

They attain the next higher level, self-consciousness, where humans are made aware of their surroundings that create the desire to acquire material things. The next level is cosmic consciousness, where through awareness, manifested bodies come to comprehend individual lives and their order of powers in the universe. This all started from the first cosmic being (Manus), which emerged with a pious nature and served as the holy soul (Āryan). With such enhancements come sacrifices that need to be made by embodied souls with prodigies of perishable heroes who destroy foes. With hymns and devotion, they serve as liberal lords. They stir up their thought processes with vigour to create an urge to control their resources and serve in a way true to the order. Serving as imperishable godly powers (Jatavedas), they come with eternal fire and become heavenly priests who serve with enlightened noble souls (Gotamas).

Progressive

According to Rig Veda, Book 1, Hymn LXXVII, victorious in the wood Agni, among mortal embodiments, persist in claiming obedience to the serving king. They are gracious and peaceful; they have mental power and sacrifice like priests. They are full of thought like enlightened noble souls (Gotamas), bearing in their hands the all-mighty creations crouched in the cavern; mighty creations struck godly power with fear.

Creations filled with understanding find the mighty powers when they sing prayers all formed in their hearts, coming as if from the unborn. They hold the broad earth up, and with the effective utterance, they fix up with the sky to reach the powers of Agni guarding the spots which loving cattle as the divine life come out from one hideout to another. Who has known dwelling approached with the stream of holy law they release with the praying sacred rites and who truly at that point announce great wealth? He who grows mightily in herbs within each fruitful mother and each babe she bears, wise, the life of all men, in the waters' home, for him, have sages built as it was a seat.

With lauded augmentation (Rig Veda, Book 1, Hymn LXXVIII), they bring magnificence with vigour to gather power that increases their influence. They, as keen and swift with priestly power (Gotamas), sing the sacred songs like imperishable godly powers (Jatavedas). They exalt their glory with a desire for eternal wealth, and they worship with songs like the best manifested avatars (Aṅgiras), who call on the winners of the spoils.

For the sake of glory, they, as evil slayers and, just for the sake of glory, shake off the father of the sky (Dasyu). They expand in the mid-air region (Rig Veda, Book 1, Hymn LXXIX) by setting golden tresses with rushing thunderstorms. They appear as raging serpents that bring the morning light to serve the honourable dames. They bring strong workers with well-winged sparkles; they appear like black bulls that create the mythical juice to bless and bring water that falls with a smile, and they make clouds put out with thunder.

They make animals produce milk, and as part of their worship, they follow the direct paths of order. They come with the godly trinity (Aryaman, Mitra, and Varuṇa), which fill the hides of milk-bearing animals serving the hindmost hips (Parijman) from where milk transforms into the mythical juice. At night, they generate power that can kill the evil powers (Rāk5asas) with sharp teeth.

Adorable in all rites, Agni brings eternal flames to aid until worshippers sing hymns to bring wealth. The eternal flame graces the eternal wealth and grants long lives to all noble souls who desire to serve as Gotamas. With songs composed with care, they are pointed like the eternal flame that manifests in mortal embodiments so they may not fear and may prosper while the keen and swift eternal flame with a thousand eyes chases the evil powers (Rāk5asas).

Exalted, eternal, manifested bodies (Rig Veda, Book 1, Hymn LXXX) are represented as cosmic fragments that travel in joy after consuming the mythical juice. They come from the heavenly region representing the mightiest thunder, all being served by Indra. They appear along with windstorms (Rudra's) as absolute reality, the supreme existence (Brahman), which protects the newly manifested mortal embodiments from the prevailing evil powers. The warmonger as the eternal manifested bodies brings the mythical fluid that gladdens their strength. They come down with thunder to strike down evil powers and cosmic vapours to free the trapped water. They create floods before they come from the sky to bring the waters and smite the evil power prevailing as terrestrial bodies.

Indra allows life-fostering waters to flow, regulated by the cosmic host (Martu's). Indra, with its wrathful bolt of thunder, crushes the foe with fierce attacks and uses water to overpower the evil. Indra, while rejoicing in the juice, comes with its hundred-jointed thunderbolts that strike them on their backs and brings prosperity to its friends. With unconquered might, Indra brings a shower of meteors and thunderbolts to smite guileful beasts.

The heroes, all seated close by Indra, watch the cosmic shower, which covers the ninety flooding rivers with might and strength. With twenty hymns of praise, they produce vibrations that come in the form of prayers. Indra, with the heroes' powers, destroys evil with the floods that shake heaven and earth; that is experienced when Indra's wrath fills the regions with trembling terror. With its thunder, Indra comes with imperial sway that generates new forms of grit to strengthen the cosmic host (Maruts), and it provides strength to the celestial and cosmic regions.

The evil powers that are not scared attack Indra generating a roar that shakes the ground like thunder. Indra attacks first with thunderbolts and then by shooting meteors that, like a thousand darts, kill the evil powers. With their mighty force, they even hit the legendary dragon. Using heavenly might, Indra sets a firm base on the ground and appears with thunder that shakes the ground. It even brings the creative powers (Tva5tar), which in wrath create earthquakes that even shake the ancient sage (Atharvan), who serves with old rites to serve as the sire of the earliest cosmic bodies (Manus).

With prayers, they unite cosmic bodies (Manus) to remove all wrath so cosmic bodies can join Indra with joy and strength and slay all evil power (Rig Veda, Book 1, Hymn LXXX). With their might, they support those performing moral and righteous deeds. Like the heroes, they provide abundant spoils. When war and battles are afoot, they lay their booty before them, and they yoke the bays, where they wilt or become subject to being slain. Indra provides such warriors riches in the form of wisdom and power that they use to enhance their physical strength. Even the sun and moon join hands and provide inspirational power for glory's sake.

They grasp the true powers of the meteors, which with iron teeth, fill the atmosphere along with steely thunderbolts. All are pressed against the brilliant light coming from the heavenly power (Surya). They serve alongside the righteous and moral warriors, who offer sustaining food. Indra lends aid and abundant wealth to those with righteous hearts who thus attain ecstasy.

They gather herds from the animal kingdom and give them treasures of many kinds that they refine, and they bring out the hidden wealth among their offspring. The heroes, all refreshed and strengthened, drink the mythical juice pouring from the bounty and serve the lord of protection (Vishnu), who regulates wealth. Indra provides for all who are worthy and makes them share their gifts with others.

Indra manifests as an avatar as the messengers (Maghavans), who are made aware of their perishable nature, are full of joy; they are told that they can solicit the powers of the sun and moon (Rig Veda, Book 1, Hymn lxxxii). They are well-fed and serve as messengers as well as perishable friends who pass away to serve as stars. They are praised with hymns while the two bay steeds, the sun, and the moon keep yoking. With reverence, the messengers look fairly on all who praise the divine will. They ride in the richly laden carriage; the constellations yoked through the powers of the sun and moon serve the mid-air region and move toward absolute truth. As tawny coursers, they experience ecstasy through extracting the mythical juice. They yoke as messengers (Maghavans) with holy prayer and pour out the mythical juice to make themselves and others happy, serving with their spouses the solar deities (Pū5ans).

Well-guarded, mortal, manifested embodiments, solar deities (Pū5ans) and Indra provide aid in attaining prosperity through the animal kingdom, including horses and cattle. Filled with such ample wealth all around, they, as the heroes, observe heavenly waters covering the ground and filling the oceans. They look down and see how far the ground is spread. They notice as pious suitors; deities are conducting delight with the love of prayer. With praise, they see the pair of manifested bodies serving as man and wife serving with the ladle.

Manifested embodiments (Pū5ans) like the ancient messenger (Aṅgirases) win eternal flames that provide the vital power needed to perform good deeds, and they use fire to create unchecked light. The embodiments prosper with the eternal laws bringing blessings and sacrifices. The embodied universal soul in water represents individual living spirits with water as the physical wealth (Pani) supporting all kinds of animals.

With the help of the ancient messenger (Atharvan; (Rig Veda, Book 1, Hymn LXXXIII), they discover the path laid by the guardian of the law (Varuna), and the powers responsible for bringing out eternal love (Mitra) appear like a bright light as their sacrifice. This setting of the straightway path drives the spiritual powers, which under the grip of intelligent demons (Uśanā, Sukracaya, and Kāvya), bring with honour life to the deathless (Yama). They attain freedom and immortal power while sitting on sacred grass, ready to aid the auspicious work; they sing hymns of praise and produce sounds all coming from the sky. Indra creates rings around manifested bodies that produce a pleasing sound filled with true spiritual powers that provides delight.

With the mythical juice (Rig Veda, Book 1, Hymn LXXXVI), Indra, as the mighty force, asks manifested embodiments to join with the cosmic host (Maruts), all filled with vigour. The sun fills the sky shield with rays of spiritual power, covering all terrestrial bodies that come to overpower everything with noble spiritual power. This brings the pair of tawny coursers (Aśvins) serving with unresisted mighty spiritual powers manifested with their immoral souls and supported by songs of praise as spiritualists (Rsis). By making sacrifices, they slay evil powers, with the sun providing direct light and the moon providing the reflected light. Supported with prayer, they, as the twin demigods, yoke and enforce morality and righteousness, the elements of spiritual power.

They perform selfless deeds by sacrificing their lives (Dadhichi) and allow their bones to be used to assemble comets with weapons (Vajasra) that, with loud vibrations, defeat evil powers and come to reclaim the newly manifested planetary system formed all coming from the underworld a part of terrestrial bodies or part of the dark matter or dormant universe. They consider no sacrifice too great to defend the defenceless from the evil powers prevailing in the underworld.

Through asteroids and meteors, they generate a sound that draws attention along with the pouring of the mythical juice as a libation. The immortal Indra provides excellent strength to bring bright streams of light flowing from the seat of the holy law. With songs of glory, Indra brings the heavenly power to offer solemn eulogies accompanied by mythical juice to bring reverence and establish their supreme powers among steeds that no charioteer has ever surpassed. Indra bestows gifts on those who resist spiritual power being offered among mortal embodiments, which become the rulers.

As rulers, they learn to crush plants with cosmic bodies to free the mythical juice, which they mix with milk and drink to attain eternal wisdom. The rulers work closely with Indra, who rejoices in their dominance over their own. Animals drink the mythical juice to establish their supremacy among their own. With reverence, they pass the wisdom on and make sure all follow the divine laws to win pre-eminence among their own by slaying the nine and ninety evil powers.

They are all yoked to the pole of order and serve like strong-spirited steers. With unrelenting spiritual power, they bestow health and long life, and they offer rich prayers and services. The sons of the heavenly power (Rudras), as swift racers, continue to support the cosmic host (Maruts) by performing mighty deeds to support the growing mid-air region. They make delightful sacrifices to overpower evil power and rule the underworld and parts of terrestrial bodies.

Spiritual Power

Heavenly powers (Rudra's) sing songs of praise (Rig Veda, Book 1, Hymn LXXXVI). As their mighty power generates vibrations, they prevail like a heavenly abode with demigods (Maruts) bringing glory to those serving along with the cosmic host. They are placed on earth as the sons of mothers (Pṛśni) and appear like their offspring and serve as the holy spirit, which shines in bright attire and is decorated with gold ornaments like holy cows. They drive away their adversaries while following the traces of corporeal bodies as they flow down with glittering spears like warriors.

The cosmic host comes fully harnessed to their carriages being pulled by spotted deer. After a fray in the terrestrial region, Indra rushes with torrents of storm clouds to wet the large planetary body (Prithvi). They bring swift coursers whose arms are extended to come and sit on the grass made with delight from the cosmic host, who brings food and strength to serve their greatness so all can grow and help build ground capable of supporting big dwellings.

The heavenly protector (Viṣṇu), along with the mythical juice, brings delight to those sitting on the ground where the holy grass attracts birds. They welcome the heroes who fight to learn eternal truth. As combatants and protectors, they seek fame before the cosmic host, and every creature lives in fear. The cosmic host, a bounteous giver, serves in joy and brings the mythical juice to shape their glorious deeds. They come to drive in the clouds and make the fountain pour the water into serving the thirsty holy sages and help them with light to fulfil their longing. They provide shelter to bestow threefold offerings among them, the same boons as the cosmic host, and they share the wealth of noble offspring with the heroes.

Serving as the best of guardians, the holy sages with mortal embodiments establish their dwelling place near water and by drinking water provided by the cosmic host (Rig Veda, Book 1, Hymn LXXXVII). The giants of the sky surpass all while listening with honour; they worship in hymns by the sages. With their embodied souls, sages vouchsafe them and have them move into a rich stable where heroes are provided with mythical juice along with daily rites.

Sitting on the sacred grass, they sing and praise the cosmic host, and with godly love, the cosmic host offers their sacrifice. Fortunate are those mortal embodiments whom the cosmic host adores and has appeared as strong heroes. They sing praise to their hearts' desire. They make great things that strike demons like thunderbolts. They drive off devouring fiends and create light only if the loud singers remain as active and strong as hot-headed males. They display themselves as the best-beloved ones wearing glittering ornaments that shine like stars.

The cosmic host moves with clouds like birds shedding rain on the corporeal realm and supports those who sing with praise (Rig Veda, Book 1, Hymn LXXXVIII). On the ground, while racing, they tremble weak and worn, and on their way, they continue to yoke their bodies for victory. They are armed with glittering spears and are admired for their might. They appear like powerful spotted steeds; they are truthful and blameless. They search for the sinless terrestrial hosts who sing divine prayers.

Speaking as the primaeval sire, they descend and stir the mythical juice. Shouting, they join Indra in drudgery when they obtain sacrificial names. Venus, representing a solid planet of love placed as the second planet from the sun, serves the strong terrestrial hosts of the sixth planet from the sun, hothead Saturn, which fears nothing. While being celebrated and praised, they possess the cosmic power to establish their beloved home in the esoteric mid-air region served by the cosmic host (Maruts).

The various godly powers together (Visvedevas) are headed by heavenly Indra. There is no dichotomy between various godly powers separating them between the noble and the evil. They are all invoked by the union of heavenly powers (Mitra-Varuna) represented by godly powers where one set of the three serves one of the three regions. Each godly power, knowing both forms, transforms from good to evil and evil to good.

The most comprehensive gathering of united godly powers (Visvedevas) comes from every side with auspicious powers that can never be deceived or resisted; they remain victorious. The auspicious power is immortal, but it can manifest as a guardian to serve mortals, where the dichotomy of good and evil comes into play.

United godly powers descend on the bounty and serve day by day by providing care like righteous gods (Rig Veda, Book 1, Hymn LXXXIX). They serve those who devoutly seek to extend their lives and live beautifully. The auspicious powers of the patron (Bhaga) from the ancient times appear as the friendly godly powers (Dak5a, Mitra, Aditi, Aryaman, Varuṇa, Soma, Aśvin's, and Sarasvatī). By bringing the wind (Vayu), they grant contentment, which transforms the life force into pleasant breath. They bring medicine from the godly mother as the earth and the godly father as the heaven. They jointly provide showers to cosmic plants (Soma), which, when pressed, provide the mythical juice to support the twin flying horses (Aśvin's), who, as the demigods, hear the voices of the immortal living spirit desiring to connect with the universal soul.

Through manifested perishable embodiments (Bṛhaspati), they invoke the living spirits controlled in mortal embodiments that serve as the lord of those who move and those who stay still. The inspiring solar deity (Pū5an) increases wealth and promotes all by keeping such creations all guarded for good. The illustrious living spirits allow the mortal embodiment (Tārk5ya) to go far and wide, serving the manifested perishable embodiments (Bṛhaspati). They vouchsafe and bring prosperity to all others in the mid-region, where they are born as the cosmic host like sons of mothers (Pṛśni). They move in glory like spotted steeds, often providing holy rites to the eternal flame serving worshippers as sages who serve manifested perishable embodiments (Bṛhaspati). They produce brilliant vibrations when they sing as splendid holy ones.

The sages learn from the splendid holy ones to use their firm limbs and other body parts to attain extended life terms. Observing a hundred autumns, they fill the space gradually by bringing the mortal embodiments facing decay or death into the same space. During transitory life, as they become ready to break, they, through Aditi, transfer from covering the mid-air and come to arrive in the terrestrial regions. They serve as offspring's of the sire (Surya) and mother (Aditi); they come to serve all godly powers by five traits that in the past manifested with auspicious power to serve the universe again and again in the same manner. The mother (Aditi), in accord with the divine laws (Varuṇa), provides guidance to the new born and, with divine love (Mitra), serves as the noble power, all serving to attain absolute truth.

According to Rig Veda, Book 1, Hymn XC, they come to know about the creator and its creation and how the members of mortality become noble souls (Aryaman). They learn to live and deal with the cycles of life and death; never deluded, they use their power to guard the holy law. They build shelters to vouchsafe the immortal powers and provide residences for the immortal living spirit. As mortal bodies, they chase away evil forces. They even mark out the paths to bliss; they are honoured and adored by the heavenly powers (Indra, Maruts, Pū5an, and Bhaga). They are protected by the sustaining powers (Vi5nu) that run their course through such paths, all enriched with hymns and provide blessings from the animal kingdom that brings prosperity to noble souls (Aryaman).

The moving wind (Vayu) with sweet puffs of mythical fluid pours out mythical fluid that fills the Soma plants that support the divine laws and divine love. They make sure the mythical juice is filled with sweetness during the night and day, where the motherly (Aditi) power and the fatherly (Surya) powers come to support all new creations by filling the terrestrial atmosphere. Even grown trees learn to exchange mythical sweetness (Soma) coming from the heavenly father (Surya) with the mythical sweetness coming from earthly power in the mythical form coming as nectar (Amrita), which comes from the moon. As a trinity, Mitra, Varuṇa, and Aryaman graciously honour the imperishable and immortal Indra, which brings the perishable mortal might (Bṛhaspati) that serves all the offspring as their ruler specially established for terrestrial bodies.

These perishable embodiments bring preeminent wisdom that, along with the mythical juice nectar (Amrita), comes to set the straightest path (Rig Veda, Book 1, Hymn XCI). For the leading godly power, they provide guidance, as did their wise forefathers (Indus), who shared their treasures among other godly powers. With insight and wisdom, they bring the physical and spiritual energies as they are possessed by all divine power or the divine will. They grant and guide such greatness among the mortals. With eternal edicts, they bring mighty powers accompanied by creative art that allow them to acquire greatness and learn and teach such glorious arts to mortal embodiments.

As the king, the ruler of the eternal laws, through its lofty rulings, brings deep glory with pure, divine love to manifest among humanity's noble souls (Aryaman). Noble souls serve the manifested holy ground (Prithvi), which was created to serve as the material world (Viraj) in the esoteric region. The holy ground among the mountains allows mortal plants to grow by joining the moving waters.

Well pleased with all this, the noble souls accept the royal oblations that, as the mythical juice are offered by the heavenly father (Surya).

The noble souls (Aryaman) serving as heroes acquire nectar with auspicious powers (Amrita) such as creative minds along with the mythical juice being provided by the mother (Aditya). The plants serve as imperishable plants; they are born but do not die, and they serve as the praise-loving lord of the plants (Soma). Such living plants support the eternal laws and bring happiness and eternal love. They give old and young the energy to serve as godly heroes.

Through these plants, the king of mortal power acquires immortal energy to kill evil powers. With loving praise and the support of the eternal laws, the lord of the plants grants happiness and provides energy for all—the old and the young—and guards them all. Such plants as the king of plants protect vegetation from all threats. Through the mythical juice, they never let harm befall friends who provide delightful aid to worshippers, and they protect those who offer praise and sacrifice imminent wishes for prosperity. Noble souls prosper being well skilled in speech; they magnify their powers through drinking the mythical juice and singing sacred songs.

As enrichers, healers of disease, and wealth finders, the noble souls drink the mythical juice to bring happiness. As do milk-producing animals, they eat grass. Such mortal souls form friendships that bring delight, just as does connecting with the mighty support of noble souls who sing sacred songs to welcome all. Serving immortal spirits residing in mortal embodiments, they develop a divine partnership that delights all and especially mighty souls. They save them from slander and distress. With the consumption of mythical juice, they polish their rough edges.

The mythical juice even creates friendly rays of light that help the noble souls prosper. With juicy nutrients generated by the eternal powers, the universal soul subdues foes with immortality. They win the highest glories from heaven through the mythical juice and win glories from the earth through pouring oblations of the mythical milk, nectar (Amrita). The honour and worship become the wealth giver that helps the heroes and their troops by sparing the brave by bringing the mythical milk to them.

Those who worship by giving the mythical milk mixed with the mythical juice provide steeds and soldiers with the knowledge needed to perform domestic duties (Karma), and when they meet the council of the holy synod (Dharma), they serve with glory their ancestral fathers in heaven. With glory, the mortal souls pour oblations to honour and worship and serve as wealth givers to those who help the heroes. Serving as a holy synod, they fight and guard camps by providing light and water provided through singing hymns. All exceedingly famous, they serve victors and bring joy with herbs, milk, the mythical juice, and water to support the firmament expanding with light that dispels darkness.

The light of dawn (Rig Veda, Book 1, Hymn XCII) makes it easy to yoke animals. The light brings distinct awareness as they sing songs to their common path. By bringing refreshment to liberal devotees, all things worship as the animals pour the milk mixed with the mythical juice. They create light for all living things. The daughters of heaven attain their wondrous splendour as they pass over the darkness with their pleasant voices. They confer their strength to their offspring— cows and horses.

The light of dawn urges them to move onward. After they gain more wealth, they become renowned as the brave sons famed for using their horses, and they carry troops and slaves. The auspicious morning light spreads widely over the world and looks west, where every living creature is moving and seeking to understand as adorers seeking truth. As in ancient days, every living creature as a seeker is born again and again. Decking out the newly born with beauty and a spirit, it seems that the auspicious goddess wastes mortal lives. Dawn shines with all her splendour, bright blessed, and extending rays like a flood rolling its water.

Never transgressing the divine commandments, dawn is enriched by sunbeams and ample wealth. It can bestow wondrous gifts to support new-borns. Moving with a radiant, sweet sound, it brings a wealth of horses and cattle. Appearing with the goddess and enriched with holy rites, it yokes their embodiments that appear like blessed and felicitous steeds. Serving as twin horses, they pull their chariot filled with material wealth. With hymns, the twin horses bring the light from heaven to invoke illumination and the mythical juice and milk to bring godly powers that can provide health to the wonderworkers born to follow the divine path.

Agni and Soma join the twins (Aśvin's) to form a mighty pair that graciously hearkens noble souls (Rig Veda, Book 1, Hymn XCIII). Such members are honoured and worshipped with special hymns.

Their ability to increase kinship among mortal souls is supported by other noble kinds. They offer holy oil with their great strength to provide extended lives for themselves and their offspring.

The pair bargains for animal food to deal with their broods and to free the waters that hold hostages. To perish, they use a single source of light from heaven that sets up many operations that they jointly reproach to free the rivers that were bound in shackles. Just like Indra's messenger (Mātariśvan), the cosmic flying bird covers the mountains and brings forth from heaven the holy prayer they use to fly, and they come down, making room for their sacrifice.

Like the messenger, they prepare oblations the mighty powers accept, and they please the union (Agni-Soma). With good protection, they grant special favours to those who sacrifice everything to acquire health and riches. With honour, they pour oil on whoever offers their oblations with godly hearts, and they protect them from distress. With inner peace, they invoke the union and serve as companions who accept the eternal wealth Indra brings. Along with ample remuneration and oblations, they are offered powers well respected by their horses and cows. By providing such eternal strength, they provide better yields and become wealthy patrons who grant power to those who use holy rites to be successful.

Holy Ground

With worthy praise and the divine will (Rig Veda, Book 1, Hymn XCIV), the immortal power (Agni) brings the messenger (Jatavedas), which as a firebird, brings distinction through eulogies that only through the minds of mortal embodiments, who serve among an assembly filled with others, are good and caring. They make sure their friendship causes no harm to other mortal embodiments.

They sacrifice, prosper, and gain heroic might that never distresses anybody. They come with their noble powers to kindle with fulfilled opinions, and they are all seated among the godly powers. They eat godly food and transformed into noble souls (Āditya's) who never harm the powers of Agni. They even bring fuel to offer Agni to burn as offerings that remind them at each festival that they must fulfil their quest to prolong their lives. Agni, with its ministers, serves as a guardian of the folk and protects the quadrupeds and bipeds with shiny rays.

The mighty power appears as a herald with the morning light presenting as the chief invoker, who was born as the purifier knowing that all priestly work is meant to serve the high priest, the sage. Lovely in form and kindness, they shine as if they were close, but they see through the darkness of night as they hear sweet speech that makes everything prosper. Through speech and thoughts acting like their weapons, they smite evil and devour demons near and far. They treat their mortal embodiments like chariots, and they yoke two red and two ruddy steeds.

Supported by the power of the air (Vayu), they move from high pressure to low pressure, thus creating changes in temperature and generating roaring sounds like a heavenly bull that comes with the smoke-banner flame to attack forests; every bird-eating grass is terrified with the sparks that fly forth. They make it easy for air to pass through the embodiment as breath without disturbing the divine friendship with Agni or suffering any harm.

The wonderful union (Mitra-Varuṇa) soothes the wrath caused by the cosmic host (Maruts), which descend with grace allowing manifested embodiments' hearts to return and try again through godly powers as friends of nature (Vasus). They make the sacrifice to bring the wondrous nature back. They dwell on their own and provide protection and grace to kindle individual spirits.

The mythical juice is sent forth with benevolent power to help worshippers gain wealth. The lord of godly riches grants them freedom from every sin and, with perfect wholeness, provides them with strength so they can evolve and become the imperishable power so that through Agni, they become the imperishable universal soul.

The immortal, universal soul and the immortal individual spirits travel in succession; one is golden and the other one bears bright colours (Rig Veda, Book 1, Hymn XCV); they produce ten vigilant daughters of Surya who, with eternal flames, have infants each representing the heavenly, ferocious fire as Agni. Within mortal embodiments, they appear on the ground, in mid-air, and in heaven.

At their place of birth, each serves in splendour. On the ground, they establish order and govern the seasons. As infants, they are brought forth with godlike natures (Astavastu). They appear in the mother's womb as astral bodies sitting in water, and they blossom like embryos. Over time, they appear in the womb as living things. They grow and become visible, fair, and bright; all are lifted from the water.

In the heavenly region with auspicious powers and reverence, the immortal, universal souls manifest spiritually wise and filled with calm, gentle, and tender powers such as lowing cows and in physical forms like lions, and each seeks its own style. Those appearing in the heavenly region learn the right ways to offer oblations by serving as the mighty powers. They bring unguent to smooth rough spots. They stretch their mighty arms like the mother goddess (Savitar), which helps them with extend borders and strives to connect the heavenly and earthly regions.

They draw new embodiments from the heavenly mother and serve in noble splendour. They are provided milk with the mythical juice, which produces their true brilliance. They learn to embellish themselves like manifested noble souls, and they go into the depths of divine wisdom and encompass all the space around them. They learn to connect with godly powers and spread widely through interstellar space. They become resplendent, sanctified, mighty powers that learn how to preserve their imperishable universal souls.

The mighty powers see mortal living things turning below on the ground, hidden in dry spots. They cut channels and send torrents of water. The universal soul moves in the region, creating food and grass. They are provided with the eternal flame that creates glory to bring out the auspicious powers that, with prayer, bring the eternal laws. They are granted the power to bring out the first trinity of godly powers representing the mother with love and serving as the trinity (Aditi, Mitra, and Sindhu), and they encompass all the esoteric regions.

They allow engendered bodies to be captivated by wisdom so they can learn to worship and become friendly with Agni (Rig Veda, Book 1, Hymn XCVI). Through the ancient process of breathing (Āyu), they acquire wisdom with the sun's and the moon's light. Passing along cosmic vapours, they provide the holy ground (Prithvi) with water and thus create the material world (Viraj).

In the holy ground, they establish progeny along with godly wealth bestowed by the eternal flame (Agni). Through worship and praise, the mortal embodiments serve the chief (Aryan). Through performing sacrifices and being constant givers, they serve as sons of strength. With Indra appearing with an illuminated soul and the eternal flame as the messenger (Mātariśvan), they guard and serve souls seeking enlightenment and paths for their offspring. The heavenly messengers offer godly blessings and eternal flame. They turn darkness into light, change the seasons, suckle milk as infants, and appear shining between heaven and earth.

This established the roots of the material world by setting places of treasures and gathering places to offer sacrifices. The suppliants' wishes are always granted to preserve their immortal spirits regulated by the eternal fire. Along with old wealth, the house is created, and what was born a foretime is guarded against what is and what will be. Agni grants eternal wealth and food to heroes and their offspring, and they establish the length of days for mortal embodiments. They are all fed with purifying fuel.

The heavenly Indra prevails in the universe with the illuminated soul, and through the sun, moon, and stars provides inner illumination. Indra create fields that remove sin and make mortal bodies pleasant homes (Rig Veda, Book 1, Hymn XCVII). They become chiefs who, by sacrifice, chase sins away and serve the worshippers with extended lives. Like the ever-conquering Agni, they send enlightenment. Their faces look everywhere to see the triumph and past foes to chase away sins like riding on a ship passing over floods.

The mighty powers regulating the celestial region serve as true invisible powers that support the battle of heavenly, unattainable rulers by providing the source of illumination (Suraya), providing the cosmic powers to regulate and control the esoteric region. Within the defeated terrestrial region, they use the cosmic host (Maruts) and Indra to eliminate evil powers serving as the destroyer (Vṛtra). They win each fight supported by heavenly powers using the stable grace of the godhead (Vaiśvānara), which continues to appear and serve all living things. Hence, the mortal embodiments, as a union of the godhead, manage the process and spring to life and protect them from the competition coming from the heavenly godhead power (Agni). The same power regulating the true source of external illumination (Suraya) prevails among all plants with the eternal flame to preserve such creation.

The godhead union brings an abundance of wealth as the eternal firebirds (Jatavedas) brings immortal heavenly power that provides the mythical juice. When consumed (Rig Veda, Book 1, Hymn XCIX), it takes over the evil powers and allows creation to avoid trouble. With the eternal flame, it removes challenges such as taking a boat across the river. It moves on paths that bring the mythical juice from heaven in cosmic vapours.

Indra and the cosmic host as demigods (Maruts) subdue foes and thus succeed over the chief heavenly messenger (Aṅgirases), serving as the friend among friends with might amid the mighty. They are honoured by most singers and worshippers for their help, along with the cosmic host, all supported by heavenly powers (Rudras) that produce winds and vibrations. This helps their offspring conquer their foes in physical battle.

The lord of the heroes and the cosmic host invoke godly powers and help them acquire inner illumination even in battle. They help folk as their guardians and provide comfort; they offer holy service like heroes appearing as the holy one. They eliminate the darkness and deliver them from ignorance. With the left hand, they check their physical qualities, and with the right hand, they evaluate their intrinsic spiritual qualities. With both qualities, they explore their eternal treasure and support their humble hearts, helping the hosts of heroes to win even more assets.

During the day, they are well known for their mighty powers, and at night, they fight and conquer even those who hate them and many on their way. They are invoked by others serving as strangers who develop kinsmen. They are all blessed in waters before they appear like sons and grandsons, bringing forth progeny through singing hymns and drinking the mythical juice. With boundless knowledge, they become fierce fiend slayers and thunder wielders, and they further evolve.

Those who have won the eternal light roar like thunder from heaven. They guard the newly created five tribes, and after receiving treasures, the tribes attend to the godhead and learn to follow the cosmic host. They come from every side and surround the five tribes, and not like heavenly gods or the celestial godhead; they appear as cosmic demigods serving as terrestrial archangels. They have limited power like the sons of the hermit. They, with blaze filled celestial riches, command high standing. They manifest as mortal embodiments serving as the ruler (Rjrāśva) who can overpower evil forces. They come in chariots drawn by stallions. Serving the hosts as joyous mortal beings, they are noted like the earthly messenger (Vār5āgiras), who sing hymns to please the mortal embodiment of the ruler. They followed celebrated devotees (Ambarī5a, Surādhas, Sahadeva, and Bhayamāna). Once they are invoked, they come to slay evil powers while mighty Indra, with its fair complexion, brings sunlight and water.

Along with those singing and praising, they make the rulers glad to serve the terrestrial bodies by driving away their sinister descendants. Those with strong right hands wield thunderbolts to invoke the cosmic host so others will become friends of Indra and come with triumphant wrath to smote down evil powers (Vyaṁsa) and transform the unrighteous (Śambara) unto Pipru, which are never satisfied as to the wondrous powers (Śu5ṇa).

Keeping intact the holy law and heavenly luminous power, they follow the cosmic host and invoke friends serving as the lord of animals as their lord (Pursan) and expert (Bhaga). The lord of all the manifested world, Brahman, who even prevailed before Indra, unveils eternal truth all brought with vibrations and has it move into every manifested body using the powers of wind (Vayu), serving as the breath, and making everything alive. As the mortal embodiment (Ṛjrāśva), Indra observes the evil ruler (Dasyus), who once invoked the valiant war; they all cast down their weapons and flee like cowards.

In the region with refulgent heavenly power (Rudras) and proceeding like the daughters of the sky covering the wide space appearing as devotees, they sing hymns of praise to the godhead and serve as friends of the cosmic host with divine delight. Covering the loftiest gathering place, they bring true rites and serve oblations. They rejoice on the sacred grass and represent themselves as a team of new born godly powers. Indra brings the bay steeds, the sun and the moon. They, with oblations, bring the eternal flame to please the cosmic host, who is serving as guards of the camp and with praise, bring the booty to Indra.

Singing hymns to the mighty ones, their desire is gratified (Rig Veda, Book 1, Hymn CII). They honour Indra with the strength by which the godly powers have feasted along with the flowing mythical juice. With the seven rivers bearing the godhead's glory coming from far and wide, they come to earth displaying themselves in their comely forms. The sun and moon bring change that is granted with similar powers to those who help conquer other embodiments. After the victory, Indra bestows joy and contentment on them. The messenger (Maghavan) fights foes and, with ascending embodiments, helps the godhead be victorious.

The glory of the messenger fills the world with inspiration. Once they see the evil powers slain, they are served by the three great elements—water, air, and earth—along with three dominions of light—the sun, moon, and stars representing the eternal fire. They turn the material world into a purified godhead without foes or magical arts and bring back in control the godly mother (Asta-Vasu).

The heavenly Indra and the living spirit (Atma) turn individual hearts to make the embodiments fight off any attack. Bringing booty back, they prevail in those great accounts and even in trifling battles. They become keen to know the powers of the mighty ones worshipped to achieve victory over any foe. Indra becomes the protector of mortal embodiments.

The highest godhead powers influence the direct messengers (Maghavan), who serve as the envoy (Rig Veda, Book 1, Hymn CIII). These messengers appear in the form of sages serving just like celestial priests, the seers. The sages and seers unite under one flag (Risi) in battle, spread throughout the terrestrial region, and fix their domicile on the holy ground (Prithvi), from where they use thunderbolts to smote evil to loosen the imprisoned waters. They strike down evil marine creatures (Ahi) and burn to death the evil powers (Rauhiṇa). They slaughter flying evil powers (Vyaṁsa). Trusting in their prowess, Indra and Agni destroy the forts of evil devotees (Dāsas) and cast darts at the evil leader (Dasyu).

The mortal powers with spirit (Ārya) increases with thunder power coming along with their might and glory; they guide and develop living beings to serve as noble souls (Āryaman). They have all seen the abundant wealth that they can possess, and with vigour, they follow trusted Indra. They, as a noble race, find cattle and horses, mountains, forests, and oceans. With their strength, they learn to perform many deeds as they serve like strong bulls. As heroes, they learn to extract the mythical juice from plants. They give their possessions to the godless and perform mighty deeds to wake them from bringing slumbering creatures; in the ocean, they let Indra manage the evil (Ahi).

Goddesses with divine delight bring joy to all the cosmic host that smites evil powers (Śuṣṇa, Pipru, and Vṛtra Kuyava). They go after hidden evil powers (Śambara), which flee like panting coursers when exposed to the divine power (Āryan), where it comes to rest. After obtaining the divine power, they even go after the horses at night and during the day, as well as the fast stallions. Semi-manifested bodies (seraphs) bring good fortune on the ground and in the water. With Indra, they cast themselves amid waters creating froth.

After their kinship with Indra is fully checked, the goddesses come to manifest by setting their roots in the ancient streams where they live as heroes. Others share sunlight and water and remain sinless; they make sure no one harms their unborn. They create paths for the roots and stems and serve as devotees. When hungry, they receive food, and when thirsty, they receive a drink. They always plead not to be slain or forsaken and not be taken away from their delight. They even pray not to split their unborn to brood. They offer Indra pressed juice to drink and oblations to be heard by the godly father.

Golden Wheel

In the esoteric region, the mighty powers establish themselves with virtue and beauteous wings that, like the golden wheel, regulate the light coming from the sun and moon that serves the expanding terrestrial region (Rig Veda, Book 1, Hymn CV). The mighty powers even use the golden wheel to regulate the existence of immortal and mortal embodiments residing in the material world (Viraj), which serve as part of the ground (Prithvi) that is in the esoteric region.

The golden wheel serves as the sun and moon, which Indra serves, as the bay steed as the embodied souls commonly observe mythical humanoids that develop an affliction to material wealth. They do not know that material wealth is an illusion (Maya), which clings to every physical embodiment. Especially when a union is established between a man and a woman, it intertwines and makes every embodiment and its offspring subject to the laws of aversion and attraction. They do not know that such laws can easily overpower eternal love and thus force mythical hominoids to resist the woes of material wealth.

The sun and moon never become attached to the laws of affliction and aversion, and, through sacrifice, they create divine bliss with which they can invoke the powers of the divine will to come from the heavenly region. In the form of brilliant light, they come from external and internal sources, always bringing contentment that removes torment. The brilliant light can also be obtained through the mythical juice produced externally by crushing plants (Soma) or generated using gland-producing nectar (Amrita). Even mighty powers consume such mythical fluid to comply with the eternal laws and eternal love. They use the fluid to spread the divine will or primordial energy wandering in all three lucid regions. They establish their temporary homes and serve as mortal or perishable bodies, all regulated by the golden wheel.

The golden wheel and the regulator of the eternal laws and eternal love (Varuna-Mitra) travel to observe any wicked actions and accordingly come to guide mythical hominoids to stay away from evil paths and foes. The noble souls (Aryaman) overpower the foes of the mythical hominoids. Noble souls sing old hymns and blossom with bliss to invoke every embodiment. Once individual embodiments receive powers, they overpower woe like wolves overpower deer. Even the ancient power, Satakratu, uses the divine will to pierce through embodiments to devour memories and remove any attachment to the material world.

Moving with the golden wheel, the Aryaman come to know wherever the seven rays as the daughters of Surya travel with the divine will; they extend virtue to make each home and every member of the family noble. As in the past, they establish the brotherhood among heavenly powers they form as solar deities (Tṛta Āptya). They stand high and appear as the five heavenly bodies (Agni, Indra, Varuna, Mitra, and Asvin's). They invoke the solar deities with devotion, prayers, and oblations to honour the godly powers that prevail in heaven like bulls but sit like birds on the path at the crossing driven by wolves serving as guides, along with the restless floods. They use all kinds of hymns to praise the godly powers (essence) that have not yet joined with the divine will before it passes through flowing floods.

Following the sun's rays, godly powers establish kinship with Agni and with all the other supreme godly powers to extend themselves to spread light all around. Agni, seated as the celestial priest, and the godly power, Indra speed onward offering their intelligence; with oblations, they pass around and spread among other noble powers.

With holy prayer, the regulator of the eternal laws finds the path into the sacred heart to reveal thoughts that could establish a safe pathway for the sun to rise from the cosmic to the heavenly region. Even with prayer, the safe pathway cannot be transgressed by immortal or mortal powers. Even the noble, godly power buried in the well, once freed by the power of solar deities (Tṛta Āptya), cannot go above until the eternal laws releases distress so godly powers can conquer.

During difficult situations, the five great heavenly bodies cannot rescue them from distress (Rig Veda, Book 1, Hymn CVI) and allow noble and godly powers to bring joy even after the conquest over their foes. They ask the mothers of the gods (Aditi) to strengthen them with the eternal laws, and the powers of Agni create Narāśaṁsa as the ruler of the mortal embodiments, including the animal kingdom. With prayer and hymns, the perishable embodiments (Brihaspati) make an easy path for those who crave to transform from their resting positions by stirring up their embodiments.

Even the mighty powers, along with the Agni's envoy, Narāśaṁsa, graciously release stress and troubles (Rig Veda, Book 1, Hymn

CVII). The mother (Aditi), along with her offspring (Ādityas), builds shelters for the godly powers (Varuṇa, Indra, Aryaman, Agni, and Savitar) and creates pleasing environments to draw the wondrous chariot of Indra and Agni to look around and watch living things coming to the golden wheel from the region. They drink libations and witness as the material world that encompasses oceans, and holy ground (Prithvi) is revealed.

Indra and Agni provide the mythical juice to drink until individual embodiments are satisfied, and in triumph, they go together as a blessed union to slay evil powers. The union stands adorned on the sacred grass that, with fire, lifts ladles to display eternal kindness. Performing brave deeds, they exploit their mighty, ancient, and auspicious bonds of friendship. With draughts of the mythical juice, they pour forth to the soul-charging reality (Brahman) to rise with rejoicing and serve as one along with the holy godhead with their dwellings in the lowest and highest regions.

The mighty lords (Brahman) drink the libations coming from heaven or earth (Rig Veda, Book 1, Hymn CIX). With the bright light (Surya) mounted in the midheavens, they generate direct light, the sun, while drinking libations. It sees the growth of mortal bodies with spirits forming a brotherhood. They all realize the importance of not breaking the cords; they petition for the powers of their forefathers. The union (Indra-Agni) fills with delight as it pours the mythical fluid from the sky along with water. Hearing about such a union makes the evil powers fall.

Like twin demigods, they exceed in greatness and spread the gap between the earth and heaven to help expand the material world. The union brings wealth to those who protect all manifested embodiments by giving them arms to wield thunderbolts. They bring sunbeams of absolute truth and serve as ancient fathers who shattered forts with thunderbolts. Singing sweet hymns to perform holy work, they celebrate praise as fully mortal bodies evolved over time as the godhood (Devata) arrived from the cosmic region (Rig Veda, Book 1, Hymn CX).

They come as large cosmic bodies (Ṛbhus) that create a crater filled with water that serves as lakes or deep oceans. These mortal bodies bring the mythical juice and produce sounds like hymns. They establish their home on the ground along with the solar deity bringing water (Savitar). With immortality, they proclaim and do not hide their identity even when they drink from the chalice of evil power (Asura). The cosmic mortal bodies (Ṛbhus) fully evolve like the children of the solar deity (Ribhu), the wind deity (Vaja), and the artisan deity (Vibhvan). Collectively, they called as the creative force (Rhibhus) and are honoured for their creative abilities and strength that many envy.

Manifested as mortal embodiments and born as innovative creations, they remain humble and kind, and they gradually become immortal superstars representing the sun's brilliant rays. They are created with luminous haloes that are associated with godly powers. As solar deities, they serve as the measuring rod like the chalice or goblet used in every oblation offered in individual sacrifices. With lauded power, they represent the powers of the immortal gods.

As heroes, they represent eternal knowledge that can help mortal embodiments rise to heaven. By providing strengthening food, they serve as mortal bodies (Ṛbhus) and serve as the messengers of Indra. They refresh their might with power and wealth, give gifts like godly powers, and provide happiness to quell attacks from those who pour forth no offerings. Once out of their membranes, they serve others as cows serve their calves. They appear as the descendants of the ancient holy sage (Sudhanvan). They acquire surpassing skills and provide aged parents with the strength needed to join immortal manifested bodies.

As descendants of the holy sage, the heroes shape their lightly rolling bodies (astral) to rise and reach the sun and moon, where they bear the powers of Indra and bring great gifts (Rig Veda, Book 1, Hymn CXI). For sacrifice, they use powers accompanied by eternal wisdom to feed the noble progeny. This grants them the power with which they protect their families. They bring prosperity to mortal embodiments, and, serving as vehicles, they bring prosperity to heroes and their steeds.

With Indra, they conquer all in battle, and with the solar deity (Ṛbhus), they help the wind deities create a unique strength (Vājas) that, like the cosmic host, brings draughts of the mythical juice. With the help of the eternal laws and the artisan deity (Vibhvan), they bring eternal love to support the twin coursers, which as demigods bring wealth, wisdom, and victory.

The solar deity (Ṛbhu), along with the wind deity (Vāja), sends for the twin demigods (Aśvins) to fight for prosperity and protect the union (Varuṇa-Mitra). With the mother (Aditi), they keep rivers flowing in all the regions representing the holy ground (Prithvi) between earth and heaven.

The twin demigods generate thoughts of rites, sacraments, and sacrifices to worship the holy ground (Prithvi) plus other regions between heaven and earth. According to Rig Veda, Book 1, Hymn CXII, they honour Agni, which brings light and hastens their approach to arrive and serve like demigods, two fast-moving horses, the ancient Aśvins that aid in the fight. The twin power among the manifested embodiments makes them think like the ancient demigods. They generate noble thoughts and use such thoughts to perform holy acts that generate, through glands, the inner libations, which as nectar (Amrita) serves the worshippers and helps noble heroes acquire eternal wisdom.

They even aid wanderers by bringing eternal wisdom to their offspring. Like a twice-mothered son, they swiftly pass through the mid-region and, with acquired triple wisdom, become sapient souls and serve like ancient, immortal, manifested bodies. They rise fast from the water, looking like illuminating light and manifesting as male (Rebha) and female (Vandana).

Both males and females are received by (Kaṇva), the messengers of Indra, who rescue them to conquer powers of time and space that establish life on the ground (Antaka). The status and qualities of spirits determine how the immortal spirits (Atma) will leave physical bodies to join the universal soul (Paramatma). If the spirit is free from the physical attachments, it leaves the embodiment dancing depicted as Shiva. When spirits not freed from their memories, their demise is depicted as Yama. Deteriorating embodiments sit in a deep pit (Bhujyu) as an active body filled with energy but failing. They comforted only by woe (Karkandhu). To help friendly immortal spirits, Vayya comes from happy home (Śucanti) and brings along a friendly sage (Atri), who guards the individual male spirit (Purukutsa) and individual female spirit (Pṛśnigu).

Both spirits received by the demigods and aided by the mighty ones to bring them as a family (Parāvṛj) to the godly powers that make the blind see and the lame walk. As it absorbs the vibrations that cause earthquakes, it brings sweet comfort to those practising yogi (Vasiṣṭha), which creates floods but never decays. With the help of three sages, working as a trinity (Triśoka), they provide help to the powerless fighting in battles of a thousand, and they move to seek booty like the legendary warrior queen (Viśpalā).

They are all guarded by friendly images of twin demigods Vaśa and Aśvas, supported by the ancient demigods (Aśvins). The clouds shed rain on the bounteous givers, merchants, and singers (Kakṣīvān), which, with praise, generate a mythical flow of moisture and humidity (Rasa). In victory, the embodiment surges like a carriage without horses. The holy sages drive forth individual embodiments holding the immortal spirit with the aid of the twin demigods. From far away, the sun scopes the ground and establishes the tasks of those serving as the lords of the land (Mandhātar) and those serving as sages (Bharadvāja).

After the demon power slain, those guarded well are honoured by sages with the mythical juice and assigned to serve with semi-mythical personages such as the legendary Vyaśva and the divine soul (Pṛthvi), which continue to support the twin demigods. They even support heroes who vouchsafe through the deliverance of ancient support coming from the majestic trinity (Śayu, Atri, and Manus). They ignite fires and help in the mighty fray to support the twin demigods (Aśvins). The messengers (Aṅgirases) with triumphed hearts liberate and create milk-bearing floods to bring along the ancient heroes (Manus) and their wives (Vimada). They freely give away the ruddy cows along with the host of godly servants (Sudās). They learn to serve as holy sages (Kṛśānu), who come through channels to help the young heroes (Manus), who move horses swiftly in the race and bring delicious honey. This helps speed the heroes as they fight for kindness and strive for the sons on the land.

They guard horses, and the manifested embodiments serve the lords of a hundred powers as sages (Kutsa) who receive noble warrior sons (Ārjuni) and strength from the father king (Turvīti) and mother queen (Dabhīti). They kindle fire to be purified and appear fully strengthened as Dhvasanti, which lends its power to Puruṣanti, which helps make an effectual speech.

With hymns, they serve as the twin demigods and become mighty wonder-workers who, in a luckless game, even call on demigods to strengthen their position on the battlefield. With undiminished blessings, as twin demigods for evermore, night and day, they protect all. Like the light that comes amid all fairness, they are born brilliant and send the night away to create a birthplace for the dawn. With fair and bright light like the white offspring of the sun, it comes as the goddess (Savitar) that removes darkness and brings similar immortal dwellings that follow each other from heaven to earth, changing their colours as they move on.

Light Waves

Light waves refer to an impulse or stimuli that are impersonal or inherited and motivate humans long before their consciousness develops. These stimuli continue to influence feelings and behaviour even after some degree of consciousness develops an instinct and before it is directed by an inner conscience. It represents unending light serving as the daughters of the sun that come to establish the path for the godly powers. They travel like light waves, fully formed and appear with different hues coming from the same mind. They bring dusk to create night and dawn to create the day.

According to Rig Veda, Book 1, Hymn CXIII, bright lights like leaders of glad sounds appear as the goddesses (Savitars) with eyes of splendid hues; they open their portals and stir up the world to show riches with the morning light and awaken every living creature. With the richness of the morning light, the goddess sets coiled-up sleepers afoot like snakes to wake up one for enjoyment, one for wealth, and one for worship while all others see little through their extended vision. All living creatures awaken with the morning light; one goes with high sway, one goes to exalted glory, one to pursue gain, and one to work. They are children of heaven who follow the young goddess as a maid in shining raiment who appears like the sovereign lady of all earthly treasure.

Goddesses (Savitars) turn on their auspicious powers by bringing the morning light as the first of endless morns come hereafter and follow the path of morns that have departed. With morning light bringing forth the rising urges among living things, she wakes even those who appear dead from their slumber, and, with morning light, they even cause Agni to enkindle the eternal flame that, like the sun's eye, reveals all creation.

All mortal embodiments are awakened to offer worship and perform godly and noble services. For a long time, they work together; morning light yearns for the former morning light, and they go forth gladly shining with the others. Gone are those who in days past looked on the rising of the morning light. Living things behold her brightness and come nigh to see her serving as evening light. The foe chaser born of law and protector of the law, the joy giver, the walker of all pleasant voices, brings auspicious food for enjoyment as the morning light shines.

From the eternal days, morning light has shone, so it will shine on days to come; immortal, it moves on in its own strength. In the sky's borders, it shows splendour as if the goddess has thrown off the veil of darkness. Awakening the world with her ornate horses pulling her chariot to bring life-sustaining blessings, she shows her brilliant lustre. As the last of the countless mornings that have vanished, she brings the first light that brings life.

Like the sun, the source of light, the goddess leaves the path to prolong the existence of those singing the praises of the morning. With hymns, they create a web for the priest and the poet to use to rise on. The goddess (Savitar) shines today as before, accompanied by a rich maid, who lauded such shining that brings to others the gift of life as their offspring. Dawns brings sons, all heroes who shine on those who bring oblations along with domesticated animals. With the ending of glad songs, astral bodies bring the mythical juice with vibrations along with the godly mother (Aditi) in the form of glory that exalts bounteous praise to make a chief among manifested embodiments. With splendid wealth brought by morning light, it blesses mortal embodiments who offer praise and worship to the union of Mitra-Varuṇa, which vouchsafes all.

The strong, with the braided hair, wild and stormy heavenly power (Rudra's), with praise songs, invites them to come and honour them as the lord of heroes who with all manifested bodies are ready to serve (Rig Veda, Book 1, Hymn CXIV). They are well-fed and reside in villages. They graciously bring them joy and reverence through serving them as well as their father (Manus). They provide health and strength to win sacrifice and gain wealth under their divine guidance from the bounteous ruler (Rudra's). With the worship of God's grace, they serve as rulers of these courageous manifested bodies serving as heroes. The ruler (Rudra's) brings to their families the sacred gift and especially for the unspoiled heroes who are impetuous and offer imperfect sacrifices. Rudra's aids, the wise ones repels godly powers, which desire grace.

Through braided hair, the ruler (Rudra's) comes down like a wild boar from the sky with hands filled with sovereign medicines that grant protection. They create shelters to secure them as their home. Appearing as the universal soul, the father (Rudra's) is addressed with hymns and is honoured for its might by the cosmic host. With a sweet song, they become immortal, grant food to the mortals, and become gracious enough to carry their immortal seed. They do not harm their seed, their progeny, or any living things, including heroes. With hymns of praise, they represent as the fathers of the cosmic host, which brings happiness and blessings. They keep all living beings far from the darts that kill, and as heroes, they bless them to become gracious and vouchsafe by themselves, providing doubly strong protection. Those seeking help adore the father and use the cosmic host to connect with higher powers.

The brilliant presence of the godly powers (Rig Veda, Book 1, Hymn CXV) as one like the ancient trinity (Mitra, Varuṇa, and Agni) come to serve as the universal soul among all that is moving or not moving, and it fills the space encompassing heaven and earth filled with sun and air. As a young one, they follow a maiden; so does the sun follow the morning as the goddess with its refulgent light, the moon, follows the evening light. They extend from pious embodiments, the holy souls, to manifest as the illuminated soul that fills generations with happy fortune. Like the sun and the bay horses, the illuminated souls with changing hues and, with shouts of triumph, meet with an attitude that shines like the sun along the sky's ridge. In a moment, they could speed around earth and heaven.

Established as the godhead with the might of illumination, they spread over any unfinished work. Like the loosened sunrays, like horses, they come from their station and spread over the darkness of night, pulling a garment over the darkness so as not to expose everything under it. While in the sky's lap, they join with the ancient union (Varuṇa and Mitra), which lets the sun and moon create day and night. After such creations, the heavenly body (Surya) ascends and sets manifested embodiments free from trouble and dishonour.

Like the ancient demigods (Aśvins), the manifested spirit (Atma) gladly invites all with the mythical juice (Rig Veda, Book 1, Hymn CXVI). They offer gifts to those on the sacred grass, singing songs to gain strength; they eat their share of food. Atma, living in a mortal embodiment, serves as the mortal twin (Nāsatyas); they move like immortal bodies (Aśvins) swifter than thought. They are driven like brave steeds that serve the mortal embodiments and abide with pious dwellings. Like the freed sage (Atri), they establish and regulate five tribes honoured from birth to evolve and serve as heroes among other manifested bodies.

They repel and baffle the mighty malignancies in succession as mighty heroes who manifest as sages (Rebha) from dreadful embodiments like horses that were wounded but saved by a wondrous power. In triumph (Vandana), they come as wonderworkers who, like buried gold, come to shine in the sun. With demigods as heroes such as Kak5īvān and Nāsatyas, they appear as wanderers who bring the sweetness of a hundred jars of honey and using guts and strength; they jump like horses. Praised by the holy sage's son (Kṛśānus) and with the praise of the holy sage (Viśvaka), they as heroes restore their sons (Vi5ṇāpū Gho5ā) and live in the dwelling of their father (Ru5atī). At pleasure and wearing many forms, they manifest as fleet-footed coursers (Pedu) with the strength to win a thousand plunders and become glorious victorious.

As bounteous givers of prayer, they praise habitation in both worlds (the illuminated and the underworld), while the sons of the powerful force (Pajra) call on the demigods (Aśvins) to send strength and nourishment to the illuminated world. They sing hymns so that the swift demigods will give them booty to burn. With the aid of demigods, they restore youth among the ancient sages with mortal embodiments (Cyavāna).

The daughters of the sun, with all glory, choose the noble embodiments, the demigods, to bear and serve in an ancient manner as the ever-youthful ones (Tugra). Like horses with wings, they fly to bring back demoralized noble powers (Bhujyu) from the sea of billows to serve as the ever-youthful ones (Tugras) who, with the powers of demigods, bring back uninjured mortal embodiments through the ocean, all filled with swift thought. They are well harnessed and can be carried off to safety by the mighty ones, just like quail saved from the wolf's devouring jaws.

After climbing through clefts and conquering the mountain's ridges, manifested embodiments experience a big massacre before they can become enlightened noble rulers (Ṛjrāśva). The demigods provide them with eternal light like sending perfect vision to the blind. With this great wealth, it cultivates noble thoughts as provided by the demigods. With prayers and sacrifice, they even turn the disabled (Yajna) into fully recovered embodiments (Purandhi). Through the mighty powers, they are liberated to serve as wonderworkers. They fill a cow with milk from emaciated, barren, milk-bearing animals (Śayu). They bring out silk from a spider. They use horses and bulls to plough ground and grow barley to feed the wonderworkers. With blasting trumpets, they push far away the evil powers and give light to create noble souls (Ārya).

The demigods give the horse's head to selfish manifested embodiments (Dadhyac) to bring out noble offspring (Atharvan). They are given the mythical juice to reveal the truth to the wonderworkers. As their embodiments are exposed to intellect, wisdom, and the secret powers, they, through creative powers, reveal absolute truth to the embodiments of holy sages. With absolute truth, their embodiments offer gracious prayers for riches, fame, and creative powers.

Accompanied by children, the demigods (Nāsatyas), through worshipping, create a liberal bounty, which out of the weaklings assemble and create worship. The heroes of the offspring come with an ultimate beginning (Hiraṇyahasta) and the ultimate ending (Śyāva). These heroic wonderworkers then exploit with demigods what can be achieved as in ancient times and support mortal embodiments. They serve the mighty powers through prayers addressed to the mighty powers. They speak and serve as brave sons.

Gracious demigods (Nāsatyas) flying with falcons bring friendly help to turn their embodiments to become wisdom swifter than any mortal mind (Rig Veda, Book 1, Hymn CXVII). They fly with the wind and serve the trinity of the three mighty powers. They prevail like living gods with triple-wheeled chariots. With the power of falcons, they fill cows with milk, bring determination to horses, and make each hero's son grow as strong as the ancient demigods. In manifested embodiments, they descend swiftly from the celestial region. Singing as wonderworkers, they come along with celestial bodies appearing as press stones (asteroids). Like the ancient sages, they remove affliction.

The demigods (Nāsatyas) let their falcons bear their chariots, and as swift eagles, they bring the banquet. The youthful and delighted daughters of the sun ascend their chariot to support the heroes. Borne with their swift wings supporting beauteous horses like the birds of ruddy hue, they raise strong wonderworkers. With great might and even-powered Vandana, they rescue noble souls (Rebha) out of the sea to save the sons of Tugra and give them again youth-producing echoes like the embodiment of an ancient sage (Cyavāna). The holy sage Atri casts down to the fire that scorched him as he made sacrifices to receive the strengthening favoured food for the demigods.

After accepting fair praises and with approval, the messengers (Kanva) give the ability to make blinded embodiments to see again with eternal truth. The demigods (Aśvins) as white horses were bestowed on Pedu and sent down by Indra to conquer the loud-neighing foe. They, with determination and spiritual powers, provide vigour to win over their thousand treasures and serve as nobly born heroes. When in trouble, they call on them for assistance, and through acceptance of their prayers and divine songs, well-being comes to them from the chariot laden with treasure and eternal love. The demigods (Nāsatyas), with the fresh, swift vigour of the falcon, bear oblations that are first invoked by the ancient demigods (Aśvins) at the first break of everlasting morning.

With rays of eternal light passing through their wondrous embodiments and generating swift thoughts that are borne like steeds with a thousand banners and carrying gifts and with prompt obedience, they bestow them on ample space (Rig Veda, Book 1, Hymn CXVIII). They move together singing hymns and covering all the regions with sweet oblations. Appearing as striving helpers, with their embodiments (Ūrjānī), they come with glory mounted on twin horses serving as demigods.

In contests, they come down the slope eager for victory to help the demoralized prince (Bhujyu) with some choice of boon that could save them from struggling in flood. They support like birds born to their parents. They help the mighty ones receive fame and aid transform into demigods, all serving as heavenly servants (Divodāsa).

These heavenly servants yoke their embodiments to show their glorious nature. They produce with two voices: one urges others to follow, and the other directs them to follow their goal. Heavenly servants (Divodāsa) form friendships like the maid of noble birth, which selects a male as a partner or companion like an emotionless husband. They save the source of their verbal and semantic roots (Rebh). Even barren cows come out of the scorching pit and turn into heavenly cows (Śayu) filled with refreshing milk that runs like a stream. This provides extended life to moths, which restore the worn-out embodiments to last at least for the length of their days.

On the ground (Rig Veda, Book 1, Hymn CXIX), the heavenly servant with extended life as a sage continues to perform wondrous deeds. Heavenly light as the source of inspiration provides marvellous help to stand up and continue to serve like bees providing sweetness to the mythical juice. Serving with the reflective light of the moon, they draw on the living immortal spirit and become animated and utter eternal wisdom. Like the twin demigods, the white horse, they provide strength to the dormant so they can attain excellence by conquering combatants. They seek fame coming from the heavens as the vanquishing arrows of Indra.

Enlightened

According to Rig Veda, Book 1, Hymn cxx, praising to win grace, the enlightened embodiments come to influence ignorant embodiments and made then serve the enlightened embodiments. Willingly, they serve those spiritless mortal embodiments. Even today, all-wise embodiments reach heaven as servants as they declare through prayer and offer wondrous godly oblations. With simple prayers to the mighty ones, they become sanctified and use mystic words, which save those not strong by gaining control of functions that make them angrier. With the hymn, the enlightened embodiments serving as Ghoṣā Bh1rgu show how the son of the sage (Pajra becomes a wise preacher by singing worship songs.

With the hearing from the enlightened embodiment (Ghoṣā Bh1rgu), they sing praise songs. They observe all the splendour with their own eyes coming forth with ample wealth to deal forth all gathered with powers of nature that guard and kept them safe. The wicked powers like wolves crave to hurt noble embodiments and hate those worshippers with domesticated animals.

Those who love noble souls gain friends and offer opulence that flows like milk from cows. With rich sacrifice and well content, the horseless carriage passes the light chariot bringing the mythical juice to living embodiments one after another. Those beholding it slumber in contempt; they enjoy not, vanish quickly, and are lost forever.

When the pious messengers (Aṅgiras) serve as guardians, they pray for children to hasten home and stride with holy sacrifice as established in heaven (Rig Veda, Book 1, Hymn CXXI). The skilful workers pour forth mythical juice with wealth, strength, and kindness to nurture self-born heroes, all supported by the mighty one and guided by demigods. Serving as the host, the guardians appear as mothers with heifers. The pious messengers come daily to invoke the red morning light as victorious and serve as a team; they establish heavenly quadrupeds and two-footed manifested embodiments.

With joy, they open the doors and, moving swiftly, start milk. They bring down the milk to the parents that provide the strengthening powers to conquest amiable gifts. They offer pure treasure where the milk from the cows is accompanied by nectar (Amrita). The sun's light shines forth, and with its power, a swift rapture is born that brings cosmic vapour serving as holy rivers such as the Indus. With the morning light, it brings water filled with the mythical juice to honour the establishment of the ground as an altar (Rig Veda, Book 1, Hymn CXXII). The altar filled with piles of wood could be used to offer worship and invoke the universal soul like bulls that bring living spirits as holy cows.

Appearing from the mighty heavenly region, imperishable and perishable bodies fight. These splendours serve as the planetary bodies and appear as asteroids and generate the milk as the mythical juice (water, milk, and honey) that strengthens. They appear as meteors from heaven that bring forth the supreme powers of causation as Indra, who is assisted by much-invoked noble warriors (Kutsa) and comes with endless deadly darts used to scope out mighty evil powers that, like snakes (Śuṣṇa), cover the ground.

They come out from heaven from clouds to unveil evil powers using their immortal weapons, lightning, and rain to firmly attack the knotted, mighty evil serpent powers that are thrown around in the esoteric region. Lightning and rain flash through the air like horse-drawn carriages without wheels but supported by joy.

The godhead powers go after the evil powers through the mighty thunder. The godhead powers as the lovers of the perishable manifested spirits guard with winged animals who pass through swift wind and serve as the twin demigods (Kāvya Uśanā) with strength gained from the gladdening powers (Brahmanas) that are mounted on old-fashioned twin demigods serving the godhead as the slayers of evil powers.

They appear as the flying horse (Etaśa), which with the sun's light, pushes the carriage of godheads without the wheels and casts forth beyond the esoteric ninety rivers and comes driving down on the ground into the godless pit, where all the embodiments with afflictions reside.

The godheads use powers of thunder arms, and flying horses land nearby in misery. With affluence, they use their chariots to vouch for safe embodiments. Using their powers, they provide the horses and cattle with food and gladness. The godheads make sure their loving-kindness never fails. The godheads bring their envoy (Maghavan) to make sure they share a liberal feast with the companions 'foes' cattle.

The envoy (Maghavan) offers sacrifice to bounteous heavenly powers (Rudras) and, with mythical juice (Rig Veda, Book 1, Hymn

CXXII), helps their fleet move far from the wrath caused by the evil ruler (Dyaus), all regulated by the malicious powers (Asura). With loaded prayer, the heavenly power (Rudras) brings noble heroes as the cosmic host (Maruts) to serve in the esoteric region. With their strength, the cosmic host exalts with invocations provided by the evening and morning light coming to show with varied aspects.

They turn barren land into the grass to help them shine. The golden splendour (Sūrya) roams with the morning light to bring with delight the wind accompanied by pouring water. With sharp wits, holy earthly sages (Parvata) appear as worshipping godhead powers that have all come to serve as the famous noble pair (Auśija) who enjoy, drink, and brighten all.

They sit before others with their offspring coming out of the floods as the winners in thunder and ascend as the noble warriors (Arjuna), serving their mothers like the beam from the famous noble pair (Auśija). After their winning for the tribe of Ghoṣā, they are invoked by the divine patron (Pūṣan) as the bounteous one with rich benevolence and serve the powers of Agni.

The union of Mitra-Varuṇa hears their invocations in the hall of worship and gives famous gifts that can be heard along the holy rivers (the Indu and Sindhu), filling fair fields. The vibrations coming in the form of hymns can listen to the flowing divine waters manifesting among mortal embodiments.

The famous moral perishable embodiment, Priyaratha, as a cow, supplies milk that is praised as a wealthy gift and enjoyed by heroes and their children. The embodiment with the chief supports other physical embodiments needing help, such as leading strong horses. The folks who hate the union and those who pour any libations lie in sickness. Those moral embodiments that perform righteous acts and worship to gain power bring fame, and among heroes, such embodiments become liberal givers and noble warriors forever. All encounters in their embodiments have mighty power. Those who hear the calling offer sacrifice, even their own lives, and are received by the kings of immortality, making such manifested embodiments become givers of joy. They move through clouds with a decree, and all receive bounty largely with fame to serve as chariot riders. With vigour, they bestow on embodiments a tenfold draught of the mythical juice and great riches. They obtain refreshment from their sacrifices and rejoice in the drink, sacred viands.

All the sea deities come with the morning light with praise for the pious and are pleased with both offerors and singers. Four youthful sons serving as the kings of Maśarśāra conquer the troublemaker child, Ayavasa, and subject him to the sun's light.

After offering personal sacrifices, the broad embodiments appear as the divine power (Rig Veda, Book 1, Hymn CXXIII) and merge with the eternal light that provides enlightenment by activating dormant spirits that become vibrant spirits. This vibrant light removes darkness and ignorance before the world is awakened to gain treasure and be revived by the morning light by removing darkness.

The young powers serve as the noble-born Savitar, which brings morning light accompanied by other noble powers that serve as godly friends. They establish their homestead and declare the morning light as a sinless embodiment. They show the path for the light, visit individual dwellings, and eagerly display the best godly treasures.

With singing, they serve the union of godly powers (Varuṇa-Bhaga), and as the sisters (Usha), they bring joy with the morning light, which weakens the evil workers and strengthens noble souls. They sing hymns to generate the holy thoughts that rise like eternal flames that burn away ignorance and help one ascend toward the morning light. As one departs, the other one comes, unlike when halves march on successively while others hide in the gloom.

Like godheads, parents shine with brilliance, pride, and beauty. Like maids, they appear divine, and with a longing to win, they meet with youthful, smiling faces. Fair as brides, they show forth in the form of blessed morning that shines even more widely than the evening light as miraculous dread (Dhushara). Morning light brings milk from cows, and evening light strengthens animals such as horses. With substantial sacrifice and devotion, they bring sunbeams that assume their accustomed forms to bring happy fortune. Being obedient to the rule of the eternal laws, they generate thoughts that bring blessings from the immortal powers that make the embodiments shine with riches and chiefs. They, with worship, generate vibrations that are swift to listen.

The light kindled by the eternal flame rises with the sun's light and produces brightness (Rig Veda, Book 1, Hymn CXXIV). The light sends forth for the goddess Savitar to support those who become active and work to serve the quadrupeds and bipeds, including manifested living spirits. In the east, the light sends forth heaven's daughter in garments of light.

To follow the path of order, the heavenly accommodations never fail. In the eastern half of the watery region, the divine Savitars spread onward and become wider and wider. Proud of their spotless form and shining brightly, they make the rivers humble and seek other sisters' rivers knowing no brother who can gather riches. Like loving matrons, they reach out to places to look at their elder sister as they depart. They shine with sunbeams appearing as women trooping to the festal meeting.

To all those sisters who now have vanished, a later one each day, they once again succeed. In the morning light, they shine on all—wealthy ones, liberal givers, the ungenerous, traffickers, and the unawakened. The young maid from the east, with her team of bright-red oxen and mother cows, sends light to bring the eternal flame that prevails in every dwelling. Like birds, they fly from their resting places, and with the eternal flame, the river rises to search for food. Liberal mortals stay home, where the divine goddess, Savitar, brings much good as mortal embodiments praise through prayer, which increases their wealth. The goddess brings love and helps win favour and wealth.

Coming at early morn with emotional tendencies as an unattached goddess, Svanaya brings treasure that only sensible ones receive and are entertained by such godly power (Rig Veda, Book 1, Hymn CXXV). This increases the lives of individual embodiments and their offspring, who, as brave sons, acquire abundant material riches, including gold and cattle. They are bestowed with great vital power and can hold onto the treasure.

They come in the morning with longing and appear as pious sons, who, like the lord of heroes, sacrifice everything from their wealth and offer the mythical juice to bring prosperity. They come singing pleasant hymns. The streams bring health like cows bring milk that profits those who worshipped and those who worship. It freely gives those who worship enough to fill corpulent streams.

On the high ridge of heaven, the corpulence stands exalted, seeking the liberal giver of godly powers. The water in the streams filled with rewards yields wisdom in abundance to those who give honey, milk, and water brought by heavenly sunshine. This makes the givers rich with immortal powers that prolong their lives and save them from sinking into sin and sorrow. Pious chiefs who worship never decay. This gives every embodiment protection, and lets affliction fall on ungenerous embodiments.

The unattached goddess (Svanaya), with lively praises, presents the physical body as the dweller (Bhāvya), which can fully attain eternal wisdom while standing on the bank of the holy river (Rig Veda, Book 1, Hymn CXXVI). The unconquered king (Kakṣīvān), eager to perform at once a thousand sacrifices, in desperation, accepts the gifts from the deathless heavenly lord of glory—a hundred thousand cows with chains.

The unattached goddess contributes sixty thousand stallions. The unconquered king with the animal kingdom follows a thousand unconquered cows. With forty bay horses pulling the master before a procession of thousands, the offspring of the unconquered king arrives on the ground with coursers (Pajra) with pearly accessories. They accepted earlier gifts of eight good milk cows along with three harnessed coursers. They, along with the wagon, serve as the great kinsman with troops who have been subjected to glory.

With its eternal flame, Agni holds them as heralds, munificent, gracious sons of strength who know all those who live, serve as holy singers of hymns (Rig Veda, Book 1, Hymn CXXVII) and know all the divine rites, godly powers that can transform bodies to stay erect to serve the godly powers. Once the eternal flame springs from the holy oil, it provides strength along with light. Heralds, mortal embodiments offer sacrifice and call on the best, oldest worshippers as the most brilliant ones (Aṅgirases) to wander along with the sky singer of hymns and come with power to invoke mortal embodiments and have them serve as earthly priests.

Nobility

As illuminated bodies with solar wind as the hair of flames, they speed far and wide to slay the demons. Serving like the bull, they become part of the ground that does not flinch even in the face of skilled archers. Like fire sticks, they give hidden gifts that unveil the hidden ferocious fire of Agni. Such power makes many things produce a fervent glow. Even rocks crunch with its might, especially near the sacrificial place, where it turns darkness into day. It gives as sure and firm a defence as a father gives his son.

With eternal fire, it enjoys things given and things not given; it comes roaring loudly like the cosmic host (Maruts) and turns deserts into fertile fields. Through worshipping as the heavenly power (Bhrgus), it brings relief as a gift. Agni, the lord of all treasures, comes in force and fills the whole region with eternal wisdom. Heavenly powers live in mortal embodiments and serve as guardians. They enjoy hymns as the guests that invoke among them the immortal sire, the spirit. The eternal flame becomes the cause of the birth of the mighty ones, who are born to serve as the godly powers. With their mighty mental power, they serve like immortals with embodiments that do not decay.

They appear like stars in the morning light. They send manifested bodies to worship Agni and offer oblations everywhere. The eternal flame beholds all and brings it into accordance with godly powers with gracious love and great riches. Agni enjoys the earth, and as one of the awful powers, it stirs up heroic might for those who praise the bounteous lord.

With the elimination of demons, the godhead of fire manifests on earth in the form of a pious priest, a skilled noble soul (Atithigva) born of the fire element that yearns to perform the holy law (Rig Veda, Book 1, Hymn CXXVIII). It hears from all who seek love, wealth, and fame. They, like the never-deceived earthly priest, sit at the holy place to serve the ancestral androgyne (Ila), the chief sexless progenitor serving the moon. They offer reverence and present food to help the skilled noble soul (Atithigva).

The messengers (Mātariśvan) are brought from far away by Indra after following the established course of order. They traverse all around the manifested ground (Prithvi) and manifest as Manus, which fly swiftly and bellow like steers. They bear their amiable seed as embryos. From the embryos, they manifest with the godly powers and observe the conqueror filled with eternal fire like Agni hiding in the wood. They use their hundred eyes to establish their homes on broad plains and reside far away among the highlands. Like Agni in the form of the eternal flame, they, as the wise heavenly priests, set their places in every house, create mental powers, generate noble thoughts, make sacrifices, and perform holy service.

With their mental powers, they identify all things needed to become priests and use enriched butter or fatty substances to produce holy oil for worship. Through the power and strength attained from the eternal flame, they serve as the cosmic host (Maruts). Heartened with boons, they mingle among all with roaring sounds to gladden and become active participants.

They accelerate wealth with greatness and rescue all from misery and woe. In the vast differentiated universe, as good messengers, they gain eternal love and fame by offering godly oblations to whoever pleads for them. With blessings from Agni, each pious man offers them to sacrifice in the place of ancestral power (Iḷā), which is preserved in many forms after discipline from the great heavenly powers of law (Varuṇa). The priest with the eternal flame begs to receive wealth from the messenger. Through hearing Indra's speech of orders, noble souls become strong and active in every fight. Even as mortal bodies, they show their strength. Indra serves the noble souls with righteous warriors protecting the blameless one (Rig Veda, Book 1, Hymn CXXIX). The heroes win the light, singers gain the prize, the strong and rich steeds become swift, coursers form fleets, clouds pour forth rain, and the heroes keep far away from wickedness with Indra. As friend's beloved by all, they form a strong alliance in wars through prayer and serve the mighty ones. With guidance from the righteous noble souls, the priests, and other blameless ones, they drive sin from mortal embodiments.

The mighty one invokes its power by releasing the mythical juice, and through awakening with prayer, they make even demon slayers worship. Mortal embodiments facing darts of death drive far from those who speak wicked and let them vanish into dust. With thoughtful invocation, they obtain great wealth and become the wealthy ones, but they use the wealth to serve other sweet heroes and their offspring. By offering sacred food and eulogies, they pacify and call on the majestic ones to inspire them with eternal truth, so they can drive off the wicked and devour fiends. Even when they are struck down, no firebrand can strike them.

Indra shows a path free of demons to those who go astray and protects them near and far away. With victorious wealth and the strong company of the godhead, they are provided with eternal love so they can serve as immortal saviours. They protect the mortal embodiments of righteous warriors even from armed thunder. Indra-Mitra saves the injured and wards off wicked powers.

The king of the noble powers and those who are conducting themselves as lords of heroes receive support from the godhead (Rig Veda, Book 1, Hymn CXXX). The lord of heroes gathers to meet with the king, who is designated by the godhead to treat heroes like sons. Mortal souls come with gifts of food and juice to gain strength like the magnanimous. The mythical juice pressed with stones is poured from the reservoir as sweet draughts to be absorbed like thirsty bulls' drink water. The light of the sun and moon helps them find heavenly treasure.

Striving to win an arcade of domesticated animals, Agni and Aṅgiras come to Indra, who kept concealed behind closed doors the thunderbolts that slaughter the evil powers holding the waters (Ahis). Endued with lordly might, it falls like an axe. Without much effort, Indra lets loose the blocked water that creates floods. Eager for riches, like a skilful craftsman, it creates manifested bodies with hymns and divine songs to attain bliss among singers. It performs deeds of might to show its strength, win the prize, and share it.

For the noble kingdom in Pūru, the boon dancers serve as heavenly servants and as holy worshippers. Along with the bolt from Indra, they shatter ninety evil forts to bring the demon (Śambara) from the mountain down and transform evil power into noble power (Atithigva). They distribute their strength and treasures to create a tribe of noble worshippers (Āryans), which later manifests as a mortal embodiment (Aryaman) ready to serve.

They turn the lawless dusky skin into embryos of manifested bodies (Manus), which are subjected to blazing eternal flame to burn away all tyrannous powers. After they have been subjected to the radiant rays and mighty powers of morning and evening light and their thought process is torn apart, they experience the bright red wheel organized by the sun and moon. With their powers of vibration, speech is removed by divine will and replaced with eager vibrations,

breath, and speech like a sage. The new manifested bodies (Manus) gain happiness each day. They sing hymns to break ancient barriers with praise by clansmen (Divodāsa), and they grow in glory like heavenly bodies.

Dyaus, the ruler of the evil powers, bows to the mighty ruler of the earth, Indra, with extended widespread tracts all covered by light and in one godly accord in front of the preeminent Indra (Rig Veda, Book 1, Hymn CXXXI). With all libations set apart, the spirits (Atma) of heroes urge spirits to win and join the universal soul by combining everyone's eternal light into a chariot pole of strength. With sacrifices of thoughts of immortal Indra, the mortal embodiments, with song and prayer, win aid that pours forth. Those who do not worship are chastised by floods on earth.

With might, they lead aspirants into battle with loud cries and achieve victory over their foes. Indra slays the foes like a hero with thunderbolts. Indra brings Maghavan to subdue mortal embodiments striving to conquer and pour the mythical juice (Rig Veda, Book 1, Hymn CXXXII). They are blessed with eternal flame as they divide the spoils after winning. All gather with good gifts and bow, offering bounteous gifts. They offer sacrifice and make it known to all who are ready to serve as allies. They see Aṅgirases giving aid to all who fight. They receive the juice, so lawless souls will give up and join the noble souls. The hero leads with a wise plan to conquer and win fame.

Their hymns find a welcome place of rest with Indra and help them serve the godly powers (Parvata) in the fight against all their foes. With sacrifice, the powers purge evil spirits from the earth and heaven (Rig Veda, Book 1, Hymn CXXXIII). All foes are slaughtered by hand. The messengers cast the sorcerers in a deep pit and destroy them. Indra crushes them with its fiery weapon. The illuminated ground (Prithvi) becomes a big concern especially having powerful weapons.

These powers can speed along with strong bolts of death. The brave heroes pour thrice-seven libations to gain wealth and conciliate the godly powers. Through pouring the mythical juice, they strive unchecked and win a thousandfold riches. This gives Indra lasting wealth it gives as gifts.

CHAPTER 3
SPIRITED DOMINION

Creation started with simple operating agents or entities that in the creative environment come to develop much more complex structures. Mortal physical embodiments with dissimilar sizes, shapes, colours, and scales, emerge from such structures in observed or unobserved structures and commonly follow identifiable and unidentifiable growth patterns. The emergence itself can be predictable or unpredictable, or even unprecedented, representing a new level in the physical evolutionary process. The complex behaviour and properties remain inseparable; even for a single entity, it remains unpredictable, which could be deduced from the behaviour of lower-level entities and, in fact, might be irreducible. Birds and fish emerge as distinct species, as do hominids, which can emerge as apes.

In the material world (Prithvi), as an integral part of the terrestrial region, the mammals diverged as far back as the cretaceous period, about 85 million years ago. In the palaeocene period, around 55 million years ago, the earliest fossils show the presence of life on the ground. The fossil records show the apes' superfamily, Hominidae, from which diverged the family Hylobatidae around 15 to 20 million years ago, and around 14 million years ago, a subfamily (Homininae) diverged to appear as Ponginae, known as the African great apes. From it arrived, the Hominini between 8 and 9 million years ago. This parted into a separate tribe as the Gorillini, which, in turn, formed subtribes (Hominins) 4 to 7.5 million years ago as humans and biped ancestors as chimp (Panini) subtribes when it started with living beings, humanity.

All objects, places, and creatures possess the inner power to perceive stimuli. These include animals, plants, rocks, rivers, weather systems, human handiwork, and perhaps even words, which reflect having life defined as animism, the world's oldest religion. Animism predates any organized religion and contains the oldest spiritual and supernatural perspective in the world. It dates to the Paleolithic Age, a time when humans roamed the plains hunting, gathering, and communing using the powers of nature. Each culture has its own mythologies and rituals, but animism describes the most common foundational thread of indigenous peoples' spiritual or supernatural perspectives.

The animistic perspective is so widely held by and is inherent to most indigenous peoples that they often do not even have words in their languages that correspond to animism; this is an ancestral mode of experience common to indigenous peoples around the world and to full-fledged religions. Animism encompasses all material phenomena; there is no hard and fast distinction between the spiritual and the physical worlds. An immortal, universal soul or immortal living spirit prevails among humans, animals, plants, mountains, and other entities of the natural environment, including even thunder, wind, and shadows.

Eternal Wind

According to Rig Veda, Book 1, Hymn CXXXIV, Vayu, as the life force (Pavana), blows breath (Prāna) that forms animated bodies that serve as the source of life (Mukhya Prāna). Generally, the eternal wind represents, with exceptional beauty, the essence generated through vibrations that create shining objects like white and purple breath that flies as two among forty-nine mighty powers or among a thousand living things.

The life force (Pavana) serves as the eternal wind (Vayu), which serves as the power of causation that supports deities that become a mighty force that serves mortal embodiments. In the form of the immortal spiritual father, the essence, it appears as the kernel of deity (Bhima), which manifests in different forms of commanders appearing as the monkey army (Hanuman), which as demigods appear in five forms covering the terrestrial region: atmospheric air (Anil), elemental air (Vyān), draft air (Vāta), cleansing air (Tanun), and purified breathing air (Prāṇa). Through regulating eternal air, they start to support flying objects such as the coursers that bring the mythical drink (Soma) through the eternal air.

Eternal air in the form of vibrations generates invisible power, an essence, which in the form of hymns uplifts and discerns individual minds (Chitta). In the individual mind, it overpowers other faculties, physical and nonphysical alike, and gratifies individual postures in terms of making sacrifices, being rewarded with gifts, attaining higher knowledge, and seeking eternal wisdom.

With the joy-giving drops of the mythical juice, it passes through the body as breath that transforms glands to prepare the embodiment to receive the efficacious heavenly powers directly. Consuming such powers generates the mythical fluid (Soma), which blended with milk brings strength, creates eternal wisdom, and generates the desire in mortal embodiments to unveil the secrets of causation. With such skilful power, they know how to reach heavenly powers and fulfil individual quests.

Along with the deity (Bhima) and its associated teams, they make prayers and grant power to those singing hymns and invoking eternal air, which yokes blood demigods, two reds and two purples, (Aśvins) running like twin horses drawing a chariot to unveil the secrets of absolute truth. With intelligence and eternal love, they make individual embodiments experience the living spirit and come to comprehend external illumination provided by the two extreme powers serving as the bay and the bull, the sun and the moon, along with scattered stars like cows filling the constellations. All represent the heavenly and earthly regions generating the lights of dawn and dusk (Uṣhas). They yield a mystic fluid as nectar (Amrita). From the esoteric region, the cosmic host (Maruts), engendered by heaven, come to support the mythical juice through the water to create bright light that, along with vibrations, fills the eternal air and creates showers filled with meteors. While the weary coward prays for luck, the cosmic host speeds away, protected by divine will that covers every world, including that of the highest gods. Those who cannot attain the eternal air do not receive the mythical juice until they free themselves from the stain of sin so they can receive the eternal air. The availability of milk from cows that yields butter provides another form of the mythical juice (Soma), which can help attain the eternal air.

The creation of atmospheric air (Anil; Rig Veda, Book 1, Hymn cxxxv) starts when the heavenly eternal air (Vayu) with a team of a thousand elements form atmospheric air, which is strewn like sacred grass to honour the deity (Bhima) with a feast that harnesses a hundred steeds. A drop of the mythical juice lifts the godly powers and, with enriched sweet juice, raises and strengthens them with joy. Similar purified mythical juice is passed through meteor showers, which filter through asteroids to fill the reservoir of mythical juice supported by the light of the moon. Portions shared among demigods and mortal, noble souls (Aditya) come like flying stallions inclined well with eternal love (Mitra) and fill living embodiments.

With the taste of the solemn rites and sacred food, the atmospheric air (Anil) learns to adjust to the direct light of the sun to create seasons offering pure juice as oblations. It can be shared among other attendant priests, who make food taste good by offering pleasant flavours to drink that bring splendid bounty. With songs and rites, Indra distributes the pressed and strained mythical juice mixed with water; it can offer great pleasure.

A unity (Vayu-Indra) enters every part of the terrestrial region with Anil and makes Indra appear as joyous maidens; jointly, they flow like melted butter offering the pleasant juice. They surround milk-bearing animals (cows) until they yield milk; thus, atmospheric air (Anil) flies like a swift stream that moves like sunbeams.

With ample adoration (Rig Veda, Book 1, Hymn CXXXVI), atmospheric air transforms to become the draft air (Vata), which serves the bounteous ones and allows them to serve as the demigods appearing like the cosmic host (Maruts). With sweet, adored streams, they serve the sovereigns at every sacrifice as they bring lubricant with praise. With imperial, high might, godheads never assail as they pass through the broad path of the holy law more widely laid by the direct light of the sun. They maintain with its rays the godly power (Bhaga), which with its eyes set firm on the heavenly trail that is travelled go to and from home with the eternal love (Mitra) and the eternal laws (Varu,)a), all serving as one the moral, manifested, noble embodiments (Aryaman).

They, like a trinity, give forth vital strength, and with merit, they praise the high power of life represented by the luminous mother, Aditi, serving as the upholder of the mortal embodiments. As the draft air comes day after day, mothers watch a sleepless, splendid might; they, with mighty powers, serve as the lords with liberal gifts and come to travel as a trinity (Mitra, Varu,)a, and Aryaman). With the drinking feasts, they share among other godly powers one accord that even today is joyfully accepted. Manifested kings, as the noble souls (Ādityas), serve with purified draft air that accomplishes what is asked of it.

While worshipping the trinity (Mitra, Varu,)a, and Aryaman), the draft air transforms to become clean air (Tanun). This air is served to support the righteous ones who carefully guard even the uninjured from distress and transform into manifested noble mortal embodiments (Aryaman). They, as liberal mortal embodiments, perform uprightly acts of beautiful divine will (Devavani). With the divine will, the professed lofty ruler (Dyaus) serves heaven and earth and follows the bounteous the eternal laws (Varul)a) with compassion (Mitra). By praising the ancient celestial trinity (Indra, Agni, and Bhaga), they as manifested embodiments (Aryaman) regulate the terrestrial region and make sure their progeny lives long with the help of the mythical juice. The celestial godhead Indra supports them with the splendid cosmic host (Maruts). The trinity (Agni, Mitra, and Varul)a) provides them with shelter and the sky, so other manifested, moral living beings can serve as earthly princes.

Activating primordial energy (Shakti) brings celestial asteroids with the supreme powers of eternal love and the eternal laws. Through a divine will, they bring morning light and the mythical juice. With glory and might, the strong solar majesty (Pū5an) is accompanied by the eternal air (Vayu) in its most purified form to serve as the life force (Prāl)a), which grants bliss to manifested bodies (Rig Veda, Book 1, Hymn cxxxviii). They draw to their hearts the godly powers of Pū5an to chase away foes. With their chants of praise, they stir no anger in battle as manifested bodies serving as the glorious ones.

In friendship with the solar majesty, Pū5an, along with eternal strength, they sing praises to attain wealth and offer prayers to the wide ruler to attain eternal wisdom. They immediately receive gifts of steeds that, like wonderworkers, serve as splendid ones whose friendship is not despised. Heard in prayer and honoured in thought, jointly, Agni and Indra represent heavenly powers.

Knowing all aspects of the eternal air (Vāyu), noble souls sing holy songs and worship the godheads. All godheads as one (Vivasvān) know absolute truth and sit with noble souls. They are beheld not with thoughts or by living spirits through physical bodies with pious eyes. They are supported by the mythical juice and appear as mortal twins (Aśvins), representing males and females offering oblations to the mighty ones. They scatter the mythical juice and come in golden chariots passing through the mid-air region and receiving blessings to vouchsafe them day and night. The juice makes individual hearts give up even great wealth.

Agni's messenger (Aṅgirases) hears magnified information; living beings are being received by the heavenly, unembodied, holy, universal soul, which brings along the living spirit placed among earthly embodied individuals to serve as godly kings. As the noble power (Aryaman), they bring milk from the holy cow that is mixed with the mythical juice. They do the joint work in heaven and on earth, performing their deeds, which never grow old. Like the bright glories of godly powers, they never decay before their time, and in every wondrous new age, they surpass whatever is hard to gain.

Using the ancient bones (Dadhyac) serving as the shining stars in the sky, they realize the ancestral powers (Aṅgiras, Priyamedha, Kal)va, Atri, and Manus), which knew all. With godly links, they know long lines of stretched birth; there is a connection among them that reaches from their high stations to those who bow with the song at low stations; all worship the powers of Indra and Agni. As the blessed invoker (Bṛhaspati), as a gift for friends, they offer choices to sacrifice animals. They use the sound of cosmic showers of meteorsto gain strength with heavenly waters to establish their resting places. Appearing as the eleven gods from the heavenly region, they dwell in the earthly region and serve with cosmic vapours from the esoteric region.

The manifestations live in seven transitory elements (Dhatus). Each layer of the embodiments represents a part of the subtle faculties, including the lymph (Rasa) system through which blood as liquid flows in arteries (Rakta). The red liquid flows through fibrous tissues (Mamsa), which support muscles; fat, mostly adipose (Medha); the skeleton (Asth), representing bone's structure. After the removal of subtle faculties, there is the spinal column (Majja), which represents soft, fatty tissues that, like marrow, represent vitality and sperm or seeds (Shukra), with which they turn progeny into life force. Together, they all represent the substrate (Sapa Dhatu), the holy base. This, as a physical structure related to the ground (Prithvi), is created and placed between the cosmic energy (heaven) and the cosmic matter (earth). Sacrifices are made to the divine will in its manifested form and, through an umbilical cord, connecting new life regulated by the supreme powers of causation (Paramatma), which links heaven and earth.

Through the splendid eternal flame (Rig Veda, Book 1, Hymn CXL), Agni comes to establish the altar above the ground (Prithvi), which serves as a home away from home for the heavenly powers. As the first step of manifestation, Agni, with its splendid eternal flame, provides eternal heat and food to transform earthly matter from the underworld into the physical energy to develop physical bodies all covered with skin serving like a robe and with a bright light that dissipates inner gloom.

Over the years, after eating nutrients, the manifested body learns and grasps its environment. The eternal flame regulates individual mortal embodiments passing through their first birth. Like the demigods (Aśvins), these embodiments, male and female, dwell as a pair. While moving in darkness or ignorance, they learn to produce offspring. They learn about the godly powers serving as friends of manifested bodies, and they learn like steeds to yoke their exasperated bodies by turning their physical power into the eternal flame and cultivate desires to be accomplished in the defined lines.

They learn to guide conflicting minds and move like a fleet on a rapid course. By dispelling the horror of black gloom and learning to fly forth with eternal flames, they make a glorious show. Moving over spacious tracts, they roar, seeking Indra. Agni stoops to embellish amid brown plants, and with a roar, they rush to provoke their might to create ferocious fire and volcanoes. Knowing that the resting place, the altar, is protected and covered, Indra knows well that the powers of the eternal flame cannot demolish them.

In the second step of manifestation to bring change as male and female, they serve the godlike power as parents or guardians and rise as divine offspring. With long hair, as maidens, they embrace the cycle of life and death. They appear as newborn physical embodiments filled with the new spirit (Atma) representing the universal soul (Paramatma). They wander far and wide and cover the blackened path with animals seeking to leave their marks with enlightenment. Wherever they go, they bring their eternal flame as their physical strength that makes them appear as wealthy chiefs.

After casting off their infant wrappings, they, with the eternal flame, fight darkness and ignorance. They make perfect prayer rather than imperfect prayer, and with pure brilliance, they learn to radiate through seeking eternal wisdom (Rig Veda, Book 1, Hymn CXLI). With eternal wisdom, they serve as wealthy princes with enlightened souls. They flow between earth and heaven, attaining long life or immortality by providing food to milk-bearing animals and serving with the morning and evening light.

With the eternal flame, they sing hymns and make sacrifices that induce the freedom to move. With nourishment, their bodies attain auspicious powers, serving all the seven motherly rivers. With powerful, eternal flames, they look for damsels to produce offspring. They grow into wondrous forms and appear as chiefs who serve with their strength. Like the ancient messenger (Mātariśvan) representing Indra, they brush forth its concealed power to flourish through creating the mythical juice (Soma).

Male and female join with splendid light and grow and expedite the birth of newborns. They, with vigour, serve as heralds. They as wise, one-minded, holy ones; they offer the morning rites supported by the eternal wind. They rise from the ground like birds to experience pure birth lifted to heaven.

The worshippers fly away before they are subjected to violence; they are helped by the trinity (Varuṇa, Mitra, and Aryaman). With mighty powers, they encompass everything around them, and with Agni, libations send them eternal wealth. The divine patron (Bhaga) makes them children of strength filled with eternal wealth. They vouchsafe their riches and learn to turn them into worthy ends. They sacrifice so they can be directed from both worlds. The glorious priest hears their joyful, radiant bodies being pulled like horses to conduct worship with hymns. They serve as wealthy chiefs and spread forth as beams of light above the rain clouds.

Kindled with its powers, Agni brings even today the eternal flame by lifting the ladle that pours out the mythical juice and deals with a sweet sacrifice (Tanūnapāt). Enriched with libations, a singer brings wondrous, sanctifying sacrifice, all accompanied by eternal wisdom. This generates and sprinkles three times a day to serve the heavenly demigods (Narāśaṁsa).

Ladle holders praise Agni and Indra, which spread over the trimmed grass to offer sacrifice to bring divine power. They throw open the divine doors that bring night and morning accompanied by loud hymns. All united look at the strong mothers who make the sacrifice for all seated together on the sacred grass.

The third step of manifestation brings holy sages who sing hymns that reach heaven and allow the eternal flame to manifest and appear as prophets (Hotrā). They sit on the sacred grass among the godly powers (Maruts, Bhāratī, Iḷā, Sarasvatī, and Mahī). They send forth for the creative powers (Tvaṣṭar) to send cosmic vapours as dew filled with wondrous gifts to increase and expand their eternal wisdom, all filled with creative powers. Serving as kinsmen for the mortal bodies, they welcome the united power Vanaspati as friends who make sacrifices. With eternal flame and eternal wisdom, they offer oblations to seek godly solar power (Pūṣan), which joins the prevailing terrestrial powers and rises to join with the cosmic host (Maruts). They jointly honour the celestial powers and, along with Indra, come to inspire with hymns to present with gifts.

According to Rig Veda, Book 1, Hymn CXLIII, Agni brings singing sons of strength, offspring of the waters serving as the goddess (Sarasvati), who creates the seasons. The seasons with new birth represent the entry of the ancient messenger (Mātariśvan), creating the highest firmament above the ground, all powered and kindled by Agni along with splendour (Surya), which creates illumination for all regions between heaven and earth. With such illumination, it brings the life force (Prana), which passes through floods and comes with Agni to rule as the sovereign appearing like the lord of wealth (Bhṛgus), which regulates all possessors serving the terrestrial world. No force can stay, even the powerful cosmic host (Maruts), which sends a dart to heaven. Agni eats such darts and sends bolts to smite foes. Agni joins enjoyment and the divine will that grants nature (Vasu) the wealth that moves with speed and prayers.

With flames, Agni wins, and as a friend, the daylight (Dyaus) promotes the eternal laws with a bright face that becomes keenly inflamed and produces reflective moonlight. With hymns, it guards nature, which never slumbers. The god of the daylight (Dyaus) serves as the patriarch of all illumination, including constellations of stars. The heavenly power (Surya), the father of all godly powers of causation, and Agni and Indra manifest as celestial bodies that protect all creation prevailing in the terrestrial region. Agni and Indra serve the father (Dyaus) and mother (Apas) of all mortal living things (Rig Veda, Book 1, Hymn CXLIV). Father and mother send earthly priests to sacrifice with hymns. As earthly priests, they move like a father abiding by the law and a mother leading the streams. They sing prayers and encompass all about the ground (Prithvi), their home immersed in the waters serving as the birthplace of godly powers where they reside. They absorb godlike powers and serve as supreme powers of causation.

Father and mother seek alternate courses to reach an end in the oceans, where they strive to win the same beauteous form. They invoke the divine patron (Bhaga) and hold on fast to the reins represented by the sun and moon having their dwelling in the same abode. They animate as mortal devotionals that call on the godly powers for help. They speed up over the land and perform deeds. They appear as the two mighty ones born of the eternal laws (Varuna) with eternal love (Mitra) sitting on the sacred grass, and Agni accepts with joy their prayers and serves as a joy giver.

They have eternal wisdom with admonition with commands for the lord of strength, the lord of power, and the lord of might (Rig Veda, Book 1, Hymn CXLV). They grasp all this with their eternal wisdom, they listen to vibrations, and they transform into oscillations to produce hymns. As newborns, they grasp whatever they see, move on with their kinfolk, and gain help from the mighty ones. They consume all in their embodiments with pleasure and great joy. They attain gifts in the water and on land. They declare the wisdom of works to their mortal embodiments, and they worship eternal wisdom.

The divine seven rays, the daughters of Surya, along with the triple-headed godly power (Trimurti), sink in flowing water and move with rivers; they come to reside in the mother's bosom and rest in the lap of the father. Both, serving as perfect parents, receive luminous dominions of heaven, filling the gap (Rig Veda, Book 1, Hymn CXLVI). Appearing as the primordial force (Shakti), it stands untouched from the far-reaching wilderness as it sets footsteps on the ground, Prithvi, with holy grass and plants.

With eternal red flames from Agni and licking the udder that provides proper heat and vigour, they come together to create a place for younglings to grow in the embodiments of the mother-like cow. Fair shaped, the younglings spread forth in all directions measuring out the paths that must be travelled. Entrusting all desires to the mighty ones with prudent holy souls, they develop in mortal dwellings. As mortal embodiments, they look at the rivers and the light coming from behind the mountain. Born as noble souls with eyes aiming to implore all life, they move far like the wealthy one (Surya) and serve as the sun, which becomes visible to progeny.

Radiant Agni fosters males and females to manifest as their offspring who enjoy godly powers while fulfilling the eternal laws (Rig Veda, Book 1, Hymn CXLVII). In their speech, they refer to the primordial life force (Shakti), which gives them the freedom to serve even as the most youthful. When Agni witnesses such activity, it preserves them from affliction (Māmateya). They preserve their faith, which helps them face foes and be safe from mistakes or mischief. The sinful man who worships not and offers nothing tries to harm mortal souls through double-dealing; their mortal embodiments are injured by fellow noble mortals with praise, but Agni saves them.

To serve as a herald representing all godheads with powerful resistance, the divine messenger (Mātariśvan) appears as a manifested figure that generates beautiful light (Rig Veda, Book 1, Hymn CXLVIII). From the homes of demigods and temples, Agni protects those who, with praise, follow divine acts and bring pleasure to all. The mighty powers and Agni accept their positions and constantly perform skilled work, all taken as part of worship. With praises, they establish their command that leads to the bearers. They bring forward many wondrous things with wind and fire. They never injure those waning devotees, lords of great riches; they hasten to the place of treasure, where cosmic and celestial bodies come like a steer to serve humanity, bringing new embodiments filled with the mythical juice.

Righteous Souls

Righteous souls appear like sunlight (Rig Veda, Book 1, Hymn CXLIX), covering the three luminous dominions: heaven, earth, and the esoteric regions. Being faithful servants of Agni for two births, the eternal fire calls on them with many gifts that provoke the great godly powers. They never seek aid like godless souls, who never bring offerings to honour the splendid singers serving the mightiest in heaven.

Nature (Prakriti), personified as motherhood and fertility and with the powers of creation and destruction, comes to serve living things (Rig Veda, Book 1, Hymn CL). Mother Earth restores mortal bodies like aquifers are restored by rain, and they return as free-flowing water bringing along the seed and embryo to continue progeny. Through a similar process, Agni produces the seasons, which give birth to the powers of attraction and aversion and gravity. They regulate surrounding bodies such as the moon that causes the tides, which fostered the evolution of life on earth.

The enlivening supreme powers of causation regulate mortal embodiments through the trinity (Trimurti). This includes the creator (Brahma), the preserver (Vishnu), and stability (Shiva), while the evil and noble powers threaten each other and create chaos. The supreme powers of causation bring peace and stability by calling up the primordial force to manifest and help loved ones.

The wise, noble souls offer sacrifice through transforming cosmic vapours into the rain to the creator (Brahma) as a manifested holy body (Brahman) and a soul-searching reality. The holy body offers mental powers that bring sacred songs as divine gifts and provide the mythical juice coming from far with extended fame (Purumīlha). Serving as the master of the house, it helps acquire eternal wisdom and shares among all folk prevailing with glorified birth to receive from heaven and celebrate life.

All singers sacrifice to gain eternal strength (Rig Veda, Book 1, Hymn CLI). Even the malicious Asuras among the evil powers prosper as they learn to acquire eternal wisdom and serve with those who proclaim the holy law and worship as the righteous ones. This all brings the heavenly powers to the ground, where living beings perform skilful work. The heavenly powers bring mighty treasure that is received by living things. All creations receive sunlight and moonlight, attracting maliciousness from the evil neighbourhood. They come like swift birds running from prey and crying to the light. Mitra and Varuṇa bring the divine will to prosper freely and serve with Agni, which brings them special gifts. Serving as the master of sages, the divine will comes singing songs and offering milk with their first prayer to all the righteous ones. This stirs individual enhanced minds (Chitta), which helps them recollect the ancient hymns. Serving heroes, they attain surpassing powers to serve as avatars of the protector (Viṣṇu) and declare the mighty deeds that use the altar above the ground to serve its congregation.

The righteous ones (Rig Veda, Book 1, Hymn Clii), like wild beasts, perform mighty deeds and provide life and serve creatures before they can become avatars of the protector (Viṣṇu). With hymn and worship, the avatar itself prevails above the altar like the bull having its dwelling on the mountains. All places below the protector (Viṣṇu) are filled with the mythical juice (Rig Veda, Book 1, Hymn CLIII) that provides eternal joy and upholds the threefold regions providing a place for all the heavenly creatures.

This well-loved mansion, where mortal godly souls find happiness, follows in Viṣṇu's footsteps (Rig Veda, Book 1, Hymn CLIV). With pleasure, they go to their new dwelling place, where many, like oxen, shine down from the sublime mansion of the heavenly bull. The great heroes (Avatars) sing songs of praise while they drink the mythical juice on lofty ridges.

The great heroes (Avatars) bring Indra to keep afar from the furious rush that the mythical juice brings all-mighty powers (Rig Veda, Book 1, Hymn CLV). Those who learn to direct such drink and avoid furious rushes manifest with godly powers that grant mortal souls mighty strength.

With the father's third-highest heavenly light, they appear as great heroes with special godly powers as Kṛśānu, which serve the Avatars to preserve and stride forth for life above ground and serve newly created dominions in the material world (Virag). With freedom and serving as the avatar, Kṛṣānu beholds mortal noble embodiments over the first two steps, and from the third step, they look at the restless light with amazement, making sure no mortal embodiment approaches the region covered by birds. Like a wheel, it moves with a swift motion. As the envoy of Viṣṇu, Kṛṣānu, before going the third step, seeks help from eternal love (Mitra) to bring the eternal flame fed with oil from Agni. This allowed eternal wisdom to expand with songs of praise offered as oblations and solemn rites.

Kṛṣānu brings together gifts for heavenly Viṣṇu, who told his spouse about his lofty birth, which in glory surpasses all his peers. This includes Kṛṣānu, Varuṇa, and the Aśvins, who regulate divine will (Devavani) as well as the cosmic host (Maruts). They, as mighty Viṣṇu's protectors, regulate the sources of illumination. They, along with their godly friends, unite the godly and form godlier affiliations that allow heavenly powers to unite with the mighty Viṣṇu and fellowship with the throne (Heraldz, Āryanz), who could serve three worlds through offering their worship and sharing the holy law.

After the luminous, heavenly body (Sūrya) awakens to support Agni, they generate the eternal flame, which with the celestial body rises and create sunlight and moonlight, which as Aśvins bring out their carriage so they can move on their course. They allow Savitar to move with folks in sundry ways, all supported by the twin demigods that bring the mythical juice mixed with honey and water. This is all accompanied by the eternal flame, which ignites the immortal primordial power (Shakti) to give birth to bodies with individual spirits serving the offspring of the immortal soul.

The immortal primordial power brings strength to win riches and spoils. The twin demigods come with a three-wheeled car with luxurious power and bestow delight and eternal wisdom. As they are drawn by steeds, they come to build elevations filled with animals and living beings moving to build civilizations. The demigods sprinkle nourishment to prolong life and wipe out those who trespass and destroy foes. They support those who are companions of godly powers and are immortal friends ready to store the embryos in female creatures. They pass through the eternal fire and establish the mighty sovereigns who send medicine that cures living things. They bring oblations that pour forth from their hearts.

The twin demigods join with nature, which along with the heavenly powers (Rudras), provides counsel and jointly grants powers to serve as the strong and strengthens (Rig Veda, Book 1, Hymn CLVIII). A generous, noble soul (Acathya) always standing beside the great helpers craves wealth. They fully understand such riches that can fulfil any longing. Just like long ago, Tugra's son was provided with a boat that was so well equipped that it could set across the sea.

Many praiseworthy monks (Ucathya) preserve such generous souls, and their offspring make sure, like the twin demigods, that they manifest as winged stallions. They do not exhaust themselves in flight. The devotees cast in most motherly streams where they could be securely bound and not subject to be devoured, especially when a league of the legend (Traitana) cleaves heads apart.

The eternal laws established to strengthen godly progeny and create the wonder-working force is empowered to bring forth the choicest boons. This all started with the invocation of the gracious mind of the godly father and the power of the godly mother (Rig Veda, Book 1, Hymn CLIX). They are the parents who regulate perishable life surrounded by imperishable life. With praise and sacrifices, they enliven the supreme powers of causation responsible for heaven and earth.

Serving as offspring male or female of prolific parents and blessed with wondrous power, they bring forth life from the two mothers. Both serve as extra-terrestrial energy over extra-terrestrial matter and produce divine will like their offspring, who knows no guile. Their offspring measure out the heavens and the earth. They understand that before their birth, they were united and came from one home. From birth, heaven reaches the depths of the oceans and maintains forever a new web that is connected through the solar deity (Savitar). It is through such a web that it generates thought processes among godly powers. They advance and now even create loving-kindness like cows. Using the same powers directed by the ultimate powers of causation, they are personified as one God who created heaven and earth and bestowed its riches on them.

The heavenly and earthly regions bestow prosperity, and through the sustainers, they regulate the middle region and fill the two bowls with manifested noble souls serving as the one, mighty, supreme power. They travel as companions (Rig Veda, Book 1, Hymn CLX), appearing among the sun and the moon, and they keep all creatures safe. Heaven and earth are filled with clothed offspring, all in godly forms. They manifest with mortal and immortal embodiments as the holy priest that serves with the power to cleanse and sanctify all living things and support milk-producing animals. The most skilled godly powers measure eternal wisdom and absolute truth; they establish pillars that will never decay between heaven and earth. The mighty pair brings great glory and gives strength to the folk.

The descended mythological powers races (Rbhuk5an) declare to the congregation about newly embodied spirits (Rig Veda, Book 1, Hymn CLXII) that have acquired special virtues and are not to slight the prevailing godly powers (Varuṇa, Aryaman, Mitra, Indra Vayu, or Maruts). They show how the new spirits turn common horses into stallions. Within the animal kingdom, many milk bearers such as goats and sheep appear to support Indra. The solar deity (Pū5an), who first led common horses to become swift horses, now accepts new creations coming after serving thrice-manifested noble spirits as goats and sheep. These with noble souls meet with Agni to seek the eternal flame that produces the mythical juice (Soma) and offer it to the priest to finish the sacrifice. They lead them to fill rivers where hard-working carvers build a caravan to prepare and serve food that sages with horses and birds rejoice about with their singers.

After proceeding from higher waters, the first springs of life come to arrive from death (Yama) and are given to a deity (Trita) to harness. They are first mounted by Indra, like a powerful flying horse, and later, they appear as a masculine spirit Gandharva, which appears as a blessed soul with musical skills that direct the powers of nature (Vasus). They are guided by the light of the sun, and as the courser, they come into existence to move away from death like swift horses supporting the noble powers (Āditya).

They are thoroughly divided, and to manage matters, they drink the mythical juice to hold together and be bound by thirty-three godly powers covering from heaven to the oceans. They are all supported by the powers of law, and as coursers, they recognize the noble spirits from afar. They come with their hooves and place them at a safe place to be groomed with the holy law. They fly below heaven in matchless glory, eager to win the food brought to the station. The coursers appear like bridegrooms who go after charming maidens.

With their horns of gold and their feet of iron, they taste oblations mounted for the courser. With symmetrical flanks and rounded haunches, the celestial coursers follow the heavenly causeway. With bodies of swift chargers that fly, they bring the spirit with their sirens as they spread abroad in all directions moving with restlessness to overcome wildernesses. Like strong steeds, they come forward, pondering with their minds directed toward godly powers, and like goats, they lead the sages and singers. They come into the noblest mansion and to their father and mother. This day, godly powers are welcome, which bring good gifts.

Resurrection

The benevolent priest (Rig Veda, Book 1, Hymn CLXIV) with old, grey hair and a back sprinkled with ashes from the ferocious fire, Agni manifests and appears as the recreator (Shiva) beholding as the

127

chief of the seven powers of causation. The seven coursers (flying horses) bear individual names. They, as offspring, draw as one seven-wheeled chariot representing the three parts of the dynamic universe. All generating vibrations serve the recreator (Shiva), which supports the newly manifested material worlds where manifested embodiments have already established their resting place. The seven-wheeled chariot in fiction pulled by seven brothers (horses) all drawn by seven sisters (cows) utter treasured praise songs that behold the living things.

They bring boneless astral bodies ready to support the physical bony structure. They acquire blood from the earth to protect the immortal, individual living spirit (Atma). They manifest to form mortal embodiments filled with unripe minds supported by the universal soul. They established on the ground (Prithvi) above the underworld or earth, a place for the godly powers to represent. They weave a web with their seven threads, each representing eternal truth, which combined represent absolute truth in terms of knowing the unknown; thus, they help ignorant beings acquire eternal wisdom.

From one who from the unborn image (astral body) links with six fixed, global continents on the manifested ground (Prithvi), they serve as individual regions of the material world. Each region includes animals as leaders, such as cows, to supply milk. This, as a mother, gives milk to offspring to serve as a leader-like father that generates spiritual thought, vigilance, and adoration and gives the ability to yoke to bring the mother as a godhead. With the mother's support, they bring through clouds where the infant rests. The recreator (Shiva), beholding as the chief of the seven powers of causation, looks upon godly powers for what to wear and how to adopt the shape to face three directions where three mothers and three fathers all stand erect and never weary. Shiva forms twelve months that help the wheels roll over all supported by Agni and regulates the ultimate illuminated body (Surya). Together, they define the twelve forms supporting the wealthy watery rivers to store water in the ocean.

The Surya, with far-seeing eyes, mounts the sun with five-spoked wheels, which regulates the planets as they revolve and influences the ground on which living creatures rest. The sun, the six-spoked body, encompasses all the regions to serve the living creatures.

The divine offspring are born with sacred souls (Rsis) to serve living beings. They bring divine gifts as the living spirit, all guided by the universal soul. With one sacred soul (Rsis) and six offspring (sages), they know all about their father and forefathers covering the lower and upper (Lokas).

They know where the mother cow bearing her calf has risen. The rising godlike spirit representing the universal soul is called on when the immortal living spirit departs from the living being. This is all directed by the powers of Indra and fully supported by the mythical juice (Soma).

Like two birds, they knit bonds of friendship in the same sheltering tree and find refuge, sing hymns, and spend a portion of their eternal lives as sacred synods. They procreate and sing holy hymns to serve Savitri as one of the consorts of the universal soul. Shiva, in its highest form, serves as a sect (Shaivism). This all appears as the omnipotent (Siddhant), which in the subtle, luminous form (Sadasiva) manifests as absolute truth.

In feminine form, the goddess (Savitri) is worshipped with hymns consisting of twenty-four syllables (Gāyatrī). From this hymn (Gāyatrī), the new hymn (Triṣṭup) is fashioned to win immortal life. From Triṣṭup and through chanting with the mythical juice, a new hymn (triplet) is formed that can measure the two or four syllables, like two in water and three in the inferno, and from them, it develops seven meters (a furlong) that measure the depth of the ocean. The oceans' tides are caused by the sun and moon, exposing the ground with moonlight (Jagatī) created to honour the ruler (Rathantara) serving the holy ground (Prithvi).

Based on the hymn (Gāyatrī), living things excel in majesty and vigour that invoke animals to produce milk and extract vigour from the eternal flame. The goddess (Savitri) brings a yearning to embodiments and invokes the individual immortal spirits like the lowing of cattle to give birth to a calf. The Aśvins help the mother yield her milk to feed her new-born.

Some younglings cling to the shoulder with cries giving mortal embodiments an experience of enlightenment. The living spirits help them never stumble on the path as they serve the father (Dyaus), the begetter of herdsman. They have kinship as their mothers do to the earth. They spread between the world's two halves. The father lays the embryo for the daughter on earth, never knowing the earth's limit or centre. The stallion's prolific seed reaches the highest heaven, where it abides through divine will. The seven sperms represent heaven's prolific seed serving as the avatar of the preserver (Viṣṇu). Endowed with wisdom, they encompass every presiding side. Being served by Dyaus, they wander when the firstborn with the holy law speaks; only a portion grasps the inherent strength, knowing the universal soul is related to immortal living spirits in mortal embodiments. The universal soul and living spirits move in opposite directions: one hits the mark while the other misses it.

No one knows what praise song will invoke the power to be fortunate. Just like cows feeding on grass, those who become eight footed extend to the sublime heaven. Others who descend in rivers become part of the world's four regions and serve as the path to universal life. Serving as the father (Dyaus), they see from far away from smoke and fire as it rises above with might. In three long ringlets, they show seasonality in order, one ending the year, one making a speech that sweeps the universe, and one that measures the four divisions regulated by the godhead. Of these four, three remain in hiding; only the fourth speaks in the form of a heavenly golden coloured bird (Gurda), which appears like a human.

These golden-coloured birds fly to the heavens and are robed in the waters to moisten the earth with their fatness. They set together 360 spokes (days) that cannot be loosened. They feed all things and give wealth to the goddess (Sarasvatī), which brings water no one can drain. Godly powers accomplish their sacrifice with the earliest ordinances. These mighty ones attain the height of heaven with God's old dwelling like Sādhyas. The rain gives life to earth, and fire reanimates heaven. The celestial birds place the seeds of plants in water that, with rain, bring delight within the season.

The new noble souls learn to participate among themselves and dwell with each other (Rig Veda, Book 1, Hymn CLXV). Manifested in the material world, they destroy evil powers created as embodiments. They express their love for eternal wealth, and they understand their abilities as heroes and serve as youthful ones following the young cosmic host (Maruts).

They fly and reach Indra, where they are greeted as the lords of the bay steeds. They sing hymns, and they can hurl forth loud with strength, all bearing with longing for libations. As strong companions with decorated bodies, they appear like mighty spotted deer with an understanding of their past, and they become godlike. They are still fierce and strong but are now bent away from the foe's weapon and come as comrades to serve with heroic valour. They achieve fully like the mightiest cosmic host and kill evil powers. They hold waters coming from Indra and his envoy (Maghavan). Among the godly powers, nothing equals them.

The lords of the bay steeds come armed with lightning to protect livestock and give bounteously serving free of ill will. They sing, and they drink the juice. They guard well along with their castles living beings, whom they love and fight against sin. They have all good things, including the strength to overpower their rivals. These bright ones journey in their chariots and hold many godly things.

With deerskins on their shoulders, they wear their knives, which spread out with glory as birds spread their wings (Rig Veda, Book 1, Hymn CLXVII). They pass as strong ones visible from afar like the stars. With pleasant tongues, they shout. As the noble-born, they come from far away to bring bounty to mothers to spread around. Even Indra never annuls the boon being bestowed on the pious man. Through their kinship with immortals, even the cosmic host (Maruts) pays attention by calling on them to vouchsafe the mortal embodiments. Hearing their wondrous deeds through prayer, the heroes display their might so they may flourish for longer through their abundant riches. The immortal cosmic host (Maruts) brings food for their offspring in abundance.

The Maruts come to help the lords' steeds by bringing their choice refreshments and precious goods (Rig Veda, Book 1, Hymn CLXVII). The most sapient souls with protection bring the best boons from heaven. As manifested embodiments, they move like swift horses to the seas' limits. In seclusion, they cling to their embodiments. The goddess Vāk, with a courtly voice, suggests they not follow brightly decked among all as mortal embodiments and learn from the universal soul. Even the fierce godly powers help spirits grow and follow them with heroic spirits and follow the clouds along with the heavenly power, Surya.

The young ones appear with glory and might invoke with hymns the universal soul and join with the cosmic host. They offer the juice and sing in worship to declare the greatness of the cosmic host. With loving spirits, they travel like happy females in their fortune. Mitra, Varuṇa, and Aryaman discover worthless sinners with the support of the cosmic host by offering them choice oblations. None of the spirits reaches the limit of their vigour, and they boldly adjust to encompass their foes like an ocean. As the dearest friends of Indra manifested spirits like Māndārya, son of the poet (Māna), worship daily the heroes (Ṛbhukṣa) with song in honour of the cosmic host that brings manifested bodies and their offspring food in abundance.

Surrounded by the young ones, the cosmic host manifests as the self-born, self-powered, divine power (Shiva). They spring to life, appearing as movers and shakers who bring food and light with praise (Rig Veda, Book 1, Hymn CCLXVII). They appear like powerful animals, and they grow as stalks of strong mythical plants (Soma) that produce the juice and come to dwell in the heart and grow like the friendly and wise.

They speedily descend from the sky; with their mighty strength, they cast down all armed and perform duties during the day. They reach the farthest regions where they cast down like chaff firmly established as a pile, from where the recreator (Shiva) generates floods. Dazzling in heavenly light, they mature like fruit that falls as a gift; victorious, they spread with immortal godly powers. Their voices bring rain that covers the earth, and they scatter with their corpulence sending through another, who fights in a mighty battle with a glittering army of the restless. The cosmic host nurtures together like the monster; when they look around for food, they sing like the poet (Māna) as they feed and gain strength.

Indra protects the young ones and grants them dear blessings (Rig Veda, Book 1, Hymn CLXIX). All mortals representing the young ones with eternal wisdom receive orders from Indra to support the cosmic host, which with its universal soul wins the spoils of battle. Indra keeps firm the cosmic host with a spear to face the trepidation caused by the ferocious fire that shines in the brushwood and holds back the land as an island filled with vegetation. Breath swells the breast with refreshing sweetness.

The cosmic host (Maruts), representing the universal soul, shows loving kindness and, as an old, godly power, tries to help all. They bring down boons with rain while Indra exerts its power to expand the terrestrial region. With speckled deer like a king's army, they stand on the battlefield as the herald and roar like the advancing cosmic host, who, in a rush, overthrow sinners and bring mortal embodiments who fight with love and give life to the living beings as universal gifts foremost among which are cattle. Such mortal embodiments are not able to comprehend the mystery of the cosmic host serving as the universal soul.

Vedic sages (Agastya) as brothers do not neglect (Rig Veda, Book 1, Hymn CLXX) their true friendship even though they droop when asked to prepare an altar to honour the immoral universal soul and immortal spirits. They serve as the lords of wealth, the true friends of Indra. The cosmic host tastes the oblations offered to the second heaven in the esoteric region serving the material world, where the unmanifested universal soul (Paramatma) asks for sacrifice for embodied spirits (Atma) to reside among all three regions. Encompassing the mighty ones, they all spread to serve the terrestrial region and produce their offspring such as air (Tri-Dasha) and ether (Vata), all with fires serving as the father (Pitta) and cosmic vapours (Kapha) serving the earth with water. In total, these thirty-three mighty godly powers extend from heaven to the deepest ocean, representing mortal embodiments as a dual power, which manifest as the twin demigods with horses' heads representing the universal soul and human heads representing Atma. With hymns, they suppress the universal soul's anger, and with prayer and worship, they allow individual spirits as the godly powers to become effective.

Praise from Indra brings universal gifts, the living things (Mānas) as cattle, the strong ones, pleasant and lovely, and they come as triumphant days (Rig Veda, Book 1, Hymn CLXXI). It removes the terror of evil powers, and the mighty power of Indra forgives all sins to bring oblations to the cosmic host.

The strong ones as living beings come to recognize the living things (Mānas) with their physical strength that comes with the morning light after passing through the fierce cosmic host to bring mighty glory to meet with Indra. With help from the strong ones, living beings are recognized as conquering heroes with wisdom and strength. The bounteous ones sing like birds as they expand like milk-giving cows and join the gods' assembly.

Priests bring twofold oblations from the holy youth, who, through circling the measuring stations, bring to the earth autumn fruit. They let the steer shout with a voice that reaches all the heralds between heaven and earth. They receive strength and, with praises, make themselves pious living beings who are wondrous in Indra's might. They come swiftly as noble demigods. They praise Indra as the truly mighty that makes their embodiments like the righteous hero warrior (Maghavan).

Stronger in war than those who fight against them, these righteous heroes as warriors surpass their greatness as Indra endues the earth to serve as their garment. Heaven serves as the godlike frontlet that guards the brave heroes. The hosts pour libations in the sea to control floods, which cheers all living things. They pray for Indra to linger as they worship and are guided by the godly power that serves as extolling princes. They help hold everything in good rule, and they receive Indra's support as they sacrifice. Indra helps them find ways to advance and lead others.

Indra speaks with those who cause mishandling to break down autumn and takes foes as prey but passes over to Purukutsa, the youthful, who remember their history. They are driven by the daylight that is much worshipped to honour Indra. They are born as powerful animals like elephants and water buffalo, which are used to till fields. They are praised by Indra, and through the greatness of their harpoons, they can rest at the station. They serve in battle mounted on bays and seize booty. Indra accepts many such manifested animals, which behave like sages (Kutsa) and serve humanity as they bring joy. They are submissive like the horses of the wind that pull chariots like the sun and fight their foes.

They generate inspiration like Indra, that causes worshippers to produce hymns and serve as followers (Dāsa). As worshippers, they cover the earth serving with noble souls. They produce moisture with three gleams: thunder, lighting, and power as they slay the demon (Kuyavāc) in his resting place. They support Indra to crush castles, eliminate the godless races, and deform the godless scorners with deadly weapons. Indra comes with stormy waters to create rivers, and with heroes Turvaśa and Yadu, they manage the floods. On occasion, Indra personally protects the gentle-hearted mortal embodiments to bring them victory over their rivals and helps them find food in abundance.

As the lords of the bay steeds, they quaff the mythical juice to gain wisdom (Rig Veda, Book 1, Hymn CLXXV). The more they drink, the stronger they become. The heroes conquer the lawless (Dasyu) with their mighty power, and with sages, they overpower magical devices (Śuṣṇa) before they bring death.

With strength, they bring storms that push away their foes, and with divine songs, they penetrate whoever is close and turn food into sacred food (Rig Veda, Book 1, Hymn CLXXVI). All the treasures rest among five peoples' hands and are deposited by Indra, which fights those who injure noble souls and even kills them with heavenly thunderbolts. The wealth of those who pour out no gifts is taken away and distributed to those who worship Indra. They obtain strength from abundant food. Manifested embodiments who cherish all people serve as the king of the five races and are blessed with fame and praise (Rig Veda, Book 1, Hymn CLXXVII).

Spiritual Birth

With assistance from Indra, manifested embodiments acquire vigour and come to serve like bay horses that travel between heaven and earth. Indra ascends, pouring the mythical juice, and comes down toward mortal embodiments bringing immortal spirits. Indra joins as Śakra, the lord of Devas residing on Mount Meru and serving the polar centre of the physical world. With mythical juice along with revolving around the sun and moon, they set the second heaven (Trāyastriṃśa) among the highest mountains from where the creator comes in contact with the long-lived, perishable, mortal embodiments serving as the ruling deity (Śakra). When, as a manifested mortal embodiment, it dies, the ruling deity, Śakra, is replaced with another perishable deity as the new Śakra, who with devotions worships like the singer (Māna) and finds food in abundance.

Indra gives graciously to those who sing its praises (Rig Veda, Book 1, Hymn CLXXVIII) even when they are disappointed with what the sun and moon bring to the dwelling. Indra provides them victory as heroes in the battle where they praise Indra. Through many autumns, the mighty protector toils and labours and lets husbands come near their wives or lets wives come near their husbands (Rig Veda, Book 1, Hymn CLXXIX). The mythical juice pardons sins, and mortal man toils and raises children with godly strength as sages. He, through prayer, obtains fulfilment as the institutor of sacrifice; they understand that the two forms of mythical juice (Soma and Amrita) are needed to connect celestial energy with terrestrial matter.

Dawn overtakes the coursers, who are flying apart, and establishes them with godly power that serves the friends of humanity. They convey the mythical juice and milk provided by the motherly cow. At first, it appears as fresh water; they fill the air with a fierce heat that makes the water sweet, and with the twin demigods' power, it brings out divine gift as milk. They serve milk with oblations as the mythical juice (Soma) to encompass the heavenly powers to comprehend the esoteric region. They move down to experience the true powers of nature, Vasus.

Through understanding the swift powers of the eternal wind (Vayu), they gain strength, and their embodiments become pious (Rig Veda, Book 1, Hymn CLXXXI). The Aśvins, along with the mighty virtuous guide, learn to unveil eternal truth. Rising with praise, music, and glory, they sacrifice to gain their share of riches. The twin demigods come to serve humanity. Whether sages are born wise or become wise, they know they must support all things in the cycle of day and night and support others (Rig Veda, Book 1, Hymn CLXXXV).

Similarly, as parents protect their offspring from danger, they come from heaven and earth. Like the Aśvins, they worship along with other living things and seek protection from danger from heaven and earth. In the material world, they are served by godly parents; they receive favour from the demigods regulating day and night.

Faring as young ones, they lie in their parents' bosom. Heaven and earth serve as mighty parents providing protection and the mythical juice such as nectar. Like the blessed pair, they are victorious no matter the sin committed against the gods; they serve as friends and chieftains and sing hymns to preserve those who seek their help. Endowed with such understanding, the truth can be heard by those who stay away from criticism.

The Aśvins bring the holy waters and light to serve the noble priest. With their purified body free of any stain or mark, they represent heaven's offspring. They glide down with golden colour to feed mortal embodiments. They send the mythical juice to all others. They, with vibrations, cause the water to help the grass grow to serve the animals. As prudent worshippers, they are honoured by the godly powers serving the region—Pū5an, Aśvins, Savitar, and Agni. With the godly queen (Viśpalā), they move like a chariot drawn by steeds and appear as heaven's sons to bless pious men (Rig Veda, Book 1, Hymn CLXXXII). The pious men, who long for the mighty powers, bring the sweet juice all carried by the Aśvins but passing over scrooges and misers. They understand praise and even offer to be accepted by both kinds of demigods—the Nāsatyas and the Aśvins.

Amid the floods, the demigods transform into divine offspring (Tugra) that appear as winged bodies. They escape through flying and bring mortal embodiments out of the mighty waters. They plunge into the waters like heroes as living beings (Mānas), and then they come to serve as envoys (Nāsatyas), and as Aśvins, they offer the mythical juice. This makes them ready to pass through like flying birds (Rig Veda, Book 1, Hymn CLXXXIII). They land on the ground and look for food. They sing the wondrous songs to welcome heaven's daughter, and they wait to serve in the morning and evening light. They ascend to approach worshippers and define their duties as they quicken mother. As offspring, they serve like heroes and as creator demigods. They also learn not to let the wolf come near their offspring and others. They invoke the ancient noble sages—Gotama, Brahmana, Purumīlha, and Atri serving as Sapatarishi—to obtain protection, bring oblations and honour, and follow their principles. They learn to go straight to the point and pass over the limit of darkness. They have the powers of the twin demigods to follow the paths of godly powers and find strengthening food in abundance.

Like priests, they break down the greed of misers and slay their egos by offering gracious hymns and invitations to work with the heroes. Nāsatyas and Pū5ans, the heroes with godly powers, set in order the illuminator, Sūrya with a bride, where giant steeds sprung from the ancient times out of waters to move on with grace to bring the eternal laws, eternal love, and the mythical juice. The poet (Māna) sings hymns that make mortal embodiment joyful, perform glorious actions, and gain heroic strength. With praise, demigods come into their house with fair adornment for the poet (Māna) and their children. They serve as holy sages and praise demigods, so they come passing over the limit of darkness to show godly illuminated paths to travel.

Enlivening the inner power related to love, mortal embodied souls, along with the offspring of the primaeval mother goddess (Aditi), support the deity of water (Savitar). They appear as the impeller, the rouser, the vivified synod, and the ever-youthful, who are personified through glad hymns (Rig Veda, Book 1, Hymn CLXXXVI). They bring together the trinity of Aryaman, Mitra, and Varuṇa that promotes welfare and preserves strength. Through singing hymns, they bring loving guests; the eternal flame eliminates slackness among friendly conquerors. They send food with the eternal laws like princes praised by godly powers.

With praise and song, they generate milk and rejoice as the great dragon of the deep, which nourishes its young in the holy rivers like Sindhu. With the help of the creative power (Tva5tar), even one-minded princes approach life with creative minds. As the ruler of mortal embodiments, Indra, as Vṛtra-slayer, serves heroes with hymns and learns to yoke horses. These hymns yield feeling among the heroes like delightful spouses serving the cosmic host (Maruts). They come with their hearts in concord and armed with mighty weapons. With their steeds, as the allies of the godhead serving as eternal love, Mitra, they destroy the foes.

They hasten their orders with a happy termination and are made known for their glory on a fair, bright day when the arrow flies over all the barren soil with missiles to sparkle. The Aśvins and the godly power (Pū5an) show their power and might. As the earthly godly powers—Vi5ṇu, Vāta, and Ṛbhuk5an—come along to make them happy with a reverent thought, they make holy whoever is inspired to dwell among mortal embodiments.

The glorified food invigorates Trita as a minor solar deity that appears as a protector from the prevailing evil power (Vṛtra) and comes to destroy it limb from limb (Rig Veda, Book 1, Hymn CLXXXVII). With great godly power, it sets in place a flag to honour the brave deeds done, including slaying the dragon. Even if the spirit is gone into the clouds, they are filled with eternal wisdom, which prepares them to receive enjoyment. They become more powerful Vātāpi with the mythical juice and remove impurity by transforming hymns.

As winners of thousands, they receive oblations from sages and envoys serving like the child of God (Rig Veda, Book 1, Hymn

CLXXXVII). They make sacrifices with wisdom by offering sustainingnourishment, sustenance, nutriment, subsistence, fare, bread, daily bread, cooking, baking, cuisine, foodstuffs, edibles, refreshments, meals, provisions, rations, stores, supplies, solids, vivers, eats, eatables, nosh, grub, chow, nibbles, scoff, tuck, chuck, victuals, vittles, viands, commons, meat, comestibles, provender, aliment, commissariat, viaticum nourishment. With prayers, sacrifice, and praise, they invoke the eternal flame that brings countless gifts coming from a thousand heroes. In glorious beauty, they shine forth and bring night and day; they perform sacrifices serving as twin sages. They, with ferocious fire (Agni), sacrifice even as the plant kingdom (Vanaspati) to provide sweet oblations of the mythical juice (Soma) by serving as agents of God.

Agni (Rig Veda, Book 1, Hymn CLXXXIX) brings astral bodies back to the godly path and leads them to new happiness by leading them from the danger associated with the material world. Once the astral bodies reach the second heaven (Trāyastrimśa), they are blessed and are sent to prosper as godly sons far from Agni; all diseases are destroyed by the prevailing deities.

The embodiments preserve the eternal flame, which with perpetual assistance brings light into the loving dwelling to show as the conqueror who, with praises, presides thereafter. They are subjected to sin brought with greed like an enemy that gives up and joins the spoiler. Agni is lauded for giving protection to mortal bodies. With its godly powers, it rescues them from all oppression. With pious speeches, it addresses the mortal soul (Māna) as the offspring blessed with the eternal flame Agni, and it gains countless riches and serves with the sages.

Praised with hymns, the perishable power (Blrhaspati), sweet-tongued and mighty, comes to listen to mortal beings who offer hymns and prayers according to the season and are set to move as the divine power lying out extended with sacrifices (Rig Veda, Book 1,

Hymn CXC). With their praise and adoration, the perishable power (B1rhaspati) brings illuminating rays from the sun that fill the region with light and wisdom. As strong as a wild beast but inoffensive with their songs of praise, they ascend from earth to heaven and with their powers manifest among worshippers appearing like coursers that draw eternal wisdom.

The B1rhaspati go into the skies as flying serpents and appear in multiple hues with godly powers forming the rainbow. Those who are wealthy sinners are punished by the B1rhaspati. While they sing songs of praise, they go forth, appearing as the wise and eager who need to be closely looked upon in water and the vessel with its mighty powers.

With perishable power, they make them go away before they are killed or observed as cruel, venomous creatures that attack manifested bodies (Rig Veda, Book 1, Hymn CXCI). They drive them off and mark them with death by sending them to hiding places such as under the sacred grass (Sara, Darbha, Kuśara, Sairya, Muñja, and Vīraṇa), where they seek protection from such venomous creatures. They even settle in animals' stalls where there is no light. The unseen insects and reptiles appear in the evening and attack mortal embodiments. Godly power protects those serving as heaven, the sire, earth as the mother, the mythical juice as the brother, and the powers of the mother; they come unseen and remain vigilant, knowing they are to support happy dwellings.

The venomous creatures vanish when the sun shines on them. The venomous will not die, but neither will the sun. Both just follow different paths until the bay horses eat them and turn them into the mythical juice. Though appearing as insects that can be crushed, they send forth venom that can kill or paralyze.

PART 2
CORPOREAL

The individual personality (Swabhava) represents orderly growth where one's interaction with the external world creates habits and makes up individual mental setups to follow through with the designated corporal impulses (Samskaras) to perform designated obligatory responsibilities (Karma). Then an entity holding these core qualities comes to encompass moral and righteous activities. These cultivate truthfulness (Swadharma) and perform divine responsibilities (Dharma). Performing such activities requires the use of subtle faculties that signal and enhance individual sensory nervous systems. Simulations shape individual abilities to learn, remember, create expectations, and cultivate powers of attention. It is through the powers that individuals identify their relationships with the ultimate reality and help build nurtured core values (essence). Spiritual reality or cultivated truthfulness pulls out core values (essence), which bring out hidden, shining glory, and it pulls out spiritual powers from a stone-like seed to support individual life.

CHAPTER 4
CULTURED DOMINION

Truthfulness

According to Rig Veda, Book 2, Hymn I, it brings out immortal spirits from mortal embodiments. It skilfully turns nonexistence into existence, which, in the form of eternal power, creates the self-governing power (Aṁśa) and transforms living mortal embodiments into noble souls.

Individual mortal embodiments become sanctified and go through a cleansing process to bring out hidden skills they need to serve as heralds and leaders who perform services to become pious. These pious leaders, with honour, serve the ground (Prithvi). Like a minister guiding mortal souls to follow divine rules and attain the spiritual reality (Brahman), they represent the ultimate creator (Brahma).

The Brahman serves with the trinity of the creator, preserver, and balancer to bring out the essence among mortal embodiments through creating priests of heaven (Brahmanaspati). It provides wealth, wisdom, and long life (Rig Veda, Book 2, Hymn II). With the powers of the essence, it imposes the eternal laws and institutes eternal love, and it implores individual skills to serve as sanctified mortal embodiments. Manifested with such powers, liberally enriched embodiments with the power of the sovereign (Aṁśa) prevail among all (Aryaman) to cultivate a uniquely cultured dominion. Using the powers of Tvasar, they bring creative power to all worshippers and help them use creative skills to cultivate kinship and fight evil powers (Asuras).

The cosmic host brings blessed food to serve mortal embodiments. Savitar protects all worshippers through godly powers, Pusan, that brings honour to worshippers. The divine patron (Bhaga) uses a select few to acquire eternal wisdom so they can assume responsibility as the rulers to guard their eternal wealth. Among mortal embodiments, the spirit serves with eternal love and becomes the ruler. As kings, they part with their wealth to ten, a hundred, and a thousand that represent their kingdom. In the kingdom, brotherhood appears through prayers that win in the bright form seeking like a son their friends, who duly worship them as a father who protects them.

Brahman prompts Agni to bring out the eternal flame along with sacrifice to burn anything to bestow essence. Then they appear among the adored cosmic body (Ṛbhu), which provides food and wealth. Through songs and hymns, Aditi brings these as gifts to honour Agni, which appears as the heavenly sage (Hotrā) to provide bodily heat that warms living beings. They, as the tribe of mortal embodiments (Bhāratī), cover a hundred winters along with Sarasvatī, which in summer makes sure cosmic vapours become water to support Indra while they fight evil. Indra and Agni jointly cherish the highest vital power to serve as the evil slayer.

They create a visible hue among the noble souls (Ādityas), which come from lofty heights to transfer the power of essence to mortal embodiments. They appear as bright ones who are sanctified as priests to offer sacrifices to Agni and Indra, which united give birth to a noble soul to cover earth and heaven. With the princely power of essence (Swadharma), they create brave embodiments that speak loudly in the assembly.

They are divine through their transcendental origins, and so they contribute their superior attributes to other things prevailing on the ground. Divine things are regarded as eternally based on absolute truth. They behave unlike material things; they are regarded as ephemeral illusions. As divinities (Narasamsa), they, as praiseworthy, represent the epithet of Agni; they bring godly power to maintain the divine will. They share their eternal love with animals, and as the messengers of Agni, they serve as the bright ones. They bring boons to the families, which are sent from the herald of heaven along with the sun and moon.

Those who have cultivated friendships and have expanded in glorified ways are identified with Mitra and come to support noble powers. The eternal wind (Vayu) turns the darkness of night into light. After acquiring such powers, the surrounding environment invites flocks of birds and helps them establish their dwellings. Demigods attain essence and regulate embodiments of the divine will with essence (Devavani).

They establish themselves as noble souls and make sacrifices to encompass their purpose. Noble souls bring plants life and help them grow. Agni surrounds all ridges so the plants with noble powers can spread into the valleys to create great wealth and serve manifested embodiments by providing dwellings to the immortal living spirit (Atma).

As an envoy, Agni comes out of the sky to support every morning by passing through closed and unclosed doors and bringing light to disperse the darkness. The bright ones serve as sovereign kings who seek eternity by offering rites to the worshippers. The divine will with essence manifests among hundreds and first starts to show among animals that join up as fearless steeds to merge with their individual spirits with the universal soul and thus transform from being mortal to being immortal.

Once the living beings comprehend the divine will with essence, they acquire knowledge, love, truth, righteousness, and justice that appear with embodied souls to shine in their domain. With bright beams, their spirits serve among living beings. They bring sacrifice and worship into their divine abode. They even serve as kings to keep the eternal wealth under control. With Agni, they produce glorious children who serve as messengers who manifest as mortal embodiments (Apris), which are widely famed as the epithet Narasamsa.

The bright light accompanied by the essence (Swadharma), serving as the divine will, manifests as Devavani, which brings soft energy as a gift (Rig Veda, Book 2, Hymn III). The mortal embodiments are subjected to a purification process that sanctifies them to serve as priests. A dew, just like the mythical juice, is discharged to serve the sacred body or the sacred place. They set an easy path to eternal truth and unveil the righteous acts that must be performed. They interweave time and space to create a web between the two knobs, earth and heaven, that transfers among them with their wisdom, sacred verses, and oblations.

Serving as the twin demigods (Bharati and Ilya), they serve as the creative power (Tvaṣṭar), which makes them pious and strong among heroes. They serve as the heavenly immolator offering heroes their oblations thrice anointed with oil mixed with fire so heroes can move to higher levels of righteousness.

The heroes observe the powers of the essence that come through oblations, and with Agni, they come with oblations to serve like its envoy (Apris) moving like the altar fire (Rig Veda, Book 2, Hymn IV). After they have served heroes, they appear free from old bondage and protect mortal embodiments from evil powers by establishing a longing for morality. They generate inner illumination to worship until they have their own mortal embodiments produce pleasant sounds to praise Agni to establish themselves as a mortal splendour.

With the water coming from cosmic vapours, they turn the ground into free soil.

Agni burns up the scrublands and creates sullied lines that bring the seasons. The assembly of heroes sings hymns to support such noble offspring fully supported by mythical powers. With the sacred principle of the kingdom, Kalapa, they use their vital powers to subdue hostility. They use eight elements—earth, water, fire, air, colour, smell, taste, and nutrition. The first four are primary qualities of nature, Vasu, and the other four as the secondary properties that derive from the primaries to prevail as the form predominant in the kingdom, Kalapa. Certain Kalapa is said to also include additional elements, including sound, sex, body, mind, and life.

Knowing all about the kingdom, Kalapa, heroes evolve to become teachers who serve as the patrons of Agni and guardians of the noble wealth, the mighty ones, and absolute truth (Rig Veda, Book 2, Hymn V). Using the powers of the essence and the divine will, they become noble warriors (Kshatriya), who, after going through purification and sanctification, reach the higher level (Brahmans). With their purified embodiments, they attain the seventh level, Loka, and seek the highest, the eighth level, Loka, and follow the command of the mighty ones.

By singing prayers and hymns, they learn to behold and grasp the absolute truth. They use their pure mental powers, pure essence, and absolute truth to follow the unchanging divine covenant. They appear along with Brahmans as the leader of services and Kshatriya, the true, noble warrior, and they all produce the eternal flame with a flaming hue representing themselves as the band of Agni. They appear graciously and wait to be accepted with prayer, songs of praise, and hymns of honour before eternal truth is unveiled. They share the essence and acquire strength.

The moving and stationary planetary bodies produce good or bad effects that, in terms of astrology, are called the sign (Rasi) and the (existence) Bhava. They, in combination, generate any of the three interdependent modes or qualities of nature, Prakriti. These are called Gunas and are defined as Sattva (goodness, constructive, harmonious), Rajas (passion, active, confused), and Tamas (darkness, destructive, chaotic). Among each mortal embodiment, these conditions establish individual positions relative to the planetary bodies consisting of nine planets, including the north node, Rahu, and the south node, Ketu, of the moon. Within the home, Grahas, they take at least forty-three positions, Poorna, and directions, Dasha, each depending on the divine will and essence that influences each individual planet and which, in turn, subjects them to the process of enactment with reverence to planetary powers of causation. Mortal embodiments regulate the quality of life and its relative benevolence in performing yoga (Raja) and meditation (Drishti).

As the noble warrior serving as the liberal prince, it drives away those who hate noble souls (Rig Veda, Book 2, Hymn VI). The liberal prince uses the power of essence (Swadharma) to bring rain from heaven to produce plentiful food. The liberal prince joins with those who sing songs of worship, and they manifest with imminence like holy heralds. They become well-skilled, surpass any friendly envoy of morality, and appear as holy sages on the grass and serve mortal embodiments.

As the tribe of noble souls (Bharata), they appear with demigods who let no malignity prevail against physical or spiritual powers (Rig Veda, Book 2, Hymn VII). They bring much-desired essence to serve with morality. As a favoured force among natural forces (Vasu), they bring forth floods that carry away adorable nature. They feed the animal and botanical kingdoms and are bedewed with excellent power to generate vital energy. The sons of noble souls, Bharatas, harness the powers of Agni; they seek liberation among the splendid, manifested, immortal spirit, Atma, prevailing in the mortal embodiments.

Morally and with compassion, they remain untouched by death or any foe; they are being served to free their spirits from attachments (Rig Veda, Book 2, Hymn VIII). In embodiments, with glory, they eulogize in the evening and proclaim in the morning. Even when the noble warriors are subjected to the fiery flame, they remain bejewelled with the godly mother (Atri). Their songs create special vibrations with the glory that sway evil powers. With the support of the trinity (Indra, Agni, and Soma), the mortal embodiments conquer those who fight them. After establishing their domicile above the earthly region, they maintain relationships with the supreme powers of causation that influence the planetary system and give birth to a duality: Asuras, the evil, and Adityas, the noble, and through duality, they regulate and transform evil into noble and vice versa.

The liberal prince employs their powers of essence (Swadarma) to serve with treasures. They strengthen themselves with the mythical juice in their fight against the legendary evil creature scaled with spewing fire (Rig Veda, Book 2, Hymn IX). They create, with water, obstructions to stop the other malevolent powers by becoming devotees (Dasa) and serving with noble powers (Adityas). They eliminate obstructions by turning water to create floods that eliminate malevolent powers.

The Adityas transform vibrations into divine music, transform malevolent powers, and accumulate noble powers. Their offspring serve the divine power and acquire essence as they attain inner joy through singing hymns. They are received by Indra and honoured by the supreme heavenly power (Rudras). The noble souls approach heavenly illumination and brilliance to provide direct light from the sun and seek support from the reflective light from the moon and stars. This brings embodiments the inner delight that they receive in addition to the support from the wind provided by Indra that fills the region and helps spirits prevail freely in embodiments.

The supreme powers of causation come to reform evil to serve as a devotee (Dasa) to noble souls and help them overcome hurdles they face in acquiring ultimate illuminating powers. The noble souls receive gallantry from heavenly power so they can overpower the yellowfin tuna at the depths of the ocean serving as the greatest mysterious enchanter. The bright ones with illuminating powers serve as astral bodies with immortal spirits that receive the power. This, as the manifested embodiment, is placed at the time between two strata: heaven and earth. The astral bodies transform from single cells to multiple cells, thus generating dual aspects such as male and female, good and bad, positive and negative.

They fly and, with loud cries, send forth essence along with physical energy transformed into spiritual energy even before they travel on land, where they appear as mortal embodiments that can survive. Their bellowing is heard on earth and in heaven like a big bang seen or visualized by embodiments through drinking the mythical juice. They receive the eternal flame, which baffles the monsters (Danava) as they see visible embodiments absorbing the mythical juice. With Indra's support, such living beings overpower evil forces while they sing praise songs and offer sacrifices to others.

The universal soul (Paramatma) transforms itself from nonexistence to existence by creating a mortal embodiment that provides a dwelling place for immortal spirits. They receive their first libations from the eternal air in the form of breath along with the cosmic host (Maruts) that causes astral bodies to manifest as physical bodies. Physical bodies realize with gladness the spiritual powers along with the divine will from the heavenly region and manifest as the divine will to manifest among moral and righteous embodiments, which are ready to help by comprehending the ultimate power in them. They pass through the material world and win battles while singing divine songs. With loud praises, the powers of essence are established among themselves to build and sustain themselves under the environments.

Physical Bodies

The place of worship provides the deathless astral bodies with a covering like skin that is kindled with the eternal flame (Rig Veda, Book 2, Hymn X). They acquire physical bodies and can hear the divine calling that brings immortal insight. Physical bodies are then drawn like ruddy cars by dark steeds and become infants in which Agni dwells with wisdom and power and watches in its manifested form without any rage. It recognizes the presence of the Devavani, which speak like the ancient power (Manus), and calls on Agni to appear with an eloquent tongue to dispense sweetness.

The physical embodiments are regulated by the stormy Rudra, which generates eternal air (Vayu), which brings the life force in the form of breath (Rig Veda, Book 2, Hymn XI). This life force agitates mountains and spreads as a big bang accompanied by the power of essence with the divine will. The manifested embodiments are shielded from these big sounds as they observe the dragon driven into its hiding places, such as caves, where water from the seven rivers flows to cover it.

Agni sets free and serves the noble warriors in battle. With such activity, even the universe itself trembles and chases away all demons. Priests seek the mythical juice until they learn to make it by pressing plants. The priests welcome the dawn, which sets two armies, immortal and mortal, against each other. Each supports its progeny, so neither can conquer the other. Indra presides over the earthly region and supports the ancient soul (Narmara) through re-creation.

Aesthetics deals with nature, art, beauty, and taste, which are appreciated as beauty. It is defined as the study of subjective and sensory-emotional values. Such embodiments surrender to divinity and monks that follow a variety of ascetic traditions (Śramaṇas). They contrast with those embodiments that serve as teachers, protectors, and sacred learners or priests who help the living being cope with the material world. At temples, Brahmins serve in socio-religious ceremonies such as weddings. Theoretically, Brahmins rank as the highest members of the Hindu social caste system, including farmers, traders, warriors, and priests. The stages of life among priests include bachelor students (Brahmacharya) and householders (Grihastha), and they renounce material desires (Sannyasa) and live simple, spiritual lives (Ahimsa).

After hearing the calling from Indra, manifested embodiments receive treasures and food. They receive flowing water to produce hymns of praise, songs of praise that even turn relentless embodiments into devotees (Dāsa). Those who deem to possess immortal powers (Rig Veda, Book 2, Hymn XII), like mortal heroes, worship Indra and Rudras with delight. They approach the wind (Vāyu), which draws near the brilliant cosmic host. As they become refined, through illumination coming from the highest heavenly power (Sūrya), they overpower their evil heritage. With their enchanting powers, they develop dwellings in the deep waters like fish and remain heavenly checked to make sure they stay in the flowing water and overcome the evil heritage of the manifested ocean bodies.

Once they have achieved great deeds, Indra allows them to hear the calling of the heavenly heralds (Sūrya) along with the bay steeds, the sun and the moon, which spread over the earthly region. They could halt clouds, but they move with the clouds filled with rain. They invite Indra to attack the evil power (Vṛtra), which is sending thunder. Those supporting Indra shout and baffle the evil powers (Dānava). The heroes fill water and land, become strong, and sing to Indra.

They meditate and, with praise, enjoy divine treasures. They become powerful and support their children. They build habitations for the cosmic host in accord with the wind that regulates the mind through breath or the life force (Prana). They learn to enjoy the divine creation's single-focused mind (Chitta) with delight, and they support all living beings. With strength and joy, they serve as sanctuary in battle. They win divine blessings and protect those who help with songs of praise.

The manifest heroes (Trikadruka) rejoice in drinking the mythical juice and serving it with the sun and moon along with Indra. With their might (Dānava), they cleave the evil powers of gold, silver, and iron, and with the noble powers that with light (Aurṇavābha) discloses their identity (Āryan), they become self-designated holy souls (Rishi). They serve Indra, which appears on their left as evil powers (Dasyu) that, with greed, sinks its power. On the right, eternal wealth evolves as mortal bodies serve as noble souls (Āryaman).

As mortal embodiments, they subdue all foes. They build a party that includes the sons of the creative powers (Tvaṣṭar) to serve the universal soul, which manifests in its omni form (Viśvarūpa).

They cast down over the space of mountains (Arbuda) and, in time, appear with vigour pouring libations like the trinity (Tṛta). They call on Indra to regulate the powers of the whirling wheel (Sūrya), and they call on Agni to come as an envoy (Aṅgirases) to overpower the evil serpent (Vala) and set free the milk-bearing holy cows to yield milk. This gives worshippers fortune that never fails and makes brave heroes speak loudly and build an assembly.

As soon as Indra enters the oceans onto the ground, they turn water into a moving state that turns streams into rivers to nourish the ground (Rig Veda, Book 2, Hymn XIII). This provides immortal power to mortal embodiments. Their bodies transform into astral bodies that can be filled with memories. The individual immortal spirit protects them from imperfections caused by the powers of attraction and aversion, which generate memories. Any imperfections are removed, and the astral bodies are not attracted by material wealth or kinship. They gain a firm hold that overpowers greed and obsession. They follow their sacred pathway free of memories. Cosmic vapours turn themselves into the water and keep the astral bodies floating and purified. The astral bodies live in manifested bodies as pure creations. They are praised and offered food and milk.

The godly powers provide things that worshippers admire and spread gifts in compliance with the eternal laws by which plants produce seeds. With the powers of the essence (Swadarma), they bring eternal wealth and food that they need to slay monsters. The heavenly power (Surya) supports a hundred noble souls who, as devotees, perform activities with immortal essence (Swadarma). They are not afraid of the evil powers (Dabhiti) or malevolent souls that seek personal gain. They do not want to be bound by evil strings (Dasyus).

They receive strength, and by making sacrifices, they overpower the shackles of the evil strings. They learn to share their wealth, and they are serviced by five spiritual faculties: conviction or belief through the offering of rites, devotional energy, persistence or perseverance (Viriya), mindfulness memory (Sati), the stillness of the mind (Samādhi), and eternal wisdom, understanding, and comprehension (Pañña). These five spiritual faculties, through the five sense organs, create a fivefold view with which they serve as heroes of the heroes (Jatuthira), who with the comprehensive eternal values of life through analogous tales have a special niche in literature (Vayya), and the art of storytelling simplifies even complex and mysterious subjects or situations (Turviti), which add the juice of entertainment to make them palatable to minds of the common man. They protect the universal soul (Paramatma) from evil.

The astral bodies bring recognition to the disabled and blind, and with worthy glorification, they receive a great bounty from nature and thus bring an abundance of eternal treasures. They give the mythical juice to living beings, which gives them joy. Regulated by the powers of the creator (Brahma), they send lightning that shakes the evil powers (Vrtra). They create water and wind to thrash evil power and so allow mortal embodiments to receive eternal wisdom.

After consuming the mythical drink, they become priests with eternal wisdom and acquire the power (Swadarma) that unveils absolute truth that lets astral bodies become a reality (Tattva). They say goodbye to worldly attachments and come back as advanced humanity. They acquire knowledge of numerology, and with vibes, they speed up their subtle faculties.

Astral bodies learn to invoke the individual power of the essence (Swadharma), unveil the truth, and comprehend the supreme powers of causation, which through the living spirit (Atma) come to regulate the dynamic universe. As mortal embodied souls, they give birth to highly evolved souls that follow physical practices such as yoga and enforce mental disciplines (Svasna). They transform learned priests (Vyasa) to transfer eternal truth by composing holy scriptures. Personified as holy sages (Rishi), they bring under control any demonic power that generates greed and creates egos (Susna), arrogance (Rudhikras), and narcissism (Pipru) by regulating their breath.

They make selfless sacrifices to produce the juice to attain enlightenment, and they serve eternal truth as messengers of Indra (Rig Veda, Book 2, Hymn XIV). With the powers of Indra, they demolish evil powers (Sambaras) and castles occupied by evil souls (Varcin). They cast down hundreds of thousands of evil spirits that could serve as malevolent souls. They are resurrected quickly to turn evil powers over to be handled by Indra. They learn all about the divine will (Devavani), obey at all times the order of ministers, and serve the holy priest (Adhvaryus). Using physical and mental disciplines (yoga and Svasna, respectively) daily and as part of worship, they offer the juice and milk and gradually acquire the powers of the divine will, which bring strength and joy.

Like the architect of creation (Trikadrukas), Indra slays the dragon and rises toward heaven into the unsupported space to establish different spheres (Lokas; Rig Veda, Book 2, Hymn XV). After they fill the mid-air region with the divine will, they declare absolute truth that creates space between earth and heaven. With compassion like fire, they burn their weapons to expose mortal souls that live as hermits (Dabhīti). With their mighty power, they make streams flow up to the place where the maidens are hiding; the maidens show themselves and stand before them. They destroy the barricades of the evil power (Vala) while they sleep, and they overwhelm the submerged powers (Cumuri and Dhuni) while they slay the manifested evil (Dasyu). They yield boons to those who, with loud praise, worship Indra.

The spiritual scholars who perform sacrifice and worship the noble powers (Adhvaryus) arc recognized as the holy devotees (Kavi) who persist as prophets. Sixteen holy souls (Rtvij) perform ceremonies to invoke the essence among living beings; four are selected to serve the chief priests, and the others serve as their assistants (Rig Veda, Book 2, Hymn XVI). They receive eulogies from Indra along with oblations, all offered with the powers of the essence and as the eternal flame (Agni). This saves their embodiments from decay and lives ever young (perishable). Without blessings from Indra, nothing exists, including the power of essence, which among living beings combines all the powers needed to support the heroes.

Their physical embodiments are strengthened by the juice, which brings them vast strength like Indra to help them attain wisdom. Higher knowledge comes from heaven without any support from illumination; this allows them to shine internally and fly many leagues. With the unwavering divine will, they serve mortal embodiments. By drinking Soma, they pass through the mighty blaze and always extract strength from the mental food (Meath) that enhances their intellects.

Like celestial bodies, they flow like the Aśvins and appear as two strong, holy embodiments (Adhvaryus) protected by Indra, who provides them weapons. Appearing from the heavens with the juice, they satisfy all embodiments and offer sacred rites that make them strong. With wealth,

it turns aside calamity like breeding heavenly cows that produce calves. With favours, husbands represent heavenly bulls, and wives represent heavenly cows that produce milk. The heavenly bulls worship as they speak, and like heroes, they build the assembly that worships Indra to bring the fortune that never fails.

Like the ancient envoys (Aṅgirases) honoured Agni, the new creations honour Indra and show its mighty powers that bring ecstasy to release divine strength (Rig Veda, Book 2, Hymn XVII). The divine will from the earliest draught displays the mighty power of the essence that increases majesty among the heroes and further stimulates them to fight righteous wars. With the powers of the divine will (Devavani), it sets in greatness, which allows heroes to share their mighty power. In time, other folks, through prayer, come with their embodiments, ready to serve Indra and the demigods.

They bring strength and power that can smooth uneven ridges and become greater and above all. Once they are born, they come blessed with eternal wisdom ready to spread like the external light coming from the sun and moon and to remove chaotic darkness. With mighty powers, they rush down with the waters to sustain life and use their wondrous skills to seek heaven.

They grasp precious wealth and powers like thunderbolts to strike their enemies. Their powers (Adhvaryus) make them young and save them from punishment as they share their wisdom to make others happy. As liberal givers, they even invoke those who share divine powers, so with great strength and labour, they assist others and serve Indra, from whom they receive more wealth.

Every morning, they become fully equipped with four yokes, three whips, and seven reins and guide as friendly embodiments representing ten-sided humankind (Rig Veda, Book 2, Hymn XVIII). They urge others to pray and transform their embodiments so their offspring can serve as priests or heralds who guide noble souls. Serving as the parents of the noble souls, they serve like the sun, the moon, and the stars. They learn to worship and serve as holy singers.

Indra brings the Aśvins as two horses that, when spiritually invoked, become four, six, eight, and then ten. Then they appear as very powerful creations in greater numbers as they drink the juice. They pray as heavenly children (Śunahotras) and connect the two earthly divisions—land and ocean. They provide libations in many places and provide divine treasure. They receive protection and get help from Indra to manifest as the heavenly cow; they, in turn, worship Indra.

As the children of illumination (Surya), they manifest as Atithigva, Kutsa, and Ayu and wield their powers (Rig Veda, Book 2, Hymn XXI). They bring thunder to conquer the embodied demons and create streams and rivers and then oceans. Since Indra has already slain the dragon (Vrtra), through worshipping, they bring all kinds of riches into the water, leaving behind only manifested noble souls to keep distress far away.

Imperishable Power

They help mortal embodiments residing in darkness appear as newly created creatures who milk cows, overcome life's struggles, and attain wisdom. They make sacrifices and appear with the ability to rise like the mythical flying horse (Etasa; Rig Veda, Book 2, Hymn XXII). They appear as the architect of creation (Trikadrukas) to serve others with eternal greatness, and they manifest as the Avatar serving as the sustainer (Vishnu). They become sanctified by the waters of the holy rivers, and as blessed souls, they manifest with the primordial power (Shakti).

Later, the primordial power (Shakti) appears to support the trinity, where Vishnu serves as the sustaining power that offers libations to overpower evil forces. They unveil the powers' wisdom and help heroes overpower malevolent power and gain wealth. They serve the heroes so they can recognize with praise the mighty powers of the divinities and deities, which as dancers demonstrate how to perform obligatory deeds (Karma) and lead them to perform altruistic deeds (Dharma).

The embodied noble souls emanate in a perishable castle (Bhangurah), which serves as the altar for sacrifices offered as gifts (Dakshna). Then a mythical figure evolves to serve as counsel to the godly powers serving as the Master of Sacred wisdom (Brihaspati). They sing hymns and offer rites to Indra. The preceptor of the gods (Brihaspati), as the earthly powers, brings the heavenly luminous bodies as the imperishable powers (Brahmal)aspati) to chase away revilers.

They bring the light that displays their power and serves mortal embodiments, which are regulated by perishable Blrhaspati. They sing hymns and receive spiritual power from the sun that quells foes and slays demons (Rig Veda, Book 2, Hymn XXIII). They help those in distress and guide them through prayer to avoid such situations. They punish haters and quell the moods of such creatures. Among those embodiments, the perishable godhead (Blrhaspati) serves those who face sorrow, distress, and foes with double tongues. They strive for higher knowledge and become true envoys of the heavenly imperishable powers that guard perishable bodies. They sing hymns that help them follow the righteous path. With blessed embodiments, they attend the banquet offered to imperishable Brahmal)aspati, the envoy of the immortal power (Brahma).

The imperishable embodiments serve alongside perishable embodiments as protectors of all embodiments. They provide essence (Swadharma) before they are made to serve as rulers, and they make sure no wicked person becomes a ruler with an immortal soul. They call on Agni to burn all demons. They act but do not seek praise from perishable embodiments, and they know how to destroy evil forces with speech and battle.

Pleased with such activities, the imperishable embodiment (Brahmal) aspati) praises them (Rig Veda, Book 2, Hymn XXIV). As noble souls, they never seek material wealth. They seek a place to rest and remain on the ground; they become inactive like dormant volcanoes (Sambawa). As needed, they overthrow demonic kingdoms but allow the perishable power to reside on the ground (Prithvi) while at all times encircling the inactive volcano (Sambawa). The demonic kings approach the perishable powers (B1rhaspati) to make their task of recovering treasure easier by causing landslides or earthquakes to expose the wealth. B1rhaspati (Rig Veda, Book 2, Hymn XXV) dispel the darkness and expose the caves where the evil powers shelter and allow water to flow out. They expose rock to bring out precious things.

The perishable powers (B1rhaspati) send out a sound that reaches the ears of the heavenly high priest supported by imperishable embodiments (Brahmal)aspati), who prepare them to attain mighty success through offering oblations (Rig Veda, Book 2, Hymn XXVI). Like the heroic sons, they become part of a moral and righteous society and, with loving hearts, know the absolute truth. As Brahmal) aspati, they gain booty for their efforts and are rewarded through their children, who serve like noble souls (Adityas), not as envoys but with respect; they are worshipped as the father of the gods. They help others serve embodied souls with morality and with full support to become free from sorrow.

The perishable powers (B1rhaspati) can excel in battle and bring forth food and wealth from the untroubled sun. They become stronger and support others; they make them leaders with gifts for those who love material wealth. The perishable powers support all mortal classes, including those coming from imperishable embodiments. This allows everyone to acquire material wealth and success and rejoice with mighty strength (Rig Veda, Book 2, Hymn XXVII).

They spread forth to other imperishable embodiments, including demigods (Aśvins), envoys (Maghavans), and noble souls (Aryaman), which observe the behaviour of perishable embodiments. They even use the divine will with essence (Devavani) to establish relationships with the ancient trinity. The B1rhaspati yoke waters and offer sacrificial flames to steeds accompanied with hymns that provide the assembly with earthly priests.

The perishable B1rhaspati with embodiments represent themselves as avatars of immortals (Brahmal)aspati) and claim that all the mighty deeds are directed from heaven to create such strength. This turns perishable B1rhaspati like cosmic vapours into water that is distributed throughout the region. With powerful prayers, the perishable B1rhaspati appear, claiming to be imperishable Brahmal)aspati.

Coming from perishable bodies (B1rhaspati), these shocks and frightens the imperishable (Brahmal)aspati) to hear such wrath being brought by its own envoy. The imperishable seeing the perishable reflecting as the leader with imperishable embodiments become the masters of material wealth.

Noble souls, not as envoys but as the father of the gods, organize a new imperishable trinity comprising the powers of causation (Mitra, Bhaga, and Aryaman) to balance the conflict between soul and body, spirit and matter, and perishable and imperishable, which perform acts of morality and appear with special powers (Adityas). The offspring of the godly mother (Aditi) manifests as the eternal power comprising the supreme powers of causation (trinity), the eternal laws (Varul)a), special skills (Dakṣa), and the God particle (Amsa). They reach an accord with the perishable supreme powers to accept the special eternal power (Adityas), which brings pure streams of water to free them from guile and blemish, all accompanied by bright light from Surya. With faith and support, the Adityas win over the material power and regulate by perishable bodies (Blrhaspati). They are blessed with many eyes that spot wickedness and are not deceived by evil powers.

With such support, the Adityas protect all that is perishable and imperishable by providing foresight coming from the universal soul (Paramatma), which is followed by the eternal laws and absolute truth. The powers of the divine balance the material power with ethereal power. The Adityas, through perishable manifested power (Aryaman), use their unmanifested imperishable power to make mortal bodies appear as enhanced living beings, humanity. In danger, the Adityas, through Aryaman, support humanity. The eternal laws and absolute truth come to smooth out rugged places and make paths free from thorns. The material power (Aryaman) continues to receive the ultimate blessing from the special power (Adityas).

The special power receives support from their mother (Aditi) as they pass through the earthly, heavenly, and mid-air regions, all supported by the powers of the trinity, whose greatness brings splendid power (Adityas) that is beheld aloft in the three regions. They provide fresh water to make sure that every member never slumbers and always serves righteously and morally. Even Varuna comes to serve new sovereigns of the trinity (righteousness, morality, and humanity) by granting them a hundred autumns. They receive gifts from the godly father and prosper with eternal wealth. They rank first in assemblies and serve as faithful heroes under the guidance of Adityas. The powers of Mitra-Varul)a forgive those who have sinned and free them from the threat as they receive protection from the celestial twin demigods (Aśvins). As highly favoured supreme powers, Mitra-Varul)a master the heavenly and earthly regions and serve as gracious beings who quell oppressors as they build their dwellings under the sky.

The supreme powers of causation declare the godly father as the mighty and supreme one (Rig Veda, Book 2, Hymn XXVIII) who operates through the eternal laws (Varul)a). Its greatness exceeds those who serve Agni and who beg for fortune in return for their services. As the eternal flame, Agni provides heat, warmth, and milk. The leader (Varul)a) rules by the eternal laws and serves many heroes like the sons of Mother Earth. They remain forever faithful and bless living beings, advanced or not. They serve as sustainers in the flowing water. Working under the supreme powers (Varul)a) along with noble souls (Adityas), they declare that all creation feels no weariness. They provide the environments for birds to fly free from sin and build bonds with other living creations, including humanity (Rig Veda, Book 2, Hymn XXIX).

This creates a link between all creations that weaves a web by producing pleasant sounds. The web allows each creation either an end or to be shattered before its time. Through prayer, it allows all living beings to be served by the powers of the eternal laws (Varuna) that remove all danger and accept every holy sovereign king. The law provides freedom but nonetheless can have some sinners exiled in darkness. Even old evil powers worship the powers of the eternal laws (Varul)a), which in its invincible form continues to move and not allow living things to suffer. No one, not even kings, should threaten the noble powers. No wolf or robber is free from the power of the law.

The noble kind is further supported by Varul)a, which witnesses the wealthy and the destitute. The eight elemental gods serving as Asta-Vasu serve as the divine power (Vasubandhu), which changes over time. Though their names change, they serve as the same such as fire (Anala), water (Dhara), earth (Anila), dawn, dusk (Usha), the sun, the moon, and the pole star (Dhruva). These eight elemental gods represent nature (Prakriti), which regulates all of them. Through their movement, they support all forms of transformation and influence the individual power affecting physical and subtle bodies as well as the digestive system and the inner flow of eternal power, the astral body.

As part of the trinity, Vishnu serves as the sustainer along with Brahma, the saviour, and Shiva, the transformer. Vishnu is identical to the formless metaphysical concept (Svayam Bhagavan).

Brahma and Shiva appear whenever the world is threatened with evil, chaos, and destruction. Vishnu is usually depicted as having a dark or blue complexion and four arms to hold a lotus flower, a sceptre, a conch, and a discus.

The beholder guardians (Adityas) remove the sins of those who bare their secrets and allow them to be supported by the powers of Varuṇa-Mitra (Rig Veda, Book 2, Hymn XXIX). The Adityas call on noble souls and remove those who hate the givers of good things. Adityas develop relationships that make them all well and happy and make sure their kinsmen remain kind.

Indra slays the evil power and removes the blockage by the creation of fish (Ahi), which allows the goddess (Savitar) to let the waters flow (Rig Veda, Book 2, Hymn XXX) above the ocean levels. Only the mother of the evil power (Vrtra) knows and helps show Indra how to remove the blockage.

The mother of the evil power (Vrtra) remembers when Indra overpowered the perishable material power (Bṛhaspati) and killed all the foes (Asuras) with a thunderbolt that pierced through the hero of evil powers (Vrkadvara). Even today, to protect people, Indra smites their foes. Indra provides eternal love and helps especially those who gain strength from the mythical juice.

Varuna-Mitra, along with the Aśvins and the trinity (Vasus, Rudras, and Ādityas), helps all other embodiments (Rig Veda, Book 2, Hymn XXXI), where Indra serves as the friend of all living things and provides them help so they can be untroubled by foes and conquer them with physical strength and eternal wisdom. All accompanied by Vishnu manifest and appear as the envoys (Iḷā and Bhaga) serving earth and heaven. To regulate the mid-air region, Vishnu appears as avatars (Pū5an and Purandhi), serving like the twin demigods (Aśvins).

From above the ground with blessings, Vishnu comes to support the trinity with cosmic vapours (Tva5ṭar, Vrtra, and Vala) to provide water and represent the celestial powers encompassing the trinity of essence (Āptya, Ṛbhuk5an, and Savitar), which come to honour all living things.

Vishnu regulates heaven and earth (Rig Veda, Book 2, Hymn XXXII), so no mighty pair allows any mortal's sin to annoy them. They think with their hearts along with divine bliss; they separate the noble from the ignoble. They use crawling, benignant minds to join with the divine will and produce an inexhaustible amount of wisdom. Those who invoke many urges that come to the divine will are day by day served, like the chargers Rākā, Sinvalt, and Kuhu, who observe their work that meets praise.

Like Rākā, with all kinds of lovely thoughts, they grant wealth and gifts. Those who come to the goddesses (Sinīvālī) of children are served by sisters of the gods who granted many sons. The children are presented sacred gifts from Sinīvālī, serving as the queen of morality who floats in five holy rivers: the Gungū, Rākā, Sarasvatī, Indrāṇī, and Varuṇānī. The gifts of adoration from the cosmic goddess (Kuhu) are provided with the ultimate celestial powers of Rudra, which yields and appears along with the Aśvins (Rig Veda, Book 2, Hymn XXXIII). As the cosmic host, the demigods plead to be allowed to pass through the strong shield of the sky. The celestial powers of Rudra allow them to pass through uninjured, and with their gracious hands, they allow the cosmic host to provide health and offer comfort to all by removing their woes and letting Indra bring eternal wisdom and water that nourishes vegetation. Through the powers of the cosmic host,

the vibrations generate an ambience that appears as bright-gold decorations commonly known in the sky as a form of Rudra, which in the form of a glow never departs from creations and helps the mighty sovereign serve new worlds. They manifest as celestial angels (seraphs) that come with bows and arrows to form many colours that bring forth the cutest worthy monsters. Appearing as slayers of trepidation, they save devotees from forest beasts. When the seraphs are not worshipped properly or praised by singers, they smite all but the host. They turn into cosmic vapours that bring water, and they give health to the sick.

Rudra bestows on a selected few among all mortal embodiments ancient living bodies (Manus) to demonstrate their craving to gain welfare for all, and they are thus empowered to turn into celestial objects—comets, asteroids, and meteors—that could give bounty or wrath. They, as Manus, carry fresh water and seeds to create life. Appearing as embryos or sperm, they create offspring that, as an act of nature (Prakriti), honours the celestial powers, listens during the assemblies of heroes, and offers no resistance to cosmic vapours.

They see impulsive nature coming forth in the eternal flame (Rig Veda, Book 2, Hymn XXXIV), giving birth to lightning, rain, and wind that help the cosmic host develop a brilliant torso from the lap of the mother, appearing as rain clouds from which springs radiance. The Maruts join the supreme powers of friendship (Mitra) and grant eternal life. Their swift drops cause riches to flow. They provide intellect from their udders and bring knowledge. Like swans, they seek their nests and arrive as mortal embodiments. With prayers and libations, they receive eternal wisdom and music filled with gracious songs.

CHAPTER 5
IMPARTIAL DOMINION

The principles of the trinity (righteousness, morality, and humanity) are represented in individual embodiments, serving as spheres of influence (Chakras). Working through the subtle body, they represent a variety of ancient meditation practices that collectively regulate inner controls (Tantras). The concept represents as five, six, seven, or even eight or more spheres of influence (Chakras). They are actually part of the physical body and regulate the mind and heart to establish spiritual fields of influence. In modern interpretations, they represent electromagnetic complexes, and they arise from negative, average, and positive fields of influence caused by individual activities.

They emerge like complex tubes, pipes, nerves, blood vessels, and pulses (Nadis) through which the life force (Prana) regulates and passes through the astral body to invoke spiritual powers that control the eternal force passing through the embodiment. In philosophical and mystical terms, they represent complex systems said to connect at special points of intensity to influence individual fields (Chakras) in the body and then pass through three principal pulses (Nadis) running from the base of the spine to the head.

Synod

By drinking the mythical fluid, the eternal flame provides physical bodies with physical strength and spiritual power. After attaining a state of ecstasy, the embodiments are taken over by the seven powers of causation directed by seven sages (Saptarishi) to form an assembly of gods. They provide immortal bliss served with the sanctified mystical force (Rig Veda, Book 3, Hymn 1). Such embodiments glow like manifested heavenly sages representing the celestial region.

The embodiments toil with bliss and offer aid through prayers and hymns with the eternal flame that burns like wood, melts like wax, and produces fatty substances that generate light. The eternal flames with rites are offered and honoured and worshipped as the assembly of gods (synod) coming from heaven as the wise and learned souls (Sarvastivada). They bring kinship between heaven and earth, and with the eternal flames, they bring Agni to provide welfare to embodiments serving as a beautiful sister (Apah) to the eternal flame (Agni). Jointly, they support physical bodies that serve as blessed spiritual souls.

As blessed souls, they establish a relationship with seven holy rivers augmented by the seven supreme powers of causation, all regulated by the seven sages (Saptarishi) that create floods. As an assembly of gods, they awaken the immortal spirit (Atma) residing in pure, unfilled, unmanifested astral bodies. The mighty powers first wash any glow out of them.

Astral bodies spread over the region to bring eternal wisdom as they fill it with purified life. After being filled with purified life, the body is robed with light that spreads abroad. With its highest and perfect glories among all, it is represented by the mighty ones. Unconsuming, unimpaired, not clothed and yet not naked, the astral bodies, both ancient and modern, dwell together and represent the seven supreme powers of causation (Septarishi) along with flowing water serving the seven rivers that manifest life in every form.

As they scatter with the flow of sweet water and milk for strengthening coming from mighty mothers, they join male partners and assume everlasting beauty. The mighty ones bring spiritual wisdom to create enhanced living beings. The bright ones, which appear as male and female, grow together. Knowing the heavenly father sets his desires in the bosom of the heavenly mother and sets the water in motion, they are blessed friends regulated by the powers of essence (Swadharma). As the young dames of heaven, they no longer stay hidden as the offspring of the creator, which alone as a child suckled many a teeming breast. They know they are guarded by the strength of the mighty ones who regulate their minds and hearts. While serving like the friendly, bright ones as their spouses, they form kinships. The minds of the new born increase and are filled with many a glorious flood providing strength. They receive from Agni the eternal flame and lie in the lap of the seven rivers.

These children of the floods appear most youthful and represent the eternal flame. They appear as infants carrying the spirit. They become strong and wondrous luminaries accompanied by the eternal flame generating boundless juice. They, with selfless sacrifice, serve all with oblations and create goodwill and friendship with others. With the powers of the divine will, they are granted grace, and, accompanied by rays of light, they guard the homestead. With the support of Agni, they follow the masters of all treasures and serve as noble offspring. In battle, they have the powers of Agni, which serves as the joy giver and knower of all secret wisdom. Mortal embodiments fulfil their sacred synods bedewed with holy oil.

They grant abundant wealth and bring good repute as they sing to advance as children of the floods offering great libations through birds serving as the messenger (Jatavedas) with the eternal flame. Through the union of godheads (Viśvāmitras), they receive perpetual spiritual strength to experience self-realization and rest forever in loving-kindness. They learn to sacrifice and serve as bright ones. They are granted abundant food by the priestly heralds, who vouchsafe wealth and holy food.

Astral bodies are filled with impurities they acquired because of their attachment to the material world, all hidden in the essence. The only way noble priests can achieve self-realization to attain essence is through purification. As from solid to liquid and then to gas, it transforms the eternal flame to become the power of essence (Rig Veda, Book 3, Hymn II). This requires a longing to seek spiritual strength and be accepted as the envoys of the patron (Bhrgus), who offer eulogies among the other invisible demigods and by recognizing the godhead that brings the powers of union (Vaiśvānara) that see themselves serving as the holy warriors.

They observe illumination coming from the heavenly region that turns the dark, dormant matter or unmanifested universe into a visible, dynamic universe. Heavenly powers (Rudras) bring along demigods to disperse shining solar winds to reach all newly created dwellings. The union of the godhead as a shining manifestation desirous of friendship makes offerings to the brilliant fire to bless the sacred ground from where the learned souls are seen as the envoys. As learned souls, they access the primordial power (Shakti), which comes to fill all open areas as it did during the genesis of heaven and earth.

From its great dominion, the heavenly power (Rudras) skilfully regulates the primordial power as it passes along such force to spread among those who motivate learned sages. They become oblation bearers who, as friends of the heavenly powers, teach mortal embodiments that must die to go through further purifying processes in order to appear as new splendours. With brightness and sacred rites, sages offer sacrificial food to share with demigods, who mount as the vital embryos to be laid down with astral bodies to cover the perishable worlds through stirring life in wombs and creating life.

After awakening (Rig Veda, Book 3, Hymn III), the newly born receive the powers of the united gods (Vaiśvānara) with goods and wealth reaching with respect coming from their ancestors, who are mounted beyond the ridge in heaven. They are greeted with skills and the ability to produce divine music and riches. As messengers, they remain perishable until they are needed to appear looking like the immortal sunlight. Once they elect to appear as messengers, they serve as perishable messengers of the imperishable Agni. They listen to the high praise offered by sages, follow the law, and serve as the beholders of the light. The messengers, along with the divine, will awaken with the morning light and appear as mortal manifestations that make sages serve as cheerful priests with no guile.

The mortal embodiments understand their surroundings, guide others, and follow certain paths as defined by the divine will. They represent the mighty powers in all forms, manifested and unmanifested, and they serve as heavenly priests who never break the everlasting laws and always honour Agni. They establish the link between the eternal fire and the universal soul.

Agni becomes the mortal envoy (Āprīs) and comes to reside buried in logs and stones like flames or sparks. They appear like a flash to bestow riches (Rig Veda, Book 3, Hymn IV) and enrich mortal bodies that offer special worship (Tanūnapāt) to serve as immortal heavenly powers (Varuṇa-Mitra). They offer worship to help mortal embodiments acquire higher knowledge and generate noble thoughts. This brings every boon that leads the manifested bodies to proceed toward their first worship as the strong one. They greet the priest of libations, offer sacrifices, and go up to the higher region, where radiant flames reach the heavenly priest and cause the barren ground to produce sacred grass.

Serving as the seven supreme powers of causation, the seven earthly priests make sacrifices to show their true hidden beauty. They come in different forms and colours from the celestial region as the twin demigods (Aśvins) to meet with the three ruling godly powers (trinity) serving in the mid-air region and represented by multiple demigods serving as cosmic hosts (Maruts). Through the celestial powers, they serve the trinity and the supreme powers of causation. These powers establish their dwelling on the earth, where they understand absolute truth and use eternal wisdom to establish a link among the feminine powers (Bhāratī, Iḷā, and Sarasvati) serving as the trinity on earth. They regulate the flowing water, which produces heavenly grass to invite the creative power to support offspring who procreate young heroes. The young heroes serve as lovers of the divine power and use their immortal, universal souls appearing among the press stones— comets, asteroids, and meteors. They invite Agni to serve as the creator and immolator, and they come to reside among the heavenly priests (Septarishi), who share the eternal wisdom they receive as part of the divine process. The mother hails all immortal powers to sit on the sacred grass and maintain a calm and worry-free environment.

As godly messengers with mortal embodiments, the demigods serve to bring things into balance and generate tranquillity. The first order of the demigods first includes the twins (Aśvins), which regulate morning light (dawn) and evening light (dusk). Jointly, they bring righteousness and enforce morality. They create the mythical state that, in time, acquires higher intelligence by removing ignorance and serves in a mystic state the divine will and transforms to appear as essence, which serves living beings as if they had their own power.

They are both shown with the coming of morning light (dawn) and the coming of evening light (dusk) to serve mortal embodiments representing the divine will with essence (Devavani). They establish themselves as the embryo, the friendly germ of waters. After joining Agni-Mitra, the celestial force, they create demigods that serve with the eternal flame and appear as the cosmic host that, as multiple demigods, establish an altar in the mid-air region. They serve as the friendly messenger who comes to earth as a bird with the eternal flame (Jatavedas). They follow the sun's rays to earth, where they manifest as physical bodies appearing as seven-headed dragons that guard the centre of the universe from where, as archangels, they serve new creations. They enjoy travelling through the regions of the dynamic universe and monitoring divine creation. They acquire eternal wisdom that they share with others.

These seven-headed dragons guard like the holy priests by bringing the mythical juice so their physical bodies can fly (Rig Veda, Book 3, Hymn V). They come along with the astral bodies without gaining weight so they can gain easy access to pass through all hurdles. They, as purified, are placed with the eternal flame to be born and help them grow. They carry the eternal flame to protect, and they reach the parents' lap. With enkindled astral bodies, they provide physical strength coming from Mother Earth and spiritual strength provided by Father Heaven.

They are Agni's envoys who bring the best of all luminaries through lofty Surya and regulate the planetary system. They appear with the eternal flame, which supports the oblation bearer (Bhṛgus), which lies in secret places to provide holy food, bring rain, and turn water into milk.

Proclamation

Agni, serving as guardian (Guardeth), generates pious nature (Rig Veda, Book 3, Hymn VI). They travel east, offering oblations to regions all the way from heaven to earth. They serve all the deities and demigods, and they provide eternal fire to the heavenly father (Surya) and the earthly mother (Aditi). They represent the immortal, universal soul (Paramatma) with seven-tongued, rolling serpents that provide individual dwellings with Atma. They establish immortal power (conscience) that commonly expresses the induction of morality, and through an inner feeling or an inner voice, they implant righteousness and guide them through such power to comprehend the covenants regulating the seven supreme powers to establish humanity.

Manifested embodiments with consciences learn to cultivate faith by offering prayers and oblations. Aware of conscience and faith, it unveils the invisible mighty powers (essence) that regulate the esoteric region. They realize the power of the Aśvins, and other demigods (Maruts) come to serve milk that passes through without any harm to the mothers to generate nectar (Amrita) that comes out of the holy adrenal glands that are quite incredible among the manifested species; they represent the primary survival organs that promote the fight-or-flight response.

The demigods teach through their kin how to perform great sacrificial deeds that find the inherent reality (Dharma). They give birth to a vast group that serves as envoys of the demigods. They scrve as leaders, all bound to the holy order. They sprinkle the holy order like birds that become strong and serve like the eternal firebirdss (Jatavedas). They gather like demigods in the mid-air region to worship corporeal bodies. They praise Agni, which takes eternal air to wide regions, all serving like the godly powers of causation, whose dwelling place is heaven.

The holy noble souls manifest to appear as three and thirty mighty powers that cover each of the three regions along with the demigods; they serve each region like holy priests. They are repeatedly worshipped with songs that cover all the regions of heaven and earth. They sacrifice, and with heavenly order, they bring the divine will and essence to serve each region.

The Maruts, backed with white rays from the heavenly power (Surya), establish a rainbow with a different colour to abide by the planetary system. They, with their hues, transform imperishable to perishable, which manifests as pairs of demigods like twin parents (Rig Veda, Book 3, Hymn VII). They manifest as living beings with mortal embodiments, male and female, as gods and goddesses. They set out to find riches mounted to guide streams bearing the eternal flame. They support their creative tasks (Tvaṣṭars) with all other members while they zoom on homes and enter them from both worlds as if they were one. They bring joy and are honoured by the heavenly powers (Iḷā), the ancient powers that come to support the two mighty parents serving as heaven, the father, and earth, the mother.

The mighty parents help them bring strength that comes from the seven holy singers who dispel darkness. They guard the planetary five birds' stations encompassing the terrestrial region—Mercury, Mars, Venus, Earth, and Pluto, where they serve like the heavenly priesthood. They rejoice with demigods as they follow their ways. They crave grace along with Agni and Indra and serve as the swift steeds (Septarishi) covering the seven planetary bodies. They speak only absolute truth, and they praise with eternal wisdom. The noble souls full of wisdom serve earth and heaven and are worshipped with their glory as they have a presence on earth.

The intermediaries between God and humanity (archangels) act and serve in manifested and unmanifested forms (Rig Veda, Book 3, Hymn VIII). They are created by the divine will with essence; they are usually depicted as living things with extraordinary beauty and often with wings and haloes. They protect, guide, and inspire embodied spirits with heavenly wisdom. As the sovereigns of the forest, they are sanctified and granted prosperity. They follow the sunlight and bring good fortune. They acquire special spiritual powers and become greater through cultivating their contemplative minds (Chita). They bring higher intelligence and become integral parts of the order of demigods. They sing and use wisdom, and their creative skills attain sanctification. They grant their inner wealth to help children. They as trees are supported by Ādityas, Rudras, and Vasus, who serve nature and protect the ground from demonic powers.

They serve as pillars arrayed in brilliant colours, and they take the sages to a higher place to meet the mighty gods. Among manifested living beings, they offer sacrifices by looking after lofty ensigns staked on the ground and appearing like circles (Chakras). Such embodiments are decked with senses that support essences (Swadharma) as well as the divine will. Their haloes invoke others and raise the sages and priests to higher levels. They expand with a hundred and then a thousand branches, ultimately reaching greatness.

Atma, being the waters' child (Rig Veda, Book 3, Hymn IX), is blessed beyond comparison with victorious powers. With Fire in wood, they are ready to become the ferocious flame witnessed from afar with smoke merging with its original source, the universal soul. As benevolent hosts, they prevail and continue their pursuits. Being water children, they find a place in floods.

They view the eternal flame brought by Agni that appears as a messenger (Mātariśvan) of Indra. They come from far away, fighting resistance, and thus are received by the demigods. They are friends of spiritually evolved souls, and they serve the swift envoys of the demigods to bring godly powers. Like the ancient, adorable youthful one, the envoys offer three times ten thousand sacrifices to invoke the powers of Agni.

Agni recognizes their sacrifices (Rig Veda, Book 3, Hymn X) and kindles the spirit in the priests, who guard the eternal laws and the divine will. This brings life to all manifestations, which gain heroic might and sacrifice to the ensign. The seven priests with loud hymns and songs receive inner light and mighty strength. They offer the best sacrifices, which bring piety and joy and drive away foes even in their wakeful state. They bear oblations and serve as immortal bodies.

While sitting on the sacred grass (Rig Veda, Book 3, Hymn XI), they create the sensation (aura) around the material bodies. They serve like heavenly priests who sacrifice with rites and oblations. They become messengers of Agni, and with their thoughts, they serve the ensign as they sacrifice. Knowing all, they hope to bring back the memorable old times. Before becoming part of the manifested tribe, they become active envoys of the archangels. They subdue all enemies and offer sacred food to mortal worshippers. They provide worshippers with inner light, and with hymns, they gain things that bring happiness.

As material bodies with inner light and sensation (aura), they honour Indra-Agni (Rig Veda, Book 3, Hymn XII), which generates a precious dew along with spiritual songs and prayers. That impels the mystic fluid (Amrita) with rites that invoke consciousness, spiritual awareness, and inner conscience among those following eternal love and wisdom. They experience bounteous strength to slay foes and win spoils. They offer sacred food that generates vibrations that can destroy evil forts where demon powers (Dāsas) live. They send demons down the sacred path to follow the eternal laws and perform holy tasks. They go out ready to perform mighty deeds and gain fame.

The demigods turn the earth into sacred ground located with heaven and earth (Rig Veda, Book 3, Hymn xiii) and call them holy places. They appoint sovereigns who are offered sacred rites and win wealth from Agni. Many with the eternal flame provide godly shelter and protect the creations from floods. Agni appoints manifested bodies to serve as teachers and offers tribute to those who serve as the invokers. The Maruts grant treasure to serve as nourishment for the children of noble powers and to provide heroes with exalted strength. The pleasant priest serving the noble synod comes with eternal truth and skills to ordain them as sons of strength that manifest and appear as physical bodies such as comets, asteroids, and meteors.

These heavenly bodies transform vibration into oscillations and create hymns (Rig Veda, Book 3, Hymn XIV). Such transformations like messages come from heaven to earth, bringing knowledge to those seated on the sacred grass. They come with triumph to serve the mid-air region and support the demigods, who support the planetary system with beams of lustre. They spread to anybody who approaches these beams with raised hands and offers adoration to fulfil longings. Those who worship like priests approach the living spirit (Atma) and attain powers to serve as the sons of strength among noble souls. Their sacrifice produces wise friends ready to serve while enjoying the company of immortal powers.

When heavenly powers (Rig Veda, Book 3, Hymn XV) becomes visible to mortal bodies and appear on earth, they become mortal envoys who dispel the terrors created by those who hate lofty powers. The mortal envoys are provided shelter to help guide mortal manifestations. They use such shelter to invoke other mortal embodiments to become noble and serve as the envoy (Avatar).

They serve as godly protectors of the ground. Being born like infants, they arrive in the form of astral bodies. They move through many mornings and evenings as stars that lead through with their noble powers acting like lords. They win the powers with the eternal flame and provide heat and thus acquire treasures. They serve as the chief leader (Avatar), skilled in guiding the wisest noble souls and offering sacrifices to serve as the youthful noble soul.

They are blessed with the power to support the demigods until they gather swag to create flawless terrestrial shelters. They appear ready to yield milk that no evil mortal power can block. The youthful souls receive milk as holy food from the gracious divine will (Devavani).

The Avatars fight foes and win wealth (Rig Veda, Book 3, Hymn XVI). They support astral bodies and wait for them to prosper before they serve as heroes. They increase their wealth before they fight evil enemies. The young heroes become bounteous ones. They present progeny in full power as they remove diseases. They are well ordered and perform godly service. Serving as bounteous ones, they work alongside the demigods to provide them heroic strength.

After being duly enkindled (Rig Veda, Book 3, Hymn XVII) with ancient customs, these bounteous ones acquire treasure, balm, and unguents, and with their flaming hair, they offer rites and worship;

they become heavenly like the eternal firebird's (Jatavedas). Offering their sacrificial blessing from the divine will (Devavani), they allow them to serve as the holy priest. They prosper through offering sacrifice, and ultimately, their astral bodies manifest like the ancient cosmic body (Manus), who has served at least three times prior to its current life.

They pass through various cycles of life and death, serving as mortal embodiments even before attaining their current lives. They know well about favours offered to help others to worship, and they then serve as the eternal firebirds. They produce vibrations that become hymns to honour the divine messenger. They serve as demigods and help move to the centre with eternal life; they serve as health givers and become well renowned for that service.

They work through Asta-Vasu, the eight natural powers before they appear with eternal beams that surround the eternal flame. They generate powers to fulfil their inner quests. They bring inner glow in the form of sons of strength and gain their conquest. They appear as loving friends (Visvāmitras). They adorn those who serve others, and their spirit (Atma) makes all happy.

They serve as priests skilled in worship, and they obtain boons by bringing strength and riches to all (Rig Veda, Book 3, Hymn XXIX). Visvāmitras offer oblations and bring good offspring who are given wealth, morality, and righteousness. They provide them with the ability to produce fair hymns. Visvāmitras worship with full brilliance and appear among all as the most youthful one. They are invited to the assembly and serve in honour as the heavenly host. They offer oblations and serve as kind defenders who even sacrifice themselves to vouchsafe the gift of glory.

They invoke Agni's eternal flame creating the dawn along with Dadhikrās, representing the twin demigods. Their sacrifices generate longing to attain the eternal flame. Their sounds delight the universal soul under three different names—deities, demigods, and archangels. They are represented as Bhaga, which leads godly people with the help of the law. They protect the demigods as they pass through troubled areas, and they are supported by the immortal powers of causation, including Savitar, Bṛhaspati, Dadhikrās, Agni, Varuṇa, Mitra, Aśvins, Bhaga, Vasus, Rudras, and Ādityas.

The first dominions of the ruler of immortal noble souls (Vishvamitra) comprehend eternal truth (Rig Veda, Book 3, Hymn XXI) and serve as earthly priests where Jatavedas, as the eternal firebirds, enjoys drinking the purifier, the mythical fluid. They bring the choicest boons and offer a godly feast as a sacrifice to the sages. These powers stream physical powers that run among the sages and are accepted with exceeding richness, and they receive from their core of the embodiment (Hridaya) a godly gift like the mystic fluid that connects their physical and astral bodies.

Agni increases the longing among earthly priests and creates the immortal dominion of noble souls that serve their devotees as prophets. Their devotees (Devaśrava) represent the ancestral powers of Indra as earthly priests who appear with thousands of devotees representing the winners of spoils and serving the terrestrial region.

This epithet of Agni serves as noble priests, and they acquire all knowledge, including absolute truth and eternal wisdom. They attain inner light that extends from heaven to earth and creates manifested bodies in the mid-air region. They create divine splendours and appear in the dominion of the sun, forming cosmic vapours that become part of the divine light, which goes beneath the surface to uncover everything buried in the ground.

Divine Dynasty

The divine light representing the immortal power appears in the form of an invisible mist (Rig Veda, Book 3, Hymn XXIII) that allows the eternal flame to reside in floods, and it produces great nourishment that becomes part of the mythical juice. It turns food into sweet nourishment such as honey and is as good as animals' milk that feeds new borns. As the leader of sacrifice, the immortal eternal firebird's acquire eternal powers and comes to serve the kingdoms of mortal bodies.

Clans of manifest mortal embodiments (Bharatas) as part of the ruling dynasty (Devaśravas) receive support from the eternal flame that drives their enemies away (Rig Veda, Book 3, Hymn XXIV). They celebrate godly feasts with libations that bring others' offerings to be accepted with joy. They come as splendour to serve with Agni and serve as the sons of strength, who worship as enlightened souls already granted wealth and eternal wisdom for them to pass on to others.

They come with the eternal flame to serve with the demigods such as earthly powers like sages, all bestowed with eternal wisdom, and they are given mighty powers and strength to extract the mythical juice and serve as the mighty ones (Rig Veda, Book 3, Hymn XXV). They call Indra to unite with Agni and supply them with the mystic nectar (Amrita) from the earth and the mythical juice (Soma) from heaven. By sharing among all the friendly minded, the mighty ones through divine light enkindle the immortal power appearing in many as manifestations.

They find an immortal spirit in their embodiments, and with eternal wisdom, they make them realize eternal truth as its hidden power (Rig Veda, Book 3, Hymn XXVI). Mortal embodiments know all about the supreme powers of causation and the ultimate primordial force (Shaki) that is responsible for the creation of immortal splendours. They gain support from the cosmic demigods (Maruts) and the celestial twins (Aswin), serving the regions between earth and heaven. The immortal spirit learns from the demigods all about vibrations, which bring support through holy vibrations that can be heard as pleasant female voices.

Such voices grant heroic strength and spiritual wealth to those who appear on earth, bringing immortal life through the union of godly powers (Vaiśvānara) that allow the living spirit (Atma) to create mighty forces that gather to go for victory. The demigods come with the eternal flame and become mighty benefactors through Rudra.

Clouds create physical embodiments covered with semi-mortal robes surrounding the perishable astral bodies. The embodiment is implored by Agni and supported by the cosmic host (Maruts), which serves as fair splendour that brings wealth. They gather and drink the nectar along with the mythical juice as they make sacrifices. They serve all the regions and light up the celestial, cosmic, and terrestrial regions. They generate purified thoughts that, like the wise ones, provide oblations that support the life force. They look abroad to discover hidden treasures in the region between heaven and earth.

They acquire streamlets through thunder and inspire others with prayers (Rig Veda, Book 3, Hymn XXVII). They bring joy by sharing the powers of causation to unveil absolute truth. They distribute divine food as they pass through the manifested regions between earth and heaven. Using godly powers, they listen to and bring gifts until they gain control over their foes with the strength they receive from Agni. They worship with ladles filled with fatty oils, and they are uplifted to attain holy powers. They receive immortal sacrifices and the power to perform mighty deeds. The rites they perform generate excellent thoughts. With Agni's power, they create a longing to become immortal manifestations by making vibrations that move like singers' voices. After sacrificing and offering food, they shine like sons of strength.

Agni knows all they accept as rich offerings in the morning, at midday, and in the evening (Rig Veda, Book 3, Hymn XXVIII). They come through skilled singers watching anxiously as the riches arrive from the immortal powers brought down by the matriarch, appearing as manifested asteroids, comets, meteors, and other heavenly bodies that ignite the eternal flame among two, all sitting like immortal embryos in the mortal female body.

The eternal flame grows to exalt the inner spirit (Atma) and appears like prolific animals that generate radiant splendour. Thus, a well-skilled embodiment is born as the son of Iḷā, which comes from the navel, the centre of material ground from where they fly like bird's (Jatavedas) carrying the eternal flame of Agni. They are accepted as the godly offerings that can reproduce themselves with the life force established with the breathing process in embodiments that create earthly sages who are perishable with very wise souls. They are fair to look at as they bring forth propitious gifts by appearing as the first ensigns of Agni. They create movement and follow the rising sunshine as they carry the eternal flame.

They appear like fire and follow the twin demigods; they appear as celestial bodies that create sparks that burn the grass to bring forth powers like the fire representing Agni. This invokes vibrations that become godly messages among embodied living beings serving as sages, who set themselves up as temples of worship. By making oblations to Agni and the demigods, they provide long life to fellow workers of the eternal flame.

As embryos with the eternal flame, they as the celestial germs born in varied shapes and forms, appear as the father (Tanūnapāt) and mother (Narāśaṁsa) and serve as the heavenly demigods (Mātariśvan). They follow the wind powered by heavenly power (Rudras) that creates and controls the breathing process, which brings the life force (Prana). In immortal form, the living spirit (Atma), through blessings as the seven priests, appears among the mother's bosom. Even those born with evil embodiments (Asuras) are brought to life. Those who, as newborn, like the cosmic host (Maruts), slay their foes. They become glorious (Kuśikas) with hymns ascending from their embodiments by the kindling of the eternal flame.

The divinity of victory (Verethragna) comes as the infant giver (Rig Veda, Book 3, Hymn XXX). Blessed with powers, it removes all the curses placed by ignoble souls and evil powers. They come as friends who pour libations that provide nourishing food and bring inner peace. With such libations, even wild animals become domesticated. In the terrestrial region, they appear with Indra like cosmic bodies bringing light and water that transform the solid ground into soft dirt. They extract from the surface elemental particles to create mortal embodiments to eliminate evil powers. With the support of the spirit (Atma), as manifested embodiments, they serve as heroes that destroy manifested immortal forms, dragons, ferocious mortal forms, snakes, and other evil powers that try to overpower the elements of nature (Vasus), which with divine powers stands firm by bringing eternal truth to the heroes so they can slay the evil powers. They chase even those who flee and bring them to promise to join with the powers of Indra and serve Indra with worship.

Indra brings gifts in the thousands to support the manifested mortal tribal power (Kunaru). Such tribes are provided with the power to crush evil creatures just as they did other evil powers (Vrtra). On the fertile, holy, terrestrial ground, as the righteous rulers (Kunaru), they establish their dwelling and sit with Indra and receive vast vigour. From the mid-air, like the heavenly bull, they arrive to slay the evil powers. They come to lift living embryos before they are driven away by floods, while Indra establishes an easy path for the embryos to manifest with praise as the life force, such as animals that bring food to meet with those forming pairs of males and females.

The demigods (Aśvins) appear on the ground serving as fast running, flying livestock. Once they have accomplished their goal, Indra lets them loose and gladly acts to set the twilight zone in the morning and evening. They are acknowledged with fully manifested glory that comes like the godly works created by the powers of Indra regulating the terrestrial ground.

With twilight zones, they give birth to splendours that bear the mythical juice. The heifers, female cows that have not given birth to calves, are accepted by Indra to serve as friends and especially those who produce rhythmic hymns that can overpower or slay malicious powers and take booty. As Indra's messengers, they shoot scorching arrows at evil steeds and eat them. They acquire cows and harness wild animals to serve as domesticated animals, such as horses, and they bring evil beings to cultivate individual longings, acquire skills, and use their generosity to build splendid societies. With the power of hymns, they extend their lives through eternal light and by offering support to the tribunal (Kuśikas).

By learning to use vibrations to produce sweet sounds and serving as holy singers, they bring a gift from the messenger (Maghavan) that bursts open the doors of the animal stables. They bring strength to win booty that brings eternal wisdom, which helps to unveil absolute truth. They gather on the battlefield and seek support from the messenger (Maghavan) in slaying the evil powers. The sonless mortal messengers are blessed with a daughter with a grandson; this brings fain to the sire as it witnesses a spirit eagerly flowing toward mortal embodiments to reside in a body made from earthen material.

The immortal spirit resides in mortal embodiments with the divine will as they serve on the ground (Rig Veda, Book 3, Hymn XXXI). The mortal embodiments are blessed with eternal powers to serve as the prolific parents guided by the trinity to promote perishable manifested embodiments. They enhance on the ground like earthly priests whose children are born in the form of Agni that produces blood, which with vibrations can be recognised as speech that demonstrates the movement of the eternal flame. The prolific parents hold the embryo, an unmanifested astral body that beholds the spirit (Atma) along with Indra, which with the sun, moon, and stars comes to serve others. Through sacrifices, they conquer a group waiting to become noble warriors and recognize their noble souls that bring eternal glow as light.

They rise with inner awakening to comprehend the power of dawn and meet with other prevailing master souls (Paramatma) set free by Indra. They built firm embodiments that provide domiciles to other astral bodies and build noble souls to manifest as the earthly seven priests (Saptarishis). With the seven priests, they find the pathway for other astral bodies to join and form the holy order while performing their deeds of worship; they share eternal wisdom with others. Like the mythical female dog (Saramā), with their manifested bodies, they go into mountain fissures to dig out all that is needed. Longing for friendship along with the noblest worshipper (Aṅgiras), they come from the hills pouring treasure for pious young followers. Making hymns on the way to eternal life, they build a steady and firm worship hall where through the gods of order, they draw milk from the ancient cow for them to enjoy as it goes up into the region between earth and heaven.

The pious young make a mansion to provide a glorious home for their parents. At the proper time, their ample goblet penetrates the vast body prevailing in earth and heaven. They unite all invincible powers through Indra, which provides support for them to overpower the evil spirits. They create the princes who are the keepers of a rich dominion.

They bring the life force and generate rhythms that support friends and create lovers. Indra excels with the heroes to precipitate with songs the eternal flame that brings the dawn. The Maruts make the cosmic vapours generate free-flowing waters. Through cleansing, they acquire knowledge and comprehend absolute truth as they acquire eternal wisdom to become holy souls.

By overpowering darkness and ignorance, they gain treasure, including water and astral bodies sanctified by heavenly power (Sūrya). Those lovely friends who fail to attain the ultimate measure of greatness continue serving with the lords as the evil slayers who are given the power to live. They become godly friends of the mighty ones like the messengers (Aṅgiras), who are honoured with worship. They chase many evil creatures by getting help from the messenger (Maghavan), which brings heaven's light to help others. They spread purifying waters to convey them across to safety.

True Disciple

The hearers and servers of eternal wisdom keep everything ascetic (Rig Veda, Book 3, Hymn XXXIV) by serving as disciples (Śrāvaka), who can be divided into males as monks (bhikkhus), females as nuns (bhikkuṇīs), and other devotees as males and females (upāsakas). Based on their spiritual accomplishments, they are referred to as the chief disciples (agraśrāvaka), great disciples (mahāśrāvaka), and ordinary disciples (śrāvaka), those who have not yet entered the path of irreversibly or emancipation and therefore are subject to rebirth.

They appear as two bright rivers—mother Vipāś and tributary daughter Sutudri. They appear like eager mares seeking each other. They form streams that rise and swell as they head for their ultimate destination, the ocean.

They create floods that cover the ground, and they build places for the pious young to worship like the following rivers. Like the holy ones, they produce sublime hymns that the pious young use to reach the holy ones, who call on Indra to bring thunder to dig up channels, so the evil powers trying to stop the rivers are hit. Savitar sends currents so Indra can smite evil power and allow the fish (Ahi) to overpower obstructers and let the water flow.

Indra and Savitar honour the sages with their loving-kindness so they can bow as they pray for them to stay on the rivers and keep the water level below carriage axles. Indra and Savitar keep water moving in rivers, so they produce vibrations as sounds like a mother nursing a child. They watch as the river bends to yield like a maiden serving her lover, and noble tribes (Bharatas) settle along the streams, where they grow far away from the rivers. They see noble tribes help when warriors cross where the river speeds up and slows down. They overcome and win favour brought by the rivers, which never allow sinless bulls to waste away.

Incited by prayers, Indra (Rig Veda, Book 3, Hymn XXXV) dispels foes trying to overpower noble worshippers. They serve as true disciples (Sravaka) and serve like the bounteous giver serving earth and heaven. They watch the water flowing with praise, sing, worship Indra, and attain immortality. They lead bands of devotees and overpower evil leaders in the forest. They serve night and day like milk-producing animals.

The noble souls protect those who serve as devotees and help them conquer hostile bands. They shine a light on evil powers and help devotees serve as heroes. They sing holy songs, generate noble thoughts, and serve worshippers in the earthly stratum. Indra rules all mortal bodies serving as wise singers who glorify with chants. They are rewarded for their achievements and are honoured as excellent conquerors (Vivasvān).

With love and devotion to Indra, all devotees rejoice in the direct light coming from the sun that provides physical power and nourishment. The manifested noble souls (Aryaman) as devotees appear to gain control by providing protection. They help others prosper with daylight and water.

The noble souls call on the messenger (Maghavan) as the best (Rig Veda, Book 3, Hymn XXXVI) avatar of Indra to help gather spoils. They appear in the sky as coursers hastening to drink the mythical juice. Indra-Soma appears like two swift horses and rearrange the method of their sacrifices by offering them drink to the fullest. Noble and wise souls drink the juice and gain absolute truth. They make sure all other worshippers stay beside them and gain vigour.

As they pass to the feast and the Soma, they approach as benevolent and imperishable souls. Sweet milk and water from the mountains support their physical bodies, strengthen their sublime bodies, and develop friendly mental powers (Chita) to know the absolute truth. Serving as the best avatars of the godhead, they accept sacrificial gifts brought to them by sages (Adhvaryu and Hotar), which are all blessed, and they serve as the holy emperor (Sakra), who calls on Maghavan to support them in the fight.

The heroes slay the evil powers and take their riches. Sakra shares oblations that help them become great as the givers of gifts. Each libation strengthens others, especially those who become renowned for their mighty achievements. They discover some who could grow with skill, use their mighty voices in battle, and gain strength that surpasses all other strengths. The Aśvins manifest like the heavenly bull and serve as heavenly sages. When they are accompanied by Indra, they appear as earthly sages who bring milk to serve offspring who are pushing along the streams flowing to the sea. As earthly sages, they carry embryos floating in the water. They develop individual dwellings with impetuousness from Indra and bring blessings to all.

Those who slay the evil powers attain the strength of a hundred powers (Rig Veda, Book 3, Hymn XXXVII). They receive praise for having eternal spirits that provide them with the vision to see through the manifested world and connect with the universal soul. They gain direct access to great glory and fame. They recite praise songs and awaken all. They make eternal power invincible and incomprehensible and become visible only as newborns appearing as manifested heavenly power. They are born as twin demigods who retain their beauty.

Indra, in its majestic form, serves the demigods as the wonder worker. They remain hidden in darkness or secretly reside in water collecting wisdom. They bring discriminating light to remove darkness and hold the mythical juice that removes misfortune. They serve the seven sages (Saptarishi), who appear along with other demigods (Navagvas) and later serve the prophets (Daśagvas). They remove evil powers and hostile mortal embodiments.

Indra accepts the strength from Rudra, which pours the juice until all are satisfied (Rig Veda, Book 3, Hymn XXXLI). Then Indra brings demigods who perform wealth-bestowing sacrifices through subtle faculties. The lord of the brave fills their dwelling place to create the mortal embodiment that can excel and generate in the belly celestial Soma, which like the mythical juice, brings eternal wisdom. The heroes come to destroy evil powers. With offerings, libations, and hymns, they worship Indra and embrace such powers as cows embrace their calves. After drinking the juice mixed with milk, the royal race (Kusikas) honours Indra as the lord of a hundred powers. The juice and milk make them unyielding. The special drink mixed with barley generates an urge to come to help the royal race (Kusikas).

Indra appears with the demigods and offers the juice to the royal race (Rig Veda, Book 3, Hymn XLII). They pass it to many people who serve as the twin demigods. This pleases demigods, who mix the juice with corn and make the royal race come and hear the messenger (Maghavan) appointed by Indra as their ruler who can give them the mythical juice as nectar so they can serve as the holy sage (Ṛṣi), which they hear about from those who reach the farthest limits to serve like Rudra.

They appear as fast falcons that bring joy among manifested embodiments, and they send cows from their stalls to serve as strong ones and gather spoils after winning in battle. Indra brings the demigods, who know how to restrain great glories, to bring out the golden heavenly hue that comes from the ground and nourishes the golden one. Indra creates the power to rule the masculine and the feminine. Indra appears like a joyous peacock. The demigods fly over deserts and break down barriers to the cosmic vapours. They land near pools that become lakes and bring down ripened fruit to satisfy individual desires. As the leader with glorious fame and strength, Indra hears praises and calls for support from mortal noble souls.

The ancient but ever youthful bull appears as the sovereign ruler who wields thunder from Indra (Rig Veda, Book 3, Hymn XLIV). The ruler gathers spoils, subdues foes, and grants rest to all embodied spirits (Atma). Surpassing all measures with brightness, the demigods serve the mid-air region. Indra carries a wealth of holy thoughts acquired through the juice.

The heroes are born and raised and sent to establish themselves as heroes with purified transcendent embodiments that aspire to get maximum happiness as they are often tempted to resort to methods that entail suffering. As holy souls (Rṣis), they understand the commitment that would enable mortal embodiments to fulfil their missions righteously. They understand that every such sacrifice requires a minimum of four levels, including reciting invocations and petitions of prayers (Hotrā); sacrificing (Adhvaryu); measuring the ground before building the altar, preparing the sacrificial vessels, fetching wood and water and fire with specialized hymns, and bringing mortal and immolate embodiments to bring out the invigorating properties; and finally, invoking the lord (Brahmā) to define the mystical priesthood that serves as the godly power of unity (Viśvāmitra).

Serving with physical sacrifice (Rig Veda, Book 3, Hymn XLVII), the heavenly bull manifests with rapture through the joy the mythical juice grants like the cosmic host. They unveil eternal truth in accordance with the cosmic host (Maruts), which serves as heroes with eternal wisdom provided by Indra to bring friendly demigods together and invite the cosmic host to share the drink with others in honour of the victory over the evil power (Vṛtra).

The cosmic host (Maruts) comes with Maghavan and helps the semi-immortal fish (Ahi) to slaughter the dragon (Sambara), which is supported by the evil mother. The demigods controlling milk-bearing mothers and cattle rejoice with the holy singers. The heavenly bull appears as a comet that follows the cosmic host and gives freedom to serve like mighty rulers who protect mortal embodiments.

The heavenly bull appears as the young earthly bull, drinks the mythical juice from plants like drinking water, and eats nourishing food produced from such plants. The heavenly father serves the mother milk for children and moves on with a great desire to exploit the varied aspects of life. With fierce vigour, they quickly conquer even the creative powers (Tvaṣṭar) and call on Maghavan to help them serve as heroes in the fight. They gather spoils and, with their eternal strength, listen to them and bring them support in their battles against evil powers.

Indra provides juice that fulfils their longing, and they attain eternal truth and continue to serve the engendered demigods in heaven and on earth (Rig Veda, Book 3, Hymn XLIX). They crush the evil powers and appearing as tawny coursers serving like the Aśvins, they subdue their foes and shorten the life of the evil warrior spirit (Dasyu) that prevails in both worlds. Serving as the father, Bhaga brings blessings of purified water like rain that strengthens them. Illumining the nights with moonlight and filled with strength and riches, they call on Maghavan, which slays the evil powers.

Like a pair of trusty steeds, they appear as the pair, male and female, that faithfully serves the ancient tradition by filling their cheeks with eternal love and fairness. They drink the juice mixed with milk and become preservers. This satisfies their longing, and with a very splendid and extended bounty, they seek the light with hymns to manifest like the royal race. Blessed with the power to become spiritual singers, they call on Maghavan and Indra to come in the fight and gather spoils.

They sing praises that reach Indra (Rig Veda, Book 3, Hymn LI), which appears on all sides spreading songs of praise and bringing the lord of a hundred powers that sets the body of water into the sea. It sets itself as the strong hero who brings booty for the winner with the powers of undivided faith or devotion. This breaks down all forts and brings ever-glorious light to remove the prevailing darkness. In the spoils that pile up and by singing praise songs, they win the power of Indra by taking care of matchless worshippers whom they find dwelling in darkness. They, with delight, bring Vivasvāns serving the transcendental spirit (Atma), which is ready to conquer the foe.

As most heroic, like the priests, they are glorified with songs and praises full of wondrous power; they conquest through worshipping Indra as the sole lord from earlier times. They give abundant gifts to mortals and provide water to help vegetation grow. Indra preserves the forests' wealth, and the lords of the bay offer prayers and songs gladly accepted through the powers of the essence. They offer assistance to those who worship Indra and drink the juice with the cosmic host under their guidance, always keeping away from mortal embodiments. The Manus eagerly drinks the desirous drink with immortal power kept exclusively for Indra and taken only with other deities adorned at birth to be invoked for the great fight.

The cosmic host brings to mortal embodiments noble gifts that are rejoiced by Indra, and it keeps together in possession while they serve as the evil slayer and offer worshippers the libation. As the lord of the affluent, this juice transforms individual embodiments to serve with a godlike nature, generate happiness, and prosper in the heavenly and earthly regions.

As part of ancient tradition (Rig Veda, Book 3, Hymn LII), Indra accepts in the morning a cake consisting of roasted corn and groats offered as part of eulogies as an oblation. This is accepted with all singing like one accepting his bride. At midday, a libation of roasted corn is offered to the sun. Third, many sacrifices accompanied by praise are offered as oblations. All such oblations are offered by sages, who invoke the wind (Vāja), so it will hold back the powerful celestial divinities (Ṛbhus). The cosmic deity (Pūṣan) is allowed to support Indra, and demigods (Aśvins) are allowed to come as flying horses along with the cosmic host (Maruts) together as archangels serving likewise heroes who offer meal cakes, and they meet quickly to serve as brave cosmic heroes.

Indra brings pleasant food to those who represent kinsmen (Parvata), brave heroes who rejoice in oblations and refine their hymns before they meet with Indra's messengers, who establish their home on the ground (Maghavan). The messengers hang around with the king's men like children grasping their fathers' garments. The king's men recognize the noble soul as the herald (Adhvaryu) representing earth and heaven. They convey eternal flame from Agni to pass through individual embodiments along with the mythical juice and depart, letting loose loud, neighing coursers that serve like brothers.

Indra and the herald find a place to rest along with the screaming gracious companion, the strong courser. When they, like messengers (Maghavan), are set free along with bounteous sons of heaven, they appear like Agni's ancient envoy (Aṅgirases), who with eternal truth (Virupas) regulates the evil powers. They also hold the noble powers (Viśvāmitra) from them as they attain wealth, spiritual wisdom, and absolute truth. With such wealth, they can prolong life, serving as noble powers (Viśvāmitra) and drinking the juice. They take on every shape embodiment can, and they serve as the holy ones.

They come from heaven in a moment like thrice-fitting prayers to serve as the mighty sage, the God-born and God-incited mortal embodiments. They look like billowing rivers where noble powers (Viśvāmitra) are escorted by the tribal king (Sudās), who was brought out of its entanglement with the tribal king (Kuśikas) serving the kingdom of Bhāratas. Pleased with the ancestral friendly growth and with songs of praise, Indra produces hymns of mythical juice as they celebrate.

All holy singers, worshipping sages, and demigods drink the juice and are filled with eternal wisdom, which sets free the tribal Kutikas from attachment and memories. From being mortal embodiments, they go forward and become very attentive as their mortal embodiments are let loose like horses, thus creating the tribal kings (Sudās), who win riches as they move east to west and then north, slaying their foes. On the ground, they offer praises to Indra to serve as a sustainer of mortal embodiments serving the heavenly and earthly regions.

Noble powers are invoked to become the noble tribal race (Bharatas), which keeps all mortal embodiments secure. They watch them sing hymns to Indra to make sure they bring water, so there is no drought. The noble powers (Viśvāmitra) evolve into another tribal race (Kikatas), who work to feed mortal embodiments and bring prosperity. They regulate water and milk-bearing animals and learn to extract the essence (Swadharma) that provides added wealth to progeny to give birth to another tribe, which understands the ultimate power (Pramaganda).

Like the ancient tribe, they worship the daughter of the sun and bring the glory (Jamadagnis) in mortal demigod embodiments, all created with deathlessness. Like the tribe (Sasarpari), they bring glory and serve the fivefold human generations created like the daughter of Paksa, which ascends as well as descends with the lunar power and at all times bestows new vital power that like the ancient deathless Jamadagnis gives the individual tribes the power to serve like strong oxen.

Indra gives mortal embodiments the strength to draw the wagon like a bull, supports seedlings, and provides the powers of essence (Swadharma) to gain strength to comprehend wisdom. It also provides a heart (Khayar) of strong lumber like mahogany, which is supported by the seven supreme powers of causation (Sinsapa), which create spines among mortal embodiments that allow them to stand and travel on two legs.

All Inclusive

Agni, like Indra, brings comprehensive powers (Rig Veda, Book 3, Hymn LIV) that, with strengthening hymns, provide unceasing support that allows all noble souls in the assembly to serve as synods. They sing their wishes, knowing well that the noble souls' synods are showing favour among the leaders of high advantage (Viśvedevas) to gain a comprehensive gathering of gods. They tell all concerned that no divinity should be omitted from praise and that the powers of causation are all taken together as a whole without any dichotomy.

They serve heaven and earth with faith and honour that comply with the eternal laws. They offer homage to Agni with great food as they pray for riches like the ancient holy sages whose words are ever true. They attain the power to find godly souls (Viśvedevas) in heaven and on earth. Any brave mortal embodiment serving as a hero fights with honour to conquer and make paths to demigods, who know eternal truth. Willingly, they declare to see them even from the lowest dwelling places in secret regions. Like sages, the Viśvedevas view mortal embodiments as those who are serving to bedew nectar (Amrita) and, with joy, find the seat of order that becomes their home. Agni and the divine will (Devavani) with essence come flying to find themselves as partners on the ground and remain young forever as sisters united by names.

All living things, though apart, are products of the same mighty gods (Viśvedevas) that are one mighty power, whether fixed or moving and serve all creation. They ponder their kinship like their mighty father, always singing with praise, whereby they are accustomed to standing with the celestial twin demigods or the cosmic body of demigods (Maruts). With blessed speech, they represent the young trinity (Agni, Varuṇa, and Mitra) and serve with wisdom and with glory like noble souls (Ādityas) that serve as the sovereign rulers after passing through heaven three times.

After completing their service to the assembly of gods with songs of praise, they appear to the goddess (Savitar), so they can serve as dexterous creative workers (Tvaṣṭar). They aid celestial bodies (Ṛbhus), who join cosmic bodies (Pūṣan) to prepare rites and adjust the paths of comets, asteroids, and meteors. Riding on their flashing armed car with spears, they appear as the sovereign rulers like the cosmic host (Maruts), serving as the sons of order, who serve as holy youths. They hear the goddess mother (Sarasvatī) and the sovereign rulers serving as noble offspring; they bring wealth like the rich (Viṣṇu) ancient prodigies.

All filled with praise songs, they go on the road to meet the primaeval power (Bhaga), who in the past served as the chieftain of the mighty stride, the godly mother of the essence (Swadharma), which manifests as young females. Knowing Indra, these young dames never disregard the divine order and always follow it and the rules. Through their heroic powers and majesty, they are filled with essence and serve the region between earth and heaven. Serving as the host of the lords of the brave the chieftain, Indra crushes forts and slays the evil powers. The lords of the brave chieftain appear with the Aśvins and seek to form kinship through offering glorious titles and sharing their riches.

They abide by the order and serve as friends of Indra like the once-invoked celestial body (Ṛbhus). They manifest with godly powers (Adityas) as the noble offspring of the mother (Aditi). They serve and worship and abide by the eternal laws (Varuṇa) and make sure the laws remain unbroken. They remove most of the childlessness and become rich in kind, with their offspring serving like the gods' envoys. They proclaim sinless many a quarter, serve in safety, and reside between earth and heaven.

As the gods' envoys, they hear about the powers of the sun and water. They manifest with purity among distilled raindrops. This allows them to rest firmly and with joy to generate freshening moisture and give birth to free-flowing springs. They hear about the cosmic host (Maruts) that grants auspicious shelters. Those who travel in friendship receive support and blessings as they pass through the eternal flame. Like a rich sea, this is filled with food provided by Agni. They offer glory combined with goods needed to conquer in battle and help foes with light and loving-kindness.

First thing in the morning (Rig Veda, Book 3, Hymn LV), they set all females as the godly mother, which provides breath (Prana) and validates the supreme powers of causation. Prana sets for them their sole dominion on the ground, which protects divine creations completely. Agni sets up its base between heaven and earth to establish the new region to be regulated by the godheads (Viśvedevas) and enforced with essence (Devavani). It serves as the universal soul (Paramatma), which flies over places and makes sure that the supreme powers of causation keep on making sacrifices to serve, such as fire.

Kindling the eternal flame, it unveils eternal truth and exposes all to the supreme powers of causation regulating heaven and earth. They establish this as the universal kingdom converted into regions, and then the holy ground is reset like a love seat on which one mother as the source of creation rests as vegetation, and another mother is lodged like old plants that feed the infants as mortal embodiments. The newborn grows and represents the universal soul (Paramatma), which without impregnation, appears as fruitful to help others grow.

The mother of two children is regulated by the divine covenant of righteousness and humanity. She speaks sweetly and addresses them as a friendly warrior in the battles of two worlds—the material and the spiritual. She appears as the living spirit (Atma) and explains each thing that comes near and is seen to commingle deep in the mortal embodiment that is worn out like the mighty envoy or is subject to death.

It goes looking through the dominion of arrayed splendour, and it pierces the veil to find the wondrous beauty from the loftiest station as the guardian of the heavenly power (Viṣṇu), who upholds its dear, immortal dwelling places and knows everything through the eternal flame provided by Agni as well as these mortal embodiments presiding as a variant pair. This variant pair, like night and day, have made themselves twin beauties—one dark and the other bright—true sisters representing the two mothers.

The mother and the daughter give milk at the seat of the eternal laws and are praised equally. Serving on the ground, they wear manifold beauties that uplift the mother cow licking her calf. Mother and daughter are treasured as the one manifest physically and mortally and the other hidden, spiritual, and immortal, but they take one pathway going in two directions—one departing and the other coming.

The universal soul yields rich nectar as the bull bellows like a thundering cloud in other regions. Another herd receives the rain showing the power of Bhaga, which serves as the sovereign king that protects living things on the ground. Through them, it declares eternal wisdom through five manifested physical and five associated subtle faculties.

Just like with creative power (Tvaṣṭar), they create omni forms that cause mortal embodiments to appear as all kinds of creatures. This is how heaven and earth remain united, where each is laden with treasure that the renowned heroes can gather. This is how mortal embodiments sustain individual dwellings appearing as the king who, with noble friends, serves as a hero and protects all. The earth serves Indra and its friends by sharing its godly treasures.

No being can impair the steadfast ordinances (Rig Veda, Book 3, Hymn LVI) serving earth and heaven. No malevolent or egotistical power can stop the holy sages from bowing to the emerging powers like the sun, which proceeds to eternal truth. The powers of the mighty ones stand near-infinite time that creates the past and the future while the now is apparent. Infinite time, like the heavenly bull, appears with the earthly cow in all shapes as a family with three udders, triple-breasted and blessed with three aspects of time: past, present, and future.

They majestically appear as the everlasting impregnator and serve as rulers in many places. When approached, it can be observed calling to the goddesses of water (Savitr), which stays to meet those who are wandering as enclosed noble powers (Adityas) appearing in three holy forms, first as the free-flowing heavenly water, rain; second as earthly water in rivers; and third, as infinite water in lakes and oceans. The goddess (Savitr) represents three forms of wisdom: intellect (lower knowledge), insight (higher knowledge), and illumination (enlightenment).

From illumination comes godly powers. First, the supreme assembly as the trinity comes from heaven three times a day with blessings. Second, the protector comes from the cosmos and brings wealth and treasure (Savitr). Third, the eternal laws and eternal love serve the region between heaven and earth and provide equilibrium by bringing water from heaven as wealth (Bhaga) and returning water to heaven as treasure (Savitr). These three bright dominions overpower evil powers (Asuras) and allow the holy and vigorous sovereigns to rule and protect mortal embodiments from injury.

With fine acumen and thoughts (Rig Veda, Book 3, Hymn LVII), even animals such as cows wander freely without herdsmen and produce nourishing milk for those who praise Indra and Agni. Mighty powers (Pū5an) drain heaven's exhaustless natural udder (Vasus) to bring blessings to all. They lend vigour to the bulls and, through reverence, bless them with the powers of embryos; as they come lowing to the cows, they create calves. They fix them with thoughts like the sacrifice made by the cosmic bodies that come with the eternal flame from heaven to earth. They provide boons to mortal embodiments in plenty so they can rise high like Agni and bring sweet tongues to the fair tastes among food. They call on the gods for the mythical juice coming through drinking water. It brings the wonderful and exhaustless supply all coming from the rain clouds, all from nature (Vasu) which is supported by messengers (Jatavedas), all showing loving-kindness that reaches mortal embodiments.

Nature (Vasu) keeps on yielding things like milk through mortal embodiments and, at times, even helps their offspring (Rig Veda, Book 3, Hymn LVIII). Like the holy sages, they seek donations as a charity (Dak5iṇā). This is received after a ritual has been performed, bringing refulgence. Like the twin demigods, with the praise offered to Usha to invoke dawn and evening and by well-ordered statutes, they offer sacred oblations to rise and serve like godly parents. They work to destroy any stingy or ungenerous feelings in their embodiments and express all this with sympathy. They appear as cosmic bodies that hear everything and serve as wonderworkers. They serve mortal embodiments passing through and invoke friendly demigods (Aśvins) as they offer the juice with milk.

They join mortal embodiments to serve as the mighty helpers who travel on godly paths and bring libations. They all come from the ancient ancestral home filled with an auspicious friendship that provides eternal wisdom to support the heroes. These heroes hold this wealth like holy sages (Jahnu), who have eternal wealth that keeps forming, again and again, an auspicious friendship that rejoices by all with draughts of the mythical juice. Like the Aśvins, they join with the wind (Vāyu) as one-minded and ever-youthful wonderworkers, the Nāsatyas. Strong as steeds, they enjoy the drink and become bounteous givers who become cosmic bodies and serve as press stones that move between earth and heaven.

Manifested, archetypal living beings turn their prevailing ghostly kinship and become desirous of wondrous art schemes to gain control and regulate eternal wealth, acquire knowledge, and meet individual needs (Rig Veda, Book 3, Hymn L). As the sons with holy souls (Sudhanvans), they learn to sacrifice and share with others. They drink milk to acquire intellects and appear like the heavenly bay steeds. Over time, they comprehend the regulating powers serving the heavenly region and the deities and demigods serving the earthly region.

Once they attain higher knowledge, they comprehend the cosmic mortal bodies serving as the friends of Indra and Agni. Once they fully acquire eternal wisdom, they know the grandsons' archetype (Manus), referred to as the first progenitor of the mythical rulers of the earth who perform obligatory responsibilities. As the children of Sudhanvan, they come to earth to win everlasting life by performing rites and noble acts. With Indra, they invoke the mythical juice, and they gloriously fulfil their and others' wishes. They serve as earthly priests as they perform good deeds, not like the heroic acts performed by celestial bodies (Rbhus).

Their acts are admired by Indra just as it admired the celestial bodies' sacrifice to serve the mighty ones. Like the messenger (Maghavan), they bring the heavenly, mythical juice and make sages become auspicious as they are guided by rhythmic song. They rejoice with the sons of Sudhanvan, appearing as Rbhu and Vāja, and with music and praise, they come with many offering the mythical juice being poured for the heroes or sages. By worshipping the godly powers, they are ordained with the eternal laws. Indra thus comes with mighty power to strengthen the worshippers and help them perform the sacrifice.

Usa accepts praise coming from the singers and bestows the mythical knowledge on living beings (Rig Veda, Book 3, Hymn LXI). It spreads forth with shining light filled with wisdom and appears as dawn riding on the sun and representing the celestial divinity (Surya) that, with a pleasant voice, awakens all. This wonderful light spreads from earth to heaven. Dawn, with hymns of praise, brings dewdrops like nectar from heaven.

The holy ones with hymns support Indra, who brings Agni. This generates refulgence while it goes forth soliciting fair riches by enforcing laws on firm ground, and it moves with the morning light. Appearing like the mighty bull, it is empowered with eternal laws and eternal love.

The mortal embodiments perform activities like faithful servants who support those loved ones serving Indra and Varuṇa jointly. They seek riches and come with the cosmic host (Maruts), which generates invocations to bring treasure. The Varūtrīs aid the rulers of the holy tribes (Bhāratī and Hotrā), who worship the immortal powers to come and regulate the morning and evening. The Bṛhaspati bring wealth and gifts and teach how to offer sacrifices with hymns and bring purity through the powers of prayer. Pū5an brings hymns and, with favour, receives all expressed in the form of a gracious song and with earnest thought. Like a bridegroom and bride, the living beings see through each other and see Pū5an.

The living beings attain power that brings forth with prayers an understanding of the earnest powers provided by Savitar that generates the craving to attain prosperity through manifesting as the singers. Those who worship Savitar build gathering places to worship. The living beings worship milk-bearing animals as the mother turns its milk into the mythical juice, which helps them conquer foes. It takes a seat of significance, serving as Mitra-Varuṇa, which with dew fills pastures with the eternal flame. The wind (Vayu) makes the regions adorable and joyful and regulated by the divine will (Devavani) that is lauded by the eternal flame (Jamadagni) song that sits in the place of the holy law.

CHAPTER 6
SHELTERED DOMINION

Being mortal, the physical body is subject to physical death. The perishable astral body can attain new life and adopt a different physical form because it is not subject to physical or biological death. However, it is subject to the doctrine of encirclement or cyclic existence (Samsara).

The astral body can be reborn in any of six major cycles (Bhavachakra). These include noble souls (Deva), evil souls (Asura), or other manifested embodiments such as animals or hungry ghosts that occupy the same physical space as living things but create hell, a place of torment as in the underworld (Naraka). The concept of rebirth is based on the performance of individual obligatory responsibilities (Karma), which can be good (Kushala) or bad (Akushala).

The supreme powers of causation direct the movement of physical embodiments and their ability to enhance their spiritual powers. Those attain greater protection by physical, meditative, and spiritual practices that lead to higher levels (Dharma) that help attain the liberation of individual spirits from the cycles of life and death—reincarnation.

Physical Body

The physical, mortal body consists of a subtle body that, through invisible channels, directs the eternal energies to reach a designated position or points in the physical embodiment (Rig Veda, Book 4, Hymn I). The state of the established points in the body determines the characteristics of the physical body. By understanding and mastering the subtle levels of reality, one can gain mastery over a sheltered dominion. The vital force (Prana) flows through a sheltered dominion to regulate the breathing process and manipulate and direct invisible channels toward specific points. The powers of causation direct the physical and spiritual powers and thus regulate the ultimate vital force in the dynamic universe. Mastering levels within the subtle body, the reality of the super perishable powers comes to comprehend the powers of causation. The creator and destroyer (Shiva) directs all manifestations and appears with its ferocious fire (Agni) to serve as the regulator of the eternal laws (Varuna) and eternal love (Mitra), which balance the powers that direct the dynamic universe.

With such knowledge, the powers of causation incarnate in the form of the trinity and serve as the rulers of all embodied, blessed, godly bodies to serve as noble souls. They designate mortal embodiments with Adityas to rule and work together like the wheels of a carriage helping to move swiftly on a wondrous course being pulled by steeds representing godly power (Adityas) supported through wondrous Agni, which brings progeny through the cosmic host (Maruts) and the twin demigods (Aśvins). Through a partnership, they manage from far with heavenly pleasure through newly created immortal powers that control any evil powers that dislike noble powers. Agni resides as an eternal flame in mortal embodiments and provides inner illumination. With immortal power, the living spirit (Atma), through awakening, supports mortal embodiments. The eternal flame, like the direct morning light of the sun (Surya) and the reflected light of the moon (Chanderma), generates creative ideas.

The powers of the eternal laws generated the mystic fluid (Amrita), which like the mythical juice, Soma, fills astral bodies with joy. Through their enhanced mental abilities, mortal embodiments attain bliss, including visionary power, the divine will, and the powers of essence to seek support from the perishable demigods, the cosmic host (Maruts) and the celestial host (Aśvins). They understand how cows transform water into milk that can become purified butter to support the eternal flame. Through comprehending, the astral body comes to experience birth in three forms: the first as actual birth, when the immortal spirit is placed in an astral body; next is when the astral body itself, holding the immortal spirit (Atma), is placed in the mortal embodiment; the third is when the astral body is freed from its mortal embodiment and, with divine powers, comes to serve the immortal embodiments which are serving the immortal powers as divinities and deities or immoral souls (Paramatma). The twin demigods (Aśvins) bring joyous food to create blood (Rakta). They are helped through an invisible umbilical cord to provide eternal power to living beings to receive the primordial energy (Shakti). With that, they know ways to attract and support the demigods and enjoy godsent riches.

The begetter appears as self-manifested (Shiva) in an abstract form that represents the primordial energy (Shakti), which comes to appear as a votary, a revered stone that supports mortal embodiments coming out of a disc-shaped platform serving as the primordial symbol (Lingam) coming from heaven. With rain or water, it disperses eternal wisdom. Concealed powers (Lingam) invoke the divine will accompanied by the essence touching the earthly bodies with the heavenly bodies. The symbol foetuses (Lingam) serve wondrously as they rise to the home of the holy order.

As they spring up and serve with mighty powers, the powers of causation (Septarishi) all as dear friends take on the role of a godly father with fain fulfilling the sacred law of worship (Varuna). They swarm with the morning light and drive milk-bearing animals out of the mountain cavern. With their splendid power, living beings take charge of the mountains that allow others to exploit earthly treasures. They come singing with newfound light and are accompanied by holy hymns of worship. With eager thoughts and good intent, they seek booty, and with celestial sounds, they throw open the solid ground to allow milk-bearing animals to come out of their confined stables and caves. They come riding from heaven to bring the dawn, which ascends by beholding good and evil deeds. They abide by the demigods (Aśvins), and they serve the union (Varul)a-Mitra) by calling on Agni to provide the eternal flame. Agni prevails in all three forms of the dynamic universe: the celestial fire of the sun, moon, and stars; the cosmic fire representing the life force (Prana) in embryos; and the Indra that protects against evil powers coming from the underworld, the terrestrial region.

As gracious birds (Jatavedas), they represent eternal fires that fill the hearth and kiln. After gaining intellect, Jatavedas come to know all about created beings. They possess knowledge about everything manifested, and they acquire higher knowledge of living beings. They attain godly riches and eternal wisdom, and they invoke inner illumination appearing as the altar fire, which is perceived by worshippers as the source of knowledge, wisdom, insight, and understanding about all existence. They comprehend all aspects of transmigrations from subtle bodies to physical bodies. In classical mythology, a group of godly powers appears as winged gods (Kamadeva).

They come with passion and love and manifest by giving birth to altruistic love and friendship. They share the eternal wealth and material possessions by performing charitable acts (Daan). As mortal embodiments, they serve the god of gods faithfully by worshipping it as the universal soul. Many faithfully serve in astral bodies the immortal spirit (Atma) and worship a mid-mortal godly power such as holy souls as manifested envoys. They offer worship accompanied by glory and appear as demigods or archangels represented as the spirit with wings (Eros).

Agni provides the eternal flame that appears through the powers of wind (Vayu) which appear as a manifested living being (Eros), the son of the vigour that during the day provides the eternal flame among the vegetation kingdoms. They harness its sublime form and help stallions fly. They appear as ruddy steeds that invoke the eternal flame, and with blessings, they pour other forms of fat that generate close-knit glory. They enforce the divine order and create immortal deities and demigods that fly like red horses on the solar wind. They represent the heavenly duality (Vishnu-Indra), support the trinity (Aryaman, Mitra, and Varul)a), and sometimes even help the cosmic demigods (Maruts) and the celestial twins (Aśvins).

Agni pulls them to bring oblations to serve folks appearing as their brave friends who offer perpetual sacrifices like cattle, sheep, and horses and provide sacred food for their offspring. They secure wealth and praise in the evening or the morning. They even offer a gold-girded courser that, as an oblation, goes to homes to rescue people from distress. Those who worship the eternal flame bring gifts and offer services; they do not allow sinners or the wicked to get close to the eternal flame, and they serve as the god of all mortal brings.

By bringing liberal gifts, they show them strengthening as adorable powers making sacrifices. They win through distinguishable sense and folly like horses with their straight and crooked backs and help them acquire prosperity and produce noble offspring who are granted plenty to keep poverty afar. By serving as sages, they never deceive even when they sit in mortal beings' dwellings. They behold them as friends and serve through the priest in providing good guidance; they help them make rapid footsteps that are wonderful and fair to look at.

Being the youngest, they pour the mythical juice and serve with joy the godly powers of the ruler. This brings splendid treasure and plentiful aid to perform hard work. The eternal flame blesses all faithful servants with wisdom and helps them manifest like the seven sages (Saptarishi). Engendered by the morning light, like the mother, these sages produce seven ordinands appearing like the ancient radiant messengers (Aṅgirases), which as the sons of heaven uncover the eternal spirit buried in the mountains.

Through worship and singing praises that split the ground, they make apparent the hidden spirit appearing like the reddish twilight. The buried spirits serve as archangels who perform devout acts like smelting ore and enkindling a new generation exalted by Indra. The new generation appears before the cattle and is ready to serve as sages (Saptarishis). They provide aid like the archangels by bringing eternal truth and love to all living ones. They incorporate essence with the divine will (Devavani), and they shed light on the worship.

With the light, they bring out perfect beauty from the eternal flame that, through individual eyes, displays godly splendour. Agni manifests as the eternal flame among the wise ones who sing praises and gladly accept the eternal flame. Manifested embodiments gain eternal and external wealth that brings boons for many. Conceited Rudra appears with thunder representing the hammer-wielding god (Thor) that can cast out any living thing from the solid earth and protects mortal embodiments. It comes with sanctifying power that brings fertility to fields. It is the ancient symbol of the divine marriage of the sky god and the earth goddess.

The earth's planetary motion is revised over its lives in terms of its revolutions, apogees, epicycles, nodal longitudes, orbital inclinations, and other parameters (Rig Veda, Book 4, Hymn III). This Mother Earth is established by Rudra to support mighty ones on the ground. This manifestation is fully supported by Agni, which brings golden colours and the eternal flame appearing with thunder, lightning, and windstorms that strike senseless creation. The mighty ones come as lovely brides and hear the hymns of heavenly priests. They are all worshipped to produce the mythical juice, and as the true knowers of the law (Varuna), they serve with solemn rites and listen to the songs that honour Agni as well as accept the support of Indra without being offended by eternal love (Mitra).

They support manifested embodiments serving as demigods; they accept the manifested (Aryaman) and benefactor (Bhaga) as the noble powers, and Agni reduces the eternal flame, which serves the altar and joins with mighty winds, thus appearing as blessed souls generating the circumambient environment. Agni, along with eternal truth, minimizes the heavenly powers (Rudras) and transforms as a manifested benefactor that serves with honour by offering oblations; instead of being destroyers, they purify them by removing sin. They allow them to travel to the celestial power as envoys of (Viṣṇu) with a lofty flag representing the powers of Agni. The cosmic host comes along like arrows gaining absolute truth.

The heavenly powers (Surya) answer any questions to free noble souls (Rig Veda, Book 4, Hymn IV). The godly powers (Jatavedas) fulfil heavenly work by teaming with holy souls representing the eternal fire where Agni sprinkles oil on all birds, terrestrial animals, and marine life to support them with the ancient envoy (Aṅgirases) along with the divine will that offer the greatest bliss by bringing water all accompanied by hymns, and they all settle among the mortal embodiments. They embrace their surroundings with the morning light, which appears as immortal goddesses that bring the reflective light from the moon. They never harm treacherous neighbours or unworthy kinsmen, but they punish false brothers who trespass. The strong coursers protect Agni with loving care as they destroy affliction and the demon. Agni helps them move but never touches the heroes' food.

Those who know Agni's mission as the disposer learn to keep secret the speeches, hymns, and understanding that constitute part of the ultimate essence and the divine will. They are filled with the eternal flame coming from the ancient powers (Angirasa), which serves as the envoy of Agni. Passing through the process of spiritual involution, they many times descend as demigods to manifest among mortal embodiments and serve as the heavenly body (Budha), which manifests to serve all mortal embodiments. They are commonly respected as a group of manifested immortal deities (Budha Graha) that manifest as part of the Surya, appearing to support terrestrial bodies appearing as the cosmic body; they provide illuminated light from the sun, moon, and stars.

They destroy traps created by evil powers and catch monsters in nets; they provide mortal embodiments with the strength to reach to join with the immortal force (Budha Graha). They put their fleet in motion as their spies who never deceive and always protect mortal embodiments. They stop evil powers from creating trouble, and with the immortal force (Budha Graha), they serve as mighty kings. Agni shoots arrows covered with blazing fire to warn those who cause mischief so they can be burned up like stubble. Agni drives off enemies with celestial vigour and fights alongside those who destroy their foes, whether kin or strangers.

They come forth like beams on godly portals with laud as an immortal force and serve as mighty kings who offer regular oblations to extend life. They provide them with strong physical bodies to serve as their individual dwellings. They are offered along with praise songs with gracious hymns with which they communicate with each other. They attract other good steeds to adorn day by day and vouchsafe their dominion. They let each one serves in the evening or morning or day by day and in honour bring contentment that brings joy.

They share their treasure and bring joy as they learn to draw from Budha Graha, their immortal force. They serve as mighty kings and noble saints like the ancient prophet (Gotama). Instead of being most youthful as mythical rulers, they, as noble souls, serve all other mortal embodiments. They are blessed through the divine will to protect and support Indra.

They are served by the unity (Agni and Indra), which manifests itself as mortal embodiments providing mighty physical and spiritual power. They jointly represent the universal soul, which presides over embodied spirits as matronymics and patronymics (Māmateya). Through the eternal laws and eternal love (Varuna-Mitra), they preserve embodiments from afflictions, including ignorance and spiritual blindness.

They pass on the eternal laws and eternal love (Varuna-Mitra) to help mortal embodiments acquire eternal wisdom and seek absolute truth. They vitalize the powers to know about the universal soul that presides as the mother of all spirits (Māmateya).

The pole star, in conjunction with the truth, represents the immovable position in the sky from where eternal truth (Dhruvsatya) is unveiled, which defines the principles of a mythical phenomenon or doctrine among the immortal group (Budha Graha). Agni establishes the immovable position that manifests as fire and lightning supporting the sun. They operate as embodiments to create the four stages of existence: ignorance, consciousness, conscience, and deep sleep. These, as sublime states, appear among all people (Vaiśvānara) as an epithet of the godhead that helps mortal bodies realize the principles that regulate mortal embodiments with righteousness. They help mortal embodiments enhance and comprehend the demigods and understand with immortal power. The process of attaining eternal truth is like a drying agent that manifests in water and merges with eternal truth.

Beyond Ground

Eternal truth manifests in two forms: one identifying with living creatures (Jataveda) and the other with the purified immortal spirit (Atma). It prevails among the manifested bodies that at all times seek to leave the physical world and live beyond in the dynamic universe.

This process is regulated by the powers of oblations (Yajana), which help the external mythical juice seek the purity of the immortal spirit and thus, with the powers of internal mystical fluid (Amrita), invoke the astral body, which allows the uncontaminated spirit to merge with the universal soul.

Agni manifests serving as the messenger in the form of the destroyer (Kravyād), which brings biological death that allows the physical and subtle body to disintegrate and merge with nature (Prakriti). The destroyer (Kravyād) does not allow the astral body to merge with nature until it has been purified of residual memory.

The mortal embodiment by itself is regulated by Vaiśvānara (Rig Veda, Book 4, Hymn V), which fully comprehends the trinity (righteousness, morality, and humanity). They make sure every living thing experiences the highest level of essence, and while they prevail among all manifested material world or ground (Prithvi), each mortal embodiment starts at the bottom of the underworld and gradually sustains stress and pressure to move up. While on the ground, they become strong and self-reliant, and they do not feel there is any need to seek union with the universal soul.

While serving, they vouchsafe and regulate discriminatingly, mainly using their eternal wisdom. Having in abundance perishable goods and strength, they remain youthful in appearance. Once they know all about the secret hidden in the hymns, they move like infertile cows in terms of acquiring eternal wisdom. Some even use hidden higher knowledge to obtain the eternal wisdom from the bounteous giver to enhance. They consume eternal wisdom and glow with the eternal flame. Complying with steadfast laws (Varuṇa) but not the commandments of eternal love, they go like youthful women without supporting others as brothers and perform evil acts. They become filled with sin and are subjected to evil powers. Agni brings strength to them and helps them seek and receive inner light and behold their heavy burdens through practising yoga and reciting hymns (Prṣṭha) to invoke the mighty profound power (Asta-Vasus).

The godly power regulates eight great elements (Asta-Vasus), which bring inner strength. Through self-identified qualities, they acquire beauties good to eat and purified thoughts to present. First, they receive the lower knowledge, and then the higher knowledge, and then eternal wisdom. They locate the place above the grassy ground, where the first protector (Vishnu)

established three steps above for heavenly children. By singing hymns, they learn all about the eight great elements and come in the form of noble souls to store milk in the udders of cows. They know that at the altar, a well-kept secret was placed by an ancient power that, with radiance, provides the mighty vision.

To comprehend their true relationship with their ancestors, they come to know the mother (Prśni), who keeps her secret treasure at the loftiest station. When the heavenly bull with its flaming tongue approaches, it tastes the reverence, the laws of divine order, and it sends eternal firebirdss (Jatavedas) to acquire whatever wealth is needed to become part of the sovereign to serve both earth and heaven. The Jatavedas use secret passages to come from far to reach such places where they can approach the sovereign. The Jatavedas establish rules to govern and reward the fleet-footed coursers who speed to win the divine will from the goddesses.

The Jatavedas come with the light from dawn and at dusk to regulate those who offer nothing to suffering living things. While great ones, as human beings, bring goods and glory to serve living things. Like holy priests (Adhvaryu), they offer rites and sacrifice and serve higher knowledge to seek absolute truth and move along with the demigods (Rig Veda, Book 4, Hymn VI). Savitar, the ruler of the cosmic vapours, provides them with water, and Agni gives them the eternal flame. Then the holy priests (Adhvaryu) lift the glowing ladle filled with oil and let the sacrificial smoke rise to heaven. The holy priests at the sacred grass kindle and tend to milk-bearing animals and noble souls that have gone through three rounds of reincarnation.

They serve as the holy priest (Adhvaryu), which manifests and runs like a vigorous horse. All other creatures are frightened to see the eternal flame that resides among living beings like lovely and dreadful Agni spreading to establish living splendours that are not covered by darkness or ignorance. They appear like enlightened human embodiments. Agni appoints such an ordained embodiment (Apnavāna) who is best at worship and praises the mighty powers (Bhṛgus) that bring bright colours.

To regulate the three parts of the dynamic universe, the highest ultimate reality represents the source of all existence and is genderless and infinite and knows eternal truth. With pervasive bliss, such ultimate reality (Brahman) is established. It becomes responsible for every change, but it never changes. It is the single binding unity prevailing behind all forms of diversity and exists in every part of the universe. As the ultimate reality, it represents true consciousness, which as bliss (Sat-cit-Ananda), is the highest reality that prevails everywhere and in all living beings. Through its powers, it connects and gives birth to inner conscience that, among all existence, serves as spiritual oneness.

They exist among luminous mortal embodiments that are fully evolved and serve with mortal embodiments appearing as envoys (Apnavāna; Rig Veda, Book 4, Hymn VII). Such mortal embodiments appear like demigods that come from heaven with sparkly illumining rays. They offer rites and serve as the envoy of Vivasvān, and they swiftly adopt as ensigns of Bhṛgu. They become the rulers over all manifested embodiments. They, with intelligence, serve as priests that bring the sanctifying flame. They, with mighty powers, rule mortal embodiments. They remain concealed in wood like the eternal flame. With the eternal flame, they fly knowing both worlds and settle on holy ground (Prithvi) between the two worlds. There are some who fly and bring each rite to the skilled ones serving as envoys and moving as the ancient divine will.

The eternal flame even travels through dark paths with light and serves as the chief of wonders. It moves with pregnant women to bring to life newly born envoys who rise as splendours that go along through the embodiments and generate breath served by tongues to consume food that creates strength. They follow the breath and drive on like swift horses.

The envoys of Agni worship the same mighty powers and know all about the heavenly force that brings eternal wisdom (Rig Veda, Book 4, Hymn VIII) to Brahman. They know all about the supreme powers of causation that bring love, morality, and righteousness and support humanity. Like the herald, they become well informed and move as gratified envoys of Agni, which brings sacrificial gifts. They bring wealth and perform heroic deeds to serve like Agni reverently. They show favour to those envoys who serve on the sacred grass, all pious immortal embodiments. They also support those who serve as messengers (Rig Veda, Book 4, Hymn IX).

Even though they are part of the mortal powers, they are not deceived; they welcome the chief priest (Brahman), who honours absolute reality (Brahma) with solemn rites and sacrifice. As the chief priest, they guide mortal bodies, celebrate with sacrifice, and bring oblations to the messengers serving as the envoys of Agni. They bring love, devotion, offerings, sacrifice, and their mortal gifts to heaven. They listen to the divine calling coming from the ancient envoy (Angiras), which appears with the divine power and guards them.

The chief priest (Brahman) receives noble strength and offers lofty sacrifice, and with rightful inner illumination, it brings love and right judgment to serve their commitments like the illumination coming from sunlight (Rig Veda, Book 4, Hymn X). With such power, living beings can be well disposed to the various aspects of the material world, and they, as living beings, receive heavenly voices in the form of a divine calling. Day and night, they receive inner glory that makes them self-dependent, spotless, brilliant, and pure as clarified butter. This eradicates any hate and mischief that has been committed by mortal beings and turns them to serve like the holy one. They come along with Agni and other demigods that bring prosperity, friendship, and kinship that connect mortals to the altar and build an eternal bond with the higher powers.

They shine brightly along with other cosmic and celestial bodies, all supporting the heavenly radiant one (Rig Veda, Book 4, Hymn XI). They illuminate even at night, and they provide food and create fair environments. Agni brings thoughts, discloses the divine calling, and praises with enthusiasm. From their thoughts and hymns with praise springs poetic wisdom, which heroes adorn as they become true-hearted living beings. They win booty, which they share. They remove neediness, sorrow, and ill will to protect those who attend.

They receive mental powers like the eternal firebirds. They bring fuel and toil to honour Agni. They slay foes and receive their wealth so they can become self-reliant and serve as the most youthful. They give mortal embodiments treasures to adore by being faithful to the mighty ones, which help remove whatever sin they have committed. In the presence of Agni, they become sinless and free of their mortal embodiments. As free souls, they grant to embryos health and strength, and thus help their offspring with a free spirit.

Mediator

According to Rig Veda, Book 4, Hymn XII, they sprinkle the radiant light of dawn and dusk among noble souls appearing as the ancient twins (Aśvins) representing the ultimate source of the heavenly power (Surya). Seeking heroes to spread their noble nature, the goddess

(Savitar) comes along, bringing with them the eternal laws and love (Varuṇa-Mitra). They regulate the light to drive away darkness and bring divine powers as illumination to serve established kingdoms which beholds the manifested dynamic universe, all regulated by the powers of causation, and spreads embryos that become mighty chargers. It purifies the black-hued mantle through the eternal flame, all accompanied by shining rays entering hiding places where evil powers hide.

Agni, in the form of firebirds, sees the thirty-three demigods (Nāsatyas) serving the three parts of the universe (Rig Veda, Book 4, Hymn XIV). Appearing with the dawn, they bring glories and observe while offering sacrifices to produce light for all the creatures of the world. Along with Savitar, they bring water to make their presence known by filling the space between earth and heaven with essence. They bring happiness that awakens mortal beings to serve as male and female, like ancient Aśvins serving at dawn with the mythical juice and eternal wisdom, they offer sacrifice to the mighty powers that guard the vault of heaven.

They, as the mediator (Shiva), emanate to serve as the destroyer (Skanda) of the demon powers (Taraka) and grant the eternal noble flame (Agni). The demon powers, which are considered to possess with strength the manifested embodiments, lead them to follow evil powers; as spinsters, they come in the middle of conflict like blocking water. The primordial powers (Shakti) come to shake up the mountains and let blocked water flow freely.

Celestial demigods lead Agni with solemn rites to bring the mighty powers such as archangels and avatars to come three times a day to offer solemn rites and bear blessed food (Rig Veda, Book 4, Hymn xv). With the round of oblations, Indra and Agni jointly give precious offerings to mighty ones as they move eastward with boons. They kindle and invoke other noble powers appearing among them as offspring serving as devotees (Devāvata) through transforming royal hermits (Sṛñjaya). The devotees with the eternal flame learn to serve as glorious ones who tame foes. As human embryos, these mortal heroes get implantations in the sky.

They, as envoys (Magavans) of Indra, come to regulate such impulsive newborns, humanity speeding to cover the ground. Manifested, mortal living beings (Rig Veda, Book 4, Hymn xvi) as humanity come to seek the mythical juice while offering worship with libations served only by the earthly priest regulating dawn and dusk (Uśanā). The envoys with hymns and praises filled with libations offer sages secret holy rites. The sages bring only those who work hard and sing hymns to bring heavenly light.

They appear among the best heroes and scatter through the darkness to support living beings. Indra supports those who can comprehend divine creation and can fill regions that cover the mortal material world (Prithvi). They exceed divine majesty even outside the regions being served by the rulers of the regions beyond heaven that are regulated by the thirty-three gods and goddesses. They appear as an epithet of Indra, who knows well all humanity and its activities. As the ruler (Śakra), they watch humanity hidden in the mountains, and they open their covers to expose their hidden living spirit.

The epithet of Indra strikes evil powers (Vṛtra) to create floods, and with inner conscience, they bring them to their senses. Like Indra, they send forth daring heroes with might to move them like rising waters from the ocean onto the ground. With much invocation, they show up like the female godly witch dog (Saramā). They guide the waters falling from mountains through newly created clefts. They have to show themselves as begging before ancient leaders of the evil power to let manifested living beings come bursting from stalls to support the heroes with physical strength serving like the envoy (Aṅgirases).

Maghavan, the envoys of Indra, bring the singers to implore in the battle aiding with sunlight to invoke. They overpower the prayerless father of evil powers (Dasyu), resolve conflict, and, if needed, they even slay the father (Dasyu) to save the noble powers (Kutsa). They eagerly win long friendship in a form that satisfies both, like having a faithful lady, the living spirit (Atma) among them. The noble powers are the goad that masters use and behold the brown steeds as their sages.

At daybreak, with a thousand hurls, they come down to see the greedy Śuṣṇa coming to become friendly with the wheel as it rolls near humanity. They bring first noble powers which destroy evil power (Dasyus) and overpower the other as sons (Vidathin and Ṛjiśvan), who reside in their solid forts of Mṛgaya and Pipru. The noble powers demolish fifty thousand dark forts and burn them like old garments. They then settle near the source of direct light, the sun, and see an elephant and the lion invested with mighty trepidation, which requires all wielded weapons. With light-producing libations, they acquire material wealth as they go to Indra. Expressing their conflict and longing to attain glory as they praise with songs while labouring, they fill their homes with nourishment. Indra listens to their requests.

They bring booty into the middle of conflict to capture and fly through, serving the faithful one and helping those with trepidation like the protector (Vamadeva). They join in conflict, and to protect their providence, they use the holy singer. They even serve and protect like the envoy (Maghavan), who manifests like humanity to serve as free givers who bring eternal love in every battle. With joy, they bring many autumns and appear like the sun's rays to crush foes.

Indra, Maghavan, and Vamadeva bring Bhṛgus with strong and mighty powers to bring moonlight to subdue the living beings as they sleep. They never withdraw from bringing their friendship from prayer, and they offer support to the living beings during conflict and bring them to sleep as the strong defenders. Indra brings powers with new hymns that swell like rivers and support noble beings. Agni manifests in an old-fashioned way and supports the victors.

The higher powers establish on the ground (Prithvi) their dominion serving the terrestrial region (Rig Veda, Book 4, Hymn XVII). Through the union of Indra-Agni, they provide vigour to slaughter evil powers on the ground. In deep waters, where dragon-built floodwalls arrest water and kill the productive ground, they provide nourishment for living beings. They create fear and displeasure among the heavenly powers, especially those serving in the cosmic and terrestrial regions. The demonic powers roar like their father (Dyaus) to shake down the foundation of the earth and even overthrow many worldly creatures. Renowned in battle, envoys (Maghavans) bring the frightened away to assemble and prepare them to fight the evil armies; they even bring booty to many loved ones and continue their friendship through conquering and slaying as necessary.

The evil powers, as part of the conflict, fight mightily and sometimes make it difficult to overpower their fear. The envoy (Maghavan), instead of winning all that is material like gold, tries to save all life in conflict. It makes unsettled humanity settle on the ground in the dust on which they stomp, and they use heaven's lightning to enrich embodied souls.

To settle the conflict, they use sanctified souls to follow an ancient pathway fully accepted by all gods and goddesses. They pass through a tough way, making sure they do not let it destroy the newborn or the mother. The divine will with essence (Devavani) passes through the hard passage using creative power (Tvaṣṭar), protecting the dwelling. They bring out the mythical juice to perform mysterious acts. Without any process to be born, they create many autumns to bring the embryo of a noble soul. Indra assumes old clothing to fill all to be born soon as a gift from heaven to earth.

Flowing like water, they appear as the holy ones asking what the floods are saying to the girdling rock from which the waters burst. The youthful mothers accept them as their own offspring to serve as noble souls (Kusava, Maghavan, and Vamadeva). All born on the ground, just like the heifer, they bring forth the strength and mighty power like the unconquerable bull. They bring forth an energetic image representing the motherly Indra.

Motherly, they call her mighty child as the child of godly powers who has gone through three cycles of birth and death and is a purified and sanctified embodiment (Amartava). It appears with its new mortal embodiment, ready to attain immortality and no longer be subject to death or the punishment of evil powers (Asura). It will live until the destruction of the dynamic universe when all mortals and immortals are predicted to disappear with the ending of the prevailing trinity.

Thunder-wielding Indra (Rig Veda, Book 4, Hymn XIX) and all the gods and their helpers come with powers to slaughter evil powers (Vṛtra). All the gods relax their efforts as absolute truth is born to serve as the ruler who besieged the waters. They, with a strong desire, extend too hard to waken those who slumber in perpetual sleep stretched like the dragon over the seven prone rivers with no joint farthest with thunder.

Indra shakes the earth and stirs the water with fury. Striving with strength and desire, they burst the firm ground and tear away the summits of the mountains. The mothers run to their offspring and, with the force of waves, set water free from all obstructed rivers. The wind (Vayu) comes to provide a breath to its offspring (Turvīti) that do not stay with the great flowing streams. They check the great rushing river and make floods easy to cross. They let the young maids, skilled in law and unwedded, appear like fountains streaming onto plains and deserts. After having slain the evil power, Indra sets free the rivers to wander the earth and create streams.

The wise man who knows all about its ancient achievements tells the deeds of might as though he has wrought them for his advantage. Indra, glorified with praises, lets powers swell high like rivers for the singer. For the new hymn, the lord of bays passes through songs and is victorious.

Indra slays foes in conflict (Rig Veda, Book 4, Hymn XX) and brings the Aśvins along with the envoy (Maghavan) to enrich living beings with thunder that stands by those who are making sacrifices in honour of Indra, who gives them strength, courage, and booty. They make their foes benevolent by giving them the mythical juice and food grown in the mountain ridges.

Indra brings water to fill the splendour like a jar. Pouring forth freely its mighty power, it vouchsafes all those enriched with godly powers. By this great might, mortal living beings become renowned and strong worshippers. The mortal souls pray to receive ample gifts as sanctification. With this new gift, with laud singing before the extolling, Indra declares with praise the mighty powers that swell high like rivers and bring a new hymn to worship Indra as the lord of bays.

Indra protects sanctified souls and praises the heroes (Rig Veda, Book 4, Hymn XXI). They are blessed with powers so they may further be refined by mighty powers and cherish the sky god (Dyaus) as the ruler of the supreme dominion. With heroic power, they become the most glorious ones by enriching others with bounty and serving the divine will with essence (Devavani) as a sovereign within the assembly and as the ruler of people and all-surpassing conquerors.

Indra brings from heaven to earth sanctified souls who have attained the power to create voices that strengthen the ground. With the help of the cosmic host (Maruts), they bring dominion with light that, from a distance, aids the seat of order. With Indra, they worship the godhead of great and lasting riches such as the wind (Vāyu), the victor that gathers humanity like herds and leads with boldness to attain higher fortune.

Helping the earthly priest, they offer many blessings and give reverence filled with the divine will. They incite humanity to worship and bring Indra into individual dwellings through meditation and drinking the mythical juice. In Samadhi's abode, they lie hidden with the power of Bhārvara, which supports singers and comes with delight. Such powers of devotion create spaces in mountains that let water out with the power of a wild ox and offer a bounty to sanctified souls.

Indra loves mortal living beings who are spiritually and physically strong (Rig Veda, Book 4, Hymn XXII). It brings its mighty thunder along with Maghavan, who brings the mythical juice. Born as the most divine and endowed with ample strength and mighty powers, they cause heaven and earth to tremble just as before their birth, the high god shook the heavens and earth, causing floods.

The strong one sings like wind coming from the mid-region. With joy, Indra and the goddesses extoll like coursers and set them free to serve with essence the divine will (Devavani) in long succession by performing heroic deeds that make it easy to conquer evil powers and destroy their weapons. They graciously listen to and pray and worship Indra and bring wisdom so they can help.

Sacred Ground

On the sacred ground, Indra comes with sunlight among the sanctified spirit (Atma) of the lovely one (Rig Veda, Book 4, Hymn XXIII). It provides through varied food the eternal laws, which helps remove sin. With glowing praise, it even opens ears to establish a foundation for the eternal laws that brings splendid beauties. The holy law produces milk that brings all the power to worship and honour the divine creation. By fixing the eternal laws in the individual body, it upholds any swift moves and helps win the booty. These the eternal laws, which belong to the deep earth and high heaven, bring the supreme law, which renders milk and allows Indra to swell like a river.

Worthy praise always brings before Indra the sons of strength who grant riches to the heroes and singers to produce hymns so people can invoke Indra to fight evil and bring comfort (Rig Veda, Book 4, Hymn XXIV); they risk their lives to protect heroes and their children and offspring.

To attain godly powers, the folk must fight their foes. Many worship Indra; hence, they let the brew succeed the meal-oblation and let the mythical juice banish those who pour not. Indra comforts those who long for the mythical juice and, with devoted spirits, becomes its friend.

A friend of humanity, the god-loving seek Indra's friendship, enkindle the eternal flame, and bring the mythical juice to serve the great protector (Aditya) with prayer bowed to Indra (Rig Veda, Book 4, Hymn xxv). Indra makes humans pious souls with the light of dawn, and they seek friendship with other pious souls. The quest for light from the mother (Aditi) and support from its offspring serving the protectors (Ādityas) establish sacred ground (Bharata), where the mythical juice is offered to all well-inclined spirits such as the trinity (Aśvins, Indra, and Agni). On the sacred ground (Bhārata), they provide shelter provided by Agni so they can look at the rising sun.

This sacred and holy ground is the same place (Rig Veda, Book 4, Hymn XXVI) where in the past, the first cosmic embodiment (Manus) appeared to represent celestial illumination (Sūrya) along with the sage (Kakṣīvān), the holy singer (Kutsa), and the son of the guru (Ārjuni), who brought the sapient light (Uśanā) to behold this holy ground. The land is further bestowed with rain to serve the noble souls who create a new race of humanity, which learns to bring oblations. This holy ground is guided by roaring waters that provide heavenly pleasure to all godly powers that come and move around in wild joy. On this ground, evil powers (Sambara) built ninety and nine forts that were demolished to support noble souls (Atithigva).

On this holy land, before the creation of the supreme falcon, all birds were ranked as they arrived with the cosmic host (Maruts). Strong-pinioned falcons with no embodiments move with rapid motion on a wide path, passing through with thoughts that as a fleet swiftly acquire the mythical juice. They bring from afar the draught that gladdens others, and they serve as friends of the gods. The mythical juice they bring is served to the bold ones representing the cosmic host (Maruts) who leave behind malignity, and as wise, and in wild joy generated by the mythical juice (Soma), they forget their foolish acts.

From the womb bearing the divine will with essence (Devavani) Rig Veda, Book 4, Hymn XXVII), they fly forth with speed; they conquer like the bold ones as archers (Kṛśānu). They come with the Maruts, who leave fiends and pass them over with winds to grow and become even mightier as thcy come down from the heavenly region. With a loud cry, as falcons, they hasten with the wind and serve with the cosmic host. With wide-ranging minds and godly power, they manifest as the archer and bring from heaven's lofty summit an embodiment (Bhujyu) that serves as the friends of Indra.

They hasten as the messenger (Maghavan) to accept a beaker of milk and the mythical juice from Indra. Allied with their friendship, they drink the juice to bring water to humanity in the form of the seven rivers as fountains after removing the obstructions and after Indra has slain the fish (Ahi; Rig Veda, Book 4, Hymn XXVIII). With its confederate river (Indu), which swiftly comes along with mighty Indra to fill with the mythical juice, they support all coming from heaven's summit, where the creator separates its great creations as noble souls from the evil souls.

Once Indra from the heavenly region smites conflict, they appear with the godhead ruling power from the sky. All seek dwellings to cast down the evil powers of Dasyus into many pieces. Besides Indra, all the evil power of Dasyus cast down miserable tribes of servants (Dāsas) who are put to death with a great vengeance as the foes look for more murder weapons. With Indra's mythical juice, heroes burst the stables of animals and set them free.

Lauded with powers and success (Rig Veda, Book 4, Hymn XXIX), Indra comes as tawny steeds (Aśvins) and bestows wealth on humanity. That makes their embodiments produce vigorous and joyful sounds filled with divine love. The mighty Indra pours forth in bounty to bestow gifts on humanity so they can all follow good roads that are safe. Those who are successful invite others to serve as the swift coursers who in hundreds and thousands come to like the messengers (Maghavan) of Indra and share riches with the princes, priests, and singers.

As the evil slayer, Indra brings together people to follow the renowned force (Rig Veda, Book 4, Hymn XXX) that gathers godly powers to conquer in war. While fighting singly, Indra overcomes all the furious godly powers and slays those who attack the supreme power and hurt mortals.

Indra helped the mighty power (Etaśa) by sending the envoy (Maghavan) to slay evil and quell all the demons. It did not smite any of heaven's daughters, who were contemplating overcoming the swift powers. Similarly, Indra does not crush the powers of deities (U5as) who are serving as the daughters of the sky. They are lifted in pride when the strong god has shattered and reunited their chariot; all affrighted powers of the deity (Usas) fled to join Indra. So the carriage of the deity (U5as) lies broken in pieces in the substratum (Vipāś).

Indra makes streams spread water over the land. Courageously, they seize the evil power (Śu5ṇa) and crush its fortresses. Indra smote down the evil power (Śambara) to free the devotees (Dāsa). The devotees coming from the hill slew more than a hundred thousand. Indra brought to death the unwedded damsel's son and cast away the mighty power. Indra brings the two Truvada and the Yadav, who feared the flood would not bring them to a safe zone. They brought both noble souls (Aryas) appearing as the kingdoms (Arṇa and Citraratha), who slew swift within rivers (Sarayu), and they wandered to the other side.

Indra does not make forlorn those who are blind or lame and makes sure none will miss the bliss produced by the heavenly servants (Divodāsa) that are offered along with oblations that conform Indra to those who helped overthrow two hundred stone fortresses. Thus, thirty thousand devotees with magic power and weapons come to set the hermit (Dabhīti) free. Even today, they do the same as they execute, so none are there to hinder. As the watchful one, Aryaman, they appear with godly power and serve along with ancient Pūṣan, Bhaga, and Karūḷatī, which as godly powers give all things fairly.

With the help of the wonderful friend in the mighty company, liberal spirits come with mythical juice so they can burst open even strongly guarded wealth (Rig Veda, Book 4, Hymn XXXI). Serving as the protector of all friends, they come with praise and provide aid to friends. They turn toward the living beings attracted by the hymns being offered by manifested embodiments.

Seeking their own stations with swift powers, they descend to share the sun's light that provides courage as they turn together with Indra and move with the sun. Among all the lords of power and might, humanity calls on Maghavan as the avatar of Indra, who, without pausing to think, gives their toils along with the juice. This gives them wealth filled with eternal power that supports great deeds. They keep hundreds and thousands safe, and as avatars, they elect the holy ground as their place for friendship and prosperity. They bring celestial opulence to all. With the powers of the sun, they bring fame, which becomes excellent among the godly powers serving as avatars coming from heaven.

Those serving Indra slay evil powers and appear as wondrous folk (Rig Veda, Book 4, Hymn XXXII). Even when they are weak, they can smite down with support from friends like Indra, which at all times remains close to those who sing divine songs and defends them when needed, like the meteor that comes as an irresistible wonder. Avatars, being friends of Indra, bring lively energy like the life force as wealth to serve domesticated animals that, through Indra's art, bring them strength by granting abundant food. As Avatars, they never turn away from those who are singing and always give wealth to noble souls (Gotamas), who praise and sing to Indra. They declare those who serve as servants (Dasa) to become devotees and serve the heroes performing noble deeds with joy.

They sing and bring praise that grows stronger with grace and makes renowned sons heroes. They gain the treasure of all kinds and praise and thank Indra for bringing them close and turning them to serve like the two bay steeds serving earth and heaven. They eat sacrificial cake and rejoice in songs like a lover to his bride.

Indra provides a well-trained force of a thousand steeds praying and bringing a hundred jars of juice. A hundred domesticated animals hasten to fill the bounty and obtain gifts from the ten gold water pitchers before they serve as evil slayers. They give much and bring much and are famed in many a place as bountiful heroes. They are praised as the pair of wise tawny steeds whose offspring give comfort to those frightened cows that are tied to posts. From there, they come shining like young girls to the bay steeds.

Indra sends for the most skilled herald (Ṛbhus) craving like a white cow and using the speed of the wind to overspread, and in an instant, it encompasses heaven (Rig Veda, Book 4, Hymn XXXIII). The herald (Rbhus) assists all like their parents, and for that, they win friendship from the godly powers. They give sages the power to carry away with them their devotion like fruit. Many of them serve as parents who grow again as young forever and serve the mythical juice to the herald three forms (Vāja) (Vibhvan), and (Ṛbhu), which join with Indra to protect with their sacrifice. The herald (Rbhus) itself provides like a cow provides milk to its offspring to help them form bodies that can provide brightness; their labours make them immortal.

They create four chalices from three and three chalices from two. In the same way, they create humans who speak the truth, and they can even act like the godly powers that follow the herald (Rbhus). They move with splendid power and are envied to this day. During this time, they go into hibernation, relaxing with joy as guests; they are never hidden as they go underground, where they work bringing rivers to grow plants, make fields fertile, and spread evenly over deserts and fill hollows with water. The skilled heralds receive in their work the same satisfaction as the godly powers while pondering in thought and mental insight; they appear as the godly expert artificer creating sounds (Vāja). They use these sounds to support Indra by appearing as Rbhuk5an and Varuṇa as Vibhvan; they make the sacrifice and, with praises, serve as the newly created, as bay steeds help them prosper.

Even to this day, they provide creations with gladdening drinks before they can generate hymns to support humanity but not without hard work; they attain friendship to serve as the godly powers. With sacrifice, Rbhu, Vibhvan, and Vāja come with Indra bringing riches and declaring all as the selfless sacrifice (Dhi5aṇā) given on the holy day or birthday when the life force (Prana) drinks the mythical juice and discloses individual births all with mortal richness and gathered to provide treasure.

The Rbhus creates seasonality (Rtus) to rejoice in the gladdening draughts that bring wisdom and provide humanity with riches stored for heroes (Rig Veda, Book 4, Hymn XXXIV). Rbhus appears like a living being, makes sacrifices, and learns to act like the two elders, who worship and serve like heroes bringing riches with a drink as they are gladly offered the third great libation as the heroes (Rbhuk5ans).

For the sake of mighty treasure, they are glorified with the draughts and at the closing of the approaches to their stables like cows. They make their sacrifice by providing them with the children of strength by invoking humble adoration, and as the wealth givers, they join Indra to receive in full accord the princes. They form close-knit bonds with Indra and Varuna by offering them the drink with hymns, and they welcome the cosmic host, who comes first to drink and to welcome seasonality and bring heavenly dames as treasures to rejoice with the noble souls (Ādityas). They come in concord with the kingdom (Parvatas) representing Ṛbhus.

In accord with Savitar, they bring floods that pour forth riches and are helped by Rbhus as they helped their parents and the Aśvins. They form pairs like the cows along with horses that serve as armour to connect heaven and earth by appearing as divine heroes. They make good offspring to have wealth in cattle and in booty among horses for the heroes to sustain with rich treasure serving as the herald (Ṛbhus), who with rejoicing still first drinks to welcome humanity.

Like the sons of strength, they appear among the children of Sudhanvan, who bring libations as their gifts to support humanity (Rig Veda, Book 4, Hymn XXXV). They approach like Indra, which provides craftsmen with skills to turn the single chalice into four and generate words to communicate with others. Through the powers of sounds (Vājas), they gain eternal life and pay homage to the godly powers.

They turn the subtle substance into reality using eternal wisdom and drinking the gladdening draughts of Soma. Using creative and cunning ways, they transform from being young to being parents, and as parents, they transform to attain rich treasures. They are fashioned like the two swift tawny steeds that support Indra. They pour out libations, producing joy, and serving as Vājas coming from mighty Ṛbhus. They have plenteous wealth to serve as heroes. At dawn, after drinking the eternal juice, they enjoy the noonday libation with the wealth being bestowed on them by the herald (Ṛbhus) with their skill to seek friendship with Indra.

They become like the godhead, and while sitting on the holy ground, they go to heaven like falcons bringing with them the riches of the children of Sudhanvan. Serving as sons of strength, they attain immortality through the third libation, which bestows treasure, they win skills, and they make one as the dexterous-handed drinker that brings delight and joy from Indra.

With other godly powers, Vājas and Ṛbhuk5ans travel a godly path (Rig Veda, Book 4, Hymns XXXVI and XXXVII). They accept splendid weather as a sacrifice to appear like the first manifested cosmic embodiment (Manus). They are asked to serve as humanity and, through offering rites, please hearts and enrich spirits (Atma). They appear like drops on cloth in oil that each day builds an abundance of mythical juice that provides power, strength, and delight.

After having gone through the threefold path established by the divine will (Devavani), by the god appointed powers of Vājas and Ṛbhuk5ans, they come near the newly created, individual mortal embodiments that, like the cosmic man (Manus), appear to offer younger folk the mythical juice. They appear with splendid cars drawn by well-fed horses, and they serve like sons of strength, representing Indra's progeny who offers delight and wealth to Ṛbhuk5ans and creates the mightiest comrade who serves and is favoured by Indra. They make sacrifices as they are fast and strong like steeds. Like free mortal beings, they sacrifice like princes and press forward to each point of heaven.

The cosmic body (Manus) as a manifested body (Trasadasyu) established honoured tribes (Pūrus) as winners of land (Rig Veda, Book 4, Hymn XXXVIII) that they plough and cultivate and grow strong to smite the evil powers (Dasyus). Like mighty powers

(Dadhikrās), they give many gifts to those who join the tribes. The tribes come like hawks and honour humanity. The tribes (Purus) move down from mountain peaks and, with rushing water, meet each living being with praise and joy. They spring forth like heroes as they fain for battle whirling their embodiments and flying like tempests. They gain precious booty in combat and win spoils.

The folks cry after the battle as if a thief had stolen their garments. They speed to glory like a herd of cattle; hungry like a falcon, they swoop down. With fain, they come forth first amid armies in a way like rows of rushing chariots and happy like a bridegroom making circles, tossing dust, and champing at the bit that holds all. They speed straight on and roar as they attack the affrighted. Humanity praises their swiftness, which gives them an abundance of strength. They overspread the fivefold humanity shining like the sun, which lightens the waters. With strong steeds, they win thousands with sweet praise. They send praise and prayers to the creator of earth and heaven.

Free Spirit

With the morning light, they move humanity to exertion and make them learn to bear safely over every trouble (Rig Veda, Book 4, Hymn XXXIX). With praise, they watch the mighty steed filled with a free spirit (Atma) become the stallion like divine horses (Dadhikrāvan) that fill the bounties of the rich. They appear with swift fleets and the eternal flame from Agni, all supported by the powers of law and eternal love forming to support the members of the tribe (Pūrus). They are honoured with their eternal flame, all kindled at dawn, and when they serve as the flying courser, they are known for one-minded souls all regulated by the powers of Varu,)a and Mitra and for being the children of the godly mother (Aditi). Freed of all transgression like the mighty (Dadhikrāvan), they are remembered as the source of food and strength and are worshipped as the trinity (Maruts, Varu,)a, and Mitra).

They receive powers from Agni and invoke welfare through Indra residing in mortal embodiments. Indra and Agni reside in living beings and, with vigour, turn into embodiments to make sacrifices. The powers of Varu,)a-Mitra grant the flying bodes of horses or birds (Dadhikrās) and guide living beings with glorified praise to serve like the Aśvins, who are honoured as conquering steeds.

By reciting praise, the divine horses (Dadhikrāvans) come in the morning and praise the goddess of waters (Sarsvati) with the dawn, which comes with the powers of Agni accompanied by Aṅgiras and Bṛhaspati bringing heavenly illumination (Sūrya; Rig Veda, Book 4, Hymn XL). The lover of the coursers (Dadhikrāvan) brings food, strength, and light accompanied by rapid runner pinions that strike from all sides.

The lover of courses lends swiftness by drawing together the windings of the path following as they fly (Haṁsa) and serving like nature (Vasu) beside the altar where the priests reside. Indra-Varu,)a (Rig Veda, Book 4, Hymn XLI) brings favour addressed with homage, which touches the free spirit (Atma). This brings elegant food to win and makes them partners, and with friendship, they slay the evil powers and foes in battle through mighty favours that make them famous. Indra-Varu,)a, as a unity, serve as friends inclined to honour them with graceful food and the mythical juice. They save them from robbers and oppressors and ration their vigour.

Indra-Varu,)a love songs and animals that provide milk to fill a thousand rivers. In the fertile fields, they give birth to worthy sons and grandsons using the sun's beauty, and they serve with gracious favours and work marvels to reduce the stress of battle or conflict. As princes of humanity, they come with ancient kindness seeking good comrades for treasure, and they build dear bonds of friendship. Supporting the most liberal heroes, they bring bliss like parents and show their strength with hymns. They support them in battle, serving as free givers, and they bring milk mixed with Soma as oblations to their devotees.

Indra-Varu,)a, with thoughts and praises, brings those who desire wealth noble thoughts and desires filled with love like fleet-footed mares eager for glory. Filled with riches and ample sustenance, they enhance their embodiments, and like the Aśvins, they labour with the newest success that brings them together as a team to gain riches. They come with their mighty success in battles, all supported by the mighty powers at times like flashing arrows that in combat bring winners in the contest.

As the royal ruler, Indra-Varu,)a sways all those obeying the godly powers (Rig Veda, Book 4, Hymn XLII) and serving the king of humanity. They first bring the divine will with essence (Devavani) to the existing high celestial powers to obey and follow the godly powers Indra-Varu,)a in their greatness covering heaven and earth. Even the creative powers (Tvaṣṭar) know that all beings hold them together through the moisture-shedding waters that flow and set firm and follow immediately in the order like the heaven and earth, and by the sons of the mother (Aditi), they implement the eternal laws and, as observers, they spread abroad covering the world measured in threefold. They are filled with heroes riding noble horses fain for battle and appearing as selected warriors who, in combat, call on the messenger (Maghavan) of Indra to come in conflict and stimulate them by stirring the dust with lordly vigour.

All this is accomplished with their godly power that is never opposed and always lauded with the mythical juice that makes them joyful, serving the unbounded regions. All the frightened, knowing the powers of the great disposer (Varuṇa), know all the renowned deeds they can use to slay the evil powers and free obstructed water to create floods.

As the fathers of humanity, they are relieved for the seventh time from captivity by the goddess Devi (Durgaha), who, with the primordial power (Shakti), offers sacrifice and appears serving as a demigod (Trasadasyu), which, like Indra, conquers foes. The spouse of the ruling king (Purukutsa) pays homage to Indra-Varuṇa and offers oblations to the demigods (Trasadasyu).

The slayer of the foes possesses riches and chants mantras, sacred texts used in spiritual practices. Like praying, chanting may be a personal or group practice. Diverse spiritual traditions consider chanting a route to spiritual development. The inspirational power of poems and music is referred to as the root meditation.

The spiritual seekers comprehend the merit of worship and take pleasure in offering homage to the divine immortal powers in the celestial region (Rig Veda, Book 4, Hymn XLIII). They try to be gracious, and they seek bliss through embodied powers that appear like rapid coursers that arrive as the elected daughters of the sun. They descend from the sky, representing Indra, and remove the stress like mighty powers. They transform vibrations into music like prayers, and they bring the demigods as twin powers (Aśvin's) whereby they invoke Atma. They confront great betrayal, bringing the sweetness of lovers (Dasras) to save mortal embodied souls.

Between earth and heaven, they travel on their chariot from heaven and reach the ocean all filled with sweetness that drops like lovers of sweetness, all dressed as dainty viands filling holy rivers with waves that bedew physical power like horses. This is observed with rapid movement that is pleasing. Like the daughters of lords (Sūrya), they gratify all together as grace is given, all filled with rich booty. Appearing as twins, they sing and praise and are directed by the demigods (Nāsatyas).

The Aśvin's, even to this day (Rig Veda, Book 4, Hymn XLIV), gather to offer praise with hymns that bring ample treasure all fitted in the heavenly body (Sūrya). The Aśvin's gain glory and are recognized as the sons of heaven. They appear with power and follow closely by appearing as bright and well-placed stately horses in the chariot.

Even today, they provide the mythical juices and offer homage. Born with their golden embodiments that are omnipresent, they offer sacrifice as Nāsatyas while they drink the mythical juice, which they give to those living beings who adore them. They come to earth from heaven in a golden chariot and make sure that worshippers suffer not.

After meeting with these wonderworkers, living beings attain exceeding richness and praise the Aśvin's. They serve ever gratified and give rich booty to protect the singers who offer praise to the demigods (Nāsatyas) and the divine will (Devavani). They, as demigods, wander as wonderworkers with light as they go up yoking their chariot and travelling around the summit, including heaven with their carriage filled with food and three kinds of embodiments— astral, subtle, and physical— all covered with skin to support their rustling minds seeking wisdom.

They bring forth the dawn (Rig Veda, Book 4, Hymn XLV), appearing with the carriage being pulled by horses all filled with rich viands and knowledge. After stripping the covering from the surrounding gloom, they spread through mid-air, bringing bright radiance coming from the sun. They drink the mythical juice and harness the wisdom like the chariot that loves and refreshes them on their way as they go following the paths of eternal wisdom like demigods (Aśvin's) to fill through the skin so the knowledge can be held in their embodiments. Like friendly swans, the richness of wisdom comes flying and brings libations that awaken like swimming in flood; as the jubilant fain of draughts, it brings cheer.

Knowing the solemn rites filled with the richness of eternal wisdom, they ignite the eternal flame among the singers accompanied in the morning by the Aśvin's. They break the day with pure hands bringing the prudent energetic priest a flow of Soma like the eternal wisdom brought out through pressed stones coming from the cosmic region. With the advancing rays, they chase the gloom away and spread through the firmament with bright radiance coming from the sun.

They pass through godlike nature, letting their paths known, and their devout thought declared with Aśvin's pulling their chariot like good steeds that last forever. They travel swiftly through the regions prompting worshippers to bring oblations.

After they drink the best draught of the mythical juice, they offer the holy rites that, through the air (Vāyu), spread to draw teams with hundreds, all helped by Indra, which travels seated in the chariot (Rig Veda, Book 4, Hymn XLVI). Flying and filled with the mythical fluid, they bring to a thousand living, bringing the dual powers (Indra-Vāyu) as their feast. Mounted on the golden-seated chariot, they aid those who want to reach heaven. From far, the dual powers bring to the givers' dwellings the gifts of mythical juice and, in accord with the godly powers, set them to journey with steeds set free to enjoy draughts of the juice.

To join the team of godly powers that is drawing the carriage to reach Indra, they drink the juice as they gather to reach the valley. The eternal air (Vāyu) brings the best of the sacrifices and holy rites to fill individual longings (Rig Veda, Book 4, Hymn XLVII). Jointly, Indra-Vāyu brings divine strength and attains success as they drink the mythical juice and become like the heroes who guide all the worshippers seeking blessing through offering sacrifice to them. As composers, worshippers enjoy the offering of the foe's wealth, all coming on refulgence and removing curses with atmospheric air, and they are drawn by the team serving Indra drinking the juice (Rig Veda, Book 4, Hymn XLVIII). The two treasuries of wealth hidden in the dark heaven and earth wear all beauties and wait to receive the air that brings the carriage yoked to nine and ninety steeds (Rig Veda, Book 4, Hymn XLIX).

Infinite Space

In astronomical texts, the lord of the sky is referred to as a planet that completes 364,220 revolutions every 4,320,000 earth years. This lord of the sky is considered to represent the fifth great element of nature, ether, that covers the infinite space beyond the other four great elements— earth, fire, water, and air—where they all lose their identity and appear as ether representing eternal tranquillity. It separates the manifested world from the unmanifested, ethereal world. Indra, famed for the laud-gladdening draught and the offering of such mighty power, serves as the perishable embodiment (Blrhaspati) and the lord of the sky infused with the lovely mythical juice. They, as a union (Indra-Blrhaspati), drink the mythical juice to rejoice and jointly vouchsafe a hundredfold riches with physical power equal to a thousandfold of horses, and they shed with songs the eternal wisdom that delight worshippers.

Perishable embodiments (Blrhaspati) with Indra's mighty thunder come to establish threefold seats encompassing all the regions, including the celestial, cosmic, and holy ground in the terrestrial regions filled with manifested embodiments (Rig Veda, Book 4, Hymn L). With pleasant tongues, they sit before the ancient sages known to perform deep thinking and serve as holy singers. The wise uninjured, accompanied by the rain, come to Blrhaspati from the remotest distance and settle down on the holy ground in its manifested forms, all filled with eternal love, the eternal laws, and eternal vision.

With tranquillity, they bring out of the mountain the sweet water by digging deep wells. Blrhaspati comes to support living beings that can attain mighty powers and manifest as strong supremacists among the heaven. With a sevenfold mouth, they produce thunder producing its seven rays that disperse the darkness. They sing loud praises and, with thunder, destroy any obstructive sounds or vibrations (Vala).

With thunder, Blrhaspati drives cattle to offer oblations and serve with sacrifices by offering gifts and homage to the godly father (Indra), who, as the lord of the steer and the lords of riches, stores noble progeny among heroes. Blrhaspati serves as the lord of the foes' possessions, well-tended to adorn the worship and cherish the foremost sharers, who in their own dwelling feel peace and comfort. Among the manifested living beings, they flow with rich, holy food and freely pay homage to Blrhaspati's manifested form (Brahman). They receive superiority over the ruler, those serving as the king or master of the riches of his subjects and above all, the hostile people.

With godly powers (Blrhaspati), they uphold the king, who seeks godly powers for favour, and they require the holy spirit (Atma) to protect the Brahman king's dwelling. Serving as the raisers of treasure, Indra-Blrhaspati rejoices in the sacrifice they offered with Soma, which allows them to sink deep within worshippers and thus vouchsafe heroes. All riches are filled with eternal wisdom.

The union (Blrhaspati-Indra) makes the Brahman king very happy as they are manifested; they allow all living beings to prosper and attain benevolence. They provide holy thoughts, wake up the spirit (Atma), and weaken the hatred of their foes and rivals. Through Brahman, the manifested holy spirit moves from darkness in the west to the east bringing splendid light as the morning dawn that brings the daughters of heaven coming for the welfare of all living beings (Rig Veda, Book 4, Hymn LI).

By the sacrifice created from the richly mounted, coloured morning light, they set planted pillars in the east as they dispel the gloom and bring wealthy mornings. They create the urge among liberal givers to present their treasures. In the darkness, unawaken traffickers who are resting see Brahman creating new morning light that brings the seven-toned vibrations to welcome the envoy of Agni (Aṅgira). They invite the wealth of the twin demigods serving as Navagva and Daśagva and bring the order of eternal goddesses, who appear as if they are harnessing horses that can swiftly move around the world.

They travel around, arousing the unawaken, with the morning light and though physical energy set them in motion. They even get help from some elders who, in the past, remained fixed on implementing Ṛbhus's regulations. At times, they followed the splendid dawns as they went forth to serve other splendours. Not wasting time, they serve all.

Blessed with the ancient dawn, the new dawn comes shining to bring success and let the truth spring from the holy order and the worshippers with praises and hymns. They travel from the east from one place to another in an indistinguishable manner by awaking all along with godlike dawns that come lowing like cattle. They go forth with undiminished colours making each morning similar and concealing in the gigantic might of darkness their shining and pure bodies.

All the goddesses serving as heaven's refulgent daughters bestow wealth in the form of children coming from pleasant places to rise as the masters of heroic vigour. Well skilled in the lore of sacrifice, they represent the daughters of heaven as dawns that are worshipped and addressed with glorious powers. Serving living beings, they are heavenly vouchsafed while serving as the earthly god.

Like the lady, they give delight to those following their shining sisters, the daughters of heaven. They show like the unfailing mother cows that appear as the red mare (Rig Veda, Book 4, Hymn LII). In the morning, they come as the rulers of wealth like the joyous thinking, ready to serve as friends of the demigods (Aśvins). They drive away hate and awaken souls as they meet with laud bright eyes, which come to behold blessed rays to serve the troops of cattle already freed to eat and come with the dawn all filled with wide vastness.

When they are filled with the refulgent light from the moon, they lay unembellished from gloom without light when nature comes to provide aid with morning light. It spreads the heavenly rays serving dear, wide region of mid-air and bringing shining lustre serving as the master or lord of the vast, holy soil of the subcontinent (Ksertrapati).

In holy scriptures, they are addressed as the lords of the people (Ganapati). Categorically, it represents a system for holy soil or the ground that has been worshipped by a sapient power (Ganesha).

Even the evil powers (Asuras) crave such a great gift that is worthy of choice, all given to noble powers and to those who are granted the water and the mythical juice. The godly power (Savitar) allows free worship to seek the defence provided directly by the heavenly powers (Surya). Through the heavenly rays of light, it provides protection and further vouchsafing by Adityas (Rig Veda, Book 4, Hymn LIII).

With heavenly sustaining powers, the Adityas establish as manifested noble souls who are put forth with their golden-coloured souls, clear-sighted minds, and far-spreading vision that fill the spacious dominion. Savitar brings forth loud bliss that fills the regions extending from heaven to earth. With their hymns, they wake up the godly powers regulating the region. This allows the godly power (Savitar) to stretch out among all with the life force (Prana). Producing movement among all the rays, it comes accompanied by pacifying power that motivates all through inner illumination.

This provides all living creatures with inner illumination that can never be deceived. It is protected by the goddess Savitar, who brings it all under one holy ordinance. This way, noble souls can stretch out their arms and cover the earth by obeying the eternal laws and following established rules.

The goddess Savitar, with thrice-surrounding mightiness covering from mid-air, serves all three regions by bringing light to all. It sets in motion all within their threefold terrains. With the eternal laws of causation and with gracious godly powers, they protect them by breaking stagnation by bringing life to gain control of the world. Serving all those who move not and move, it provides them with the shelter to vouchsafe the godly powers of the goddess (Savitar). This brings tranquillity to life by setting a triple bar against distress.

Throughout the seasons, Savitar helps individuals prosper and provides them food to make their noble offspring become invigorated. With praise and honour, they call on Savitar to bring wealth to all those representing the progeny of ancient cosmic manifestations (Manus) like humanity. They grant them excellent riches (Rig Veda, Book 4, Hymn LIV). They offer thanks to immortality, which comes to serve through the holy, godly powers. It brings them the nobility in the form of a gift that provides them with the opportunity to exist through succeeding lives. They seek from the godly powers forgiveness for sin caused by their weakness through thoughts that generate greed and insolence.

The goddess Savitar manifests among the demigods as well as among living beings to make sure no one can impede her godly power. She maintains tranquillity in the manifested world, and like the fair-fingered godly powers, she makes sure the earthly powers expand like the heavenly powers, and they grow to stand firm and provide the long-term sustainability of all creation.

From the lofty hills of heaven, they send forth Indra to come and fix abodes on earth and from there to support the divine power of creation to establish their homes on earth. The goddess Savitar always draws them apart, serving as a firm stratum standing still and obeying the moving divine will with essence (Devavani) serving as the eternal command of the powers of causation.

From these firm strata, they pour the mythical juice three times a day as libations, and day after day, they are blessed by Indra, which brings support to serve the heavenly and earthly regions along with the holy ground in the middle that is blessed with flowing rivers such as the Sindhu, which provides shelter fully supported by the mother (Aditi), the father (Surya), and their noble offspring serving divine creations (Ādityas).

The powers of nature (Vasus) protect and preserve all through the powers of the eternal laws regulating by Varuṇa, the laws of eternal love regulating Mitra and serving heaven and earth (Rig

Veda, Book 4, Hymn LV). They jointly support the strong godly powers to bring comfort to those offering sacrifices. They all command respect for their loud ancient statutes. Serving shining light as separators with order, they regulate perpetual ordinations and appear as beams of light. They generate holy thoughts that serve as the wonderworkers (Aśvins).

The goddesses serve as housewives and implore friendship among the unobstructed between night and morning. They appear during the day and provide protection on the pathway already disclosed by the powers of the eternal laws (Varuna) and guarded by the lord of strength (Agni), which travels with noble souls (Aryaman). Glorified with physical strength and protected by Indra-Viṣṇu, they grant powerful spiritual strength to defend them and their shelter.

Implored by favour, the cosmic host (Maruts) serves as the earthly king of mountains (Parvata) to rescue living beings from trouble through the patron (Bhaga). They come with the power of eternal love (Mitra) to save all friends from woe. The goddesses (Ahibudhnya) offer oblations to worship heaven and earth, which are responsible for the creation of Vaishnavism, which gives birth to currents that spring in the vast sea that bring a win to win.

The mother (Aditi), as the saviour, comes to defend those who provide constant care through godly powers serving as the mighty powers of heaven and earth and meet them with honour (Rig Veda, Book 4, Hymn LVI). With light and gleaming splendour, they fix those vast stretches apart most extensively with steers that roar loudly in the far-reaching courses. The goddesses and gods pour out exhaustless rain on the faithful and the guileless, serving as God's children and leaders of sacrifice with shining splendours who in the worlds filled with skilful craftsman produced the regions apart from earth and heaven.

With wise power, they bring both realms to expand to create a spacious realm reaching depths. Together with all well-fashioned and fully supported and unsupported with one accord promoting, with high protection as of queens, other of welfare, far-reaching, with the universal soul serving as the guard with carriage borne singing through the victorious song where both bring a lofty song of praise and as Pure One's they glorify both and sanctify individual form with their own proper might to rule and observe the Law. Furthering and fulfilling, ye, Mighty, perfect Mitra's Law as they sit around offering sacrifice. Through the Master of the Field, even as through a friend, they obtain nourishment for cattle and steeds (Rig Veda, Book 4, Hymn LVII). As the cow yield milk and pour freely, the Lord of the Field brings with the wave that bears sweetness distilling meath, like well-purified butter. This let the Lords of Holy Law be gracious to allow sweet be the plants from the heavens, the waters, and full of sweets for us be air's mid-region. The Field's Lord, full of sweetness, follow uninjured and happily work with steers and manifested living being as they plough furrow happily be the traces bound happily ply the goad like a way of coming the Sun (Śuna) and way of going the Moon (Sīra) are both welcome with laud milk and heavenly, mythical juice the bedew both this earth and heaven. Auspicious Moon (Sītā) comes near and worships and blesses to prosper and bring abundant fruits. Indra presses the furrow down to Pūṣan to guide them on the right course. May she, as rich in milk, be drained for us through each succeeding year. Happily, let the shares turn up the plough-land, happily go ploughs with the oxen. With distilled meath and milk, it makes the deity of rain (Parjanya) happy to grant prosperity through the Sun (Śuna) and Moon (Sīra).

It springs forth from the ocean like a wave of sweetness appearing with the mythical juice (Soma) and turns it into nectar (Amṛta), which allows physical power to come from the true centre of the glands, transforming embodiment (Rig Veda, Book 4, Hymn LVIII). Declared nectar to be clarified butter which helps the holy manifested soul (Brahman). They hear as an offer of sacrifice for which they pay homage and with praise accept them as the spoken divine words, like those emanating from ungulates: cattle, bison, buffalo, yaks, and many other spiral-horned antelopes. This all appears within the skulls of two-footed, two-handed, triple-bonded mortal embodiments, all passing through with the mighty godly powers enter physical bodies in triple-decker shapes eternal flame, discovered within emollient, serving as the godly powers among the Holy Cow, all concealed from bargains and misers, especially those who sparingly offer sacrificial oblations.

From an inmost reservoir in the embodiment, godly powers flow through countless channels, coming down like rivers that no foe can behold. Streams of nectar (Amṛta) descend through the spinal column filling with libations, all running as rivers within individual embodiments. They flow together and cleanse the individual heart (astral body) and individual spirit (Atma). The stream of a holy emollient as the nectar (Amrita) pours swiftly down like wild beasts fleeing the bowman over the rapids of a river.

The stream of holy emollient bursts through any blockage and fence, and like women at a gathering fair, they gently smile as they attain the eternal flame, all receive joyfully like the firebird (Jatavedas). Like a maiden, the holy emollient is adorned and joins the bridal feast. The mythical juice offered with milk bestows excellent possessions to bear to the gods when offered with streams of pure nectar. The dynamic universe depends on divine, mighty power that prevails in the heart like a vast sea and the living spirit (Atma) confined within the individual body.

In the world, the godly powers manifest like skilful craftsmen, which, like twain horses (Aśvins), invoke eternal wisdom that brings together both dominions and fills the spacious, unfathomable space. They as well fashioned and unsupported, stay intact, following and promoting with one accord and serving as the ruler and queens, providing protection and offering welfare to all prevailing in the far-reaching dynamic universe filled with holy souls that guard all.

Travelling as victors riding on carriages through heaven on the top and earth at the bottom, bringing praise through lofty song. They purify and glorify each other's form as they are sanctified by the mighty eternal rule created by the ancient law (Varuna). They observe established covenants to fulfil perfect laws to bring eternal love (Mitra), making sacrifices to establish friendship among all.

The master of the field, the 'Tutelary Deity' (Ksetrapati), provides nourishment to all cows and steeds, so they produce milk that bears the sweet distilling wisdom (Soma) and generates purified nectar (Amrita) used to honour the lords of the holy law (Varuna). From the mid-region, they fill plants with water and, with the sweetness of the air, help all serve the lord of the fields without being injured.

Happily working with steers, living beings plough furrows with traces bound with layers using pokers. They welcome the milk made in heaven and the dew made on earth. The auspicious moon

(Sīrā) brings abundant fruit where Indra presses down the furrow and guides the noble powers (Pūṣan) on the right course so they can attain rich milk drained for them through each succeeding year. They happily share with all who plough with oxen. With food and milk, this makes the rain deity (Parjanya) happy as they are given prosperity by the powers of the sun and moon.

Based on the worthy clan of ancestors (Brahmin), the evidence of God's existence is expressed through Lingam, a symbol of masculinity and the divine generative primordial energy (Shiva), which is worshipped as iconography found at archaeological sites where it appears in simple cylinders as rounded pillars set in the feminine part (Yoni) sometimes referred to as an aniconic representation of the goddess Pindika with carvings with one or more faces (Mukha).

PART 3
LEGACY

Anatomically, the realistic representations of the male phallus (Gudimallam), a part of divine procreative energy, is conventionally represented by a circular stone, and the feminine part, the vaginal opening, represents part of divine procreative energy that is conventionally represented as a vulva. Together as the lingam (Yoni), they are regarded as forms of spiritual iconography. Together, they symbolize the merging of the micro-cosmos and the macro-cosmos as the eternal process of creation and regeneration through the union of the feminine and the masculine.

The feminine part is conceptualized as the gateway for all births. In the mysterious practices (Kaula and Tantra), the lingam (Yoni) is interpreted literally to mean the female organs of generation. The highest elders (Pravaras) are proclaimed to be the descendants who, with open minds, take a sacred oath to establish their affiliation to serve as adorable sages. With the mighty powers of enlightenment, they offer homage to ancestors. They sing praises that reach the mighty powers, and with rising powers invoked from the Surya pantheon, they generate a golden light from the sun that is illuminated by the powers of the eternal flame, Agni. That is sent to the middle esoteric region, where it meets with reflective light coming from the moon; thus, comes individual cosmic power that, in conjunction with the terrestrial powers, prevail on the holy ground (Prithvi).

According to the elders (Pravara), specific embodiments with the highest mythological powers inhabit three, five, or seven clans. They, through multiple relationships, come to be represented as tribes. All are expressed through taking sacred oaths tied with knots in the name of the highest elders, which belong in one or more of the seven heritages (Gotras). All are classified according to the names of specific elders—Agastya, Angirasa, Atri, Bhrigu, Kashyap, Vashista, and Vishvamitra. Each elder is associated with a stellar system associated with seven specific mythical powers, all influenced by the position of the planets.

Serving through a spiritual process, the highest elders who compose hymns are personified by individual heritages (Gotras), representing one of the Septa Rishis. These spiritually enlightened souls can unveil absolute truth. They bring the golden light, which appears as Gavisthiras accompanied by the ferocious fire, Agni, travelling through the heavenly regions. When they appear near the surface of the earth (Prithvi), they join the morning light (dawn), bringing its mighty powers to fill the udders of milk-bearing creatures. With its soft light, elders understand that it is needed to turn dormancy into life; they germinate like the seed that ends up sending up plants and trees, which, like flames, rise toward heaven.

CHAPTER 7
HEREDITARY DOMINION

Anointed

On the ground (Prithvi), awakened sages with their radiance coming from the heavenly region come to serve mortal embodiments who change from inner darkness and turn themselves into anointed creations (Rig Veda, Book 5, Hymn I). They stir up the milk from feminine creatures to provide the purest nutrients. By licking their younglings and spreading eternal love, they offer divine gifts that are observed with the radiance of pious spirits, creating different hues.

At daybreak, the sun's radiance is born and turns the moving horses into flying horses, all appearing red in the sky and invoking the eternal flame, which, rich with treasures, moves among all living embodiments. Seven elders (Pravaras) bring progeny as the most skilled offering given to all those who are seated on the surface of Mother Earth (Prithvi).

They produce sweet-smelling, young, faithful sages who can sing and are excellent composers serving at every sacrifice like the divine messenger (Gavisthira). They are easily distinguished among folk who are being offered glorious homage as one of the youngest earthly sages. They, through hymns and words, help spread the essence with the divine will (Devavani) floating between the worlds, and as a balm it strengthens another faithful steed, so they never fail. These young faithful as messengers become house friends; they come like bulls with a thousand horns ready to honour the most auspicious guest (Gavisthira).

They quickly pass over all others and appear as wondrously fair and adorable envoys representing Agni. They manifest as the darling guests of all and serve as youthful divine messengers who come from near and far to bring tribute and sing songs to be used in every prayer. They are extolled highly as auspicious, divine messengers coming from the constellations to establish their shelters on the moon travelling in the mid-air. They bring oblations as they attend the heavenly feast.

The youthful divine messengers know eternal wisdom and absolute truth (Rig Veda, Book 5, Hymn II), which they keep secret as they remain close to their mother (Prithvi). Until they are ready to serve, they never yield to their father (Surya) in heaven. Serving as divine messengers, they arrive like unborn babes (astral bodies) with unfading features into the arms of motherly ground (Prithvi).

Their appearance as astral bodies is seen from afar like bright-coloured stars passing through many autumns and launching the immortal weapon (Atma) like a gold tooth.

Filled with the mythical juice and nectar (Amlrta), they become free to observe, and they see all rays passing through the sun. With brilliant and radiant bodies, they increase as they keep moving like a herd around the moon. As astral bodies, they remain concealed from the shining object, but they keep on driving toward physical embodiments like the mortal godless herds ready to serve as mortal embodiments. Like the mid mortal king, the seven great elders (Pravaras) receive offerings and prayers that bring to life the ultimate, youthful divine messenger with free immortal spirits. They come to reside in the embodiments that manifest as holy sages ready to serve the ground (Prithvi).

Through representing the seven great elders (Pravaras), they establish themselves as the most auspicious mortal embodiments (Gavisthira). They keep on returning without letting loose their positions, especially during solar eclipses (Śunaḥśepa). The seven great elders make sure the young sages remain bound to their commitments like the elder (Atri), which goes through thousands of autumns to pass through while other elders (Pravaras) eat to make their dwellings strong. They protect and make sure that the true link between the individual spirit (Atma) and the universal soul (Paramatma) remains intact. Both prevail in all manifested splendours; they, as messengers, do not break their union even when the heavenly power, Agni, is angry. They still protect the eternal bond among the races. Those serving as messengers maintain the eternal bond with Varuna-Mitra, which is jointly regulated to serve as a mother (Atri) serving the messengers.

Other great elders (Pravaras) come from far away with splendour like the sun, which brings bright light from Surya. This makes apparent all things that cannot be conquered by godless and malign attractions, such as the gore with sharpened horns (Rakṣas). From above, with loud roaring sounds, they even make Agni bring immortal lightning like a keen-edged weapon to support the auspicious mortal embodiments (Gavisthira). They destroy the demons and, using the eternal flame of Agni, burst forth through the mythical juice passing through the cosmic manifested splendour and bringing ecstasy. While the godless and demons press around, these powers cannot stay because they lack the skill to produce hymns and serve and please the mighty one and support the elders.

Agni spreads the eternal flame that produces holy grass and holy plants. With the help of worshippers, they build grand shelters such as temples and worship halls where mortal embodiments with oblations honour the divine powers.

As a band, the divine powers are seen in the night sky as stars that cannot be individually distinguished by the naked eye. They

255

appear to be setting the path (Aryamṇáḥ Pánthāḥ) for the noble souls (Aryaman). These noble souls manifest as omniscient friends who appear in the sky flying horses as companions that protect the path being created by the heavenly bodies, the galaxy, and the Milky Way. They, as omniscient souls, travel with other godly powers (Varuna-Mitra, Bhaga, and Blrhaspati), serving as both souls, the noble (Adityas) and the evil (Asuras). They follow the same path to invoke the living spirit (Atma) placed in mortal living embodiments.

Agni, with its radiant power, supports such regulators as the divine law (Varuna), which cultivates bonds of friendship with divine love (Mitra). Within the terrestrial region, they serve as support and are ruled by Indra. They offer sacrifices to transform from the mid mortal noble powers (Adityas) to demigods to serve as mortal, self-sustaining bodies. As friendly powers, they appear like females who soothe their counterparts, males. Jointly guided by the cosmic host (Maruts), they serve as demigods in the esoteric mid-air region.

These males and females are empowered by the heavenly power (Rudras) and gain support from the radiant divine splendours operating during the day by the sun (Surya) and during the night by the moon (Chanderma). They guard all while they are placed in the newly created biosphere, which is a secure and sacred area protected by the sky shield (Akasha) covering all the ground. This biosphere is further supported by the mid mortal heavenly power (Vishnu), which serves as the godly father coming from heaven to protect the sacred godly mother coming from the earth. This is all supported by demigods appearing as the cosmic host (Maruts), which come along to support the glorious astral bodies created for new generations. These astral bodies encompass the infinite, unbound, universal soul (Paramatma), which resides as the living spirit (Atma) among individual physical embodiments.

The astral bodies are thus assigned finite mortal dwellings like houses. The mortal embodiments (Aryaman) as omniscient bring pleasure and better life along with the eternal flame from Agni before they appear in the terrestrial region. The Aryaman, who are blessed with eternal wisdom, serve as messengers as they share eternal wisdom. As a guest, the immortal spirit (Atma) is aided by Agni as fully empowered to conquer its encumbered mortal state and seek freedom and ultimately join the mid mortal embodiments, the demigods (Paramatma).

To attain such freedom, the omniscient with mortal embodiments guided by offering proper oblations attain inner awakening and are made to understand the purpose of illusions (Maya) created to provide pleasure and happiness. They learn to comprehend all this and thus become sons of strength. They serve as youthful envoys who overpower plotters, sinners, slanderers, and those using double-dealing to injure other noble souls.

The youthful envoys receive support from the ancient godly fathers who come at dawn to serve by offering wealth and enkindling good things that save noble souls. Agni, serving as ancient godly fathers, count on them as their own sons who serve as sapient powers. They make them skilled in the holy law. In adoration, they give such sapient powers many titles, so each is blessed and acquires mighty powers to serve with bliss.

The youthful envoys offer sacrifices with delight and face fierce attacks as mortal embodiments (Rig Veda, Book 5, Hymn IV). They obtain long lives to fight like rulers. Agni allows noble souls to serve with strength and provides them with the ability to behold the far-reaching powers prevailing in nature. As envoys, they maintain themselves with abundant glory, and they keep their households and use fire to cook, always measuring their intake.

Serving as mortal sages, they produce balm to purify their bodies. As omniscient, their mortal embodiments serve all godly things and win in accord with a divine calling (Iḷā). They learn to choose what to enjoy. They always strive in rivalry with beams of light coming from Sūrya. They change their feminine voices to masculine voices when they serve as the chief progenitors. Among the mid mortal demigods, they serve as mortal godly power (Jātavedas).

Offering oblations, they become friends of the house. With the taste of oblations, they are welcomed into dwellings as guests. Among disseminated assailants, who bring the foes (Dasyu), including weapons, they drive away evil powers. With vital power, they develop desires and become sons of strength. They come ready to protect heroic powers and serve Agni.

They, as the sons of strength, bestow wealth on others. They make sacrifices and offer oblations. They dwell in all three regions with reverence. They serve as demigods protecting triply guarded shelters. They travel and protect others from woe and danger like Jātavedas. They are praised as the sons of the godly mother (Atri). Serving as the guardians of mortal embodiments (Pravaras), they remember the great immortal spirit residing in their mortal embodiments. They acquire pious embodiments with pleasure and wealth for their offspring and animals.

The omniscient Aryaman, serving the seven legendary sons of the creator (Brahma), appear as the heavenly priests (Rig Veda, Book 5, Hymn V). The enlightened souls, as the sons of the mother (Atri), use eternal wisdom to compose hymns, songs, and prayers. They express absolute truth learned from leading members of ancestral communities (Brahmin, Prajapatis, Kshatriya, and Vaishya).

With the enkindled flame (Jātavedas), they generate the nectar (Amrita) that produces heavenly fire (Narasimhan) to invoke the universal soul. Like Saptarishis, they offer their adoration to Agni and Indra. This helps to place the individual living spirits (Atma) in a safe place with the universal soul. With holy hymns generating vibrations, living spirits spread among the universal soul. It spreads like mist within the fine soft fibre and creates grass away from the oceans filling the ground (Prithvi). They create a beautiful open space where the demigods come from the heavenly region to provide aid.

On the ground, the living spirit (Atma) is commonly placed at special locations like waterfronts from where it can spread like grass to fill other regions. Aditi guides in the morning and night by regulating the individual life force (Prana). To strengthen and supplicate when needed, Aditi manifests as the goddesses serving the holy rivers (Iḷā, Sarasvatī, and Mahī). These rivers cover the sacred ground without harming the holy grass.

Under mysterious godly names (Vanaspati), rich in physical skills and knowledge of absolute truth, they serve as the ruler of the plant kingdom. This mysterious Vanaspati is known to wait to free the living spirit by burning itself and leaving behind its mortal parts as ashes (Svaha). Through such sacrifice, the mysterious Vanaspati invoke the ancient divine powers (Agni, Varuṇa, and Indra) along with the demigods (Maruts), who, as their envoys, come to support as archetypal rulers.

The first archetypal rulers with individual cyclic lives came to manifest as the offspring of divine power, Brahma, which established and populated the newly created biosphere with the sky as a shield (Akasha) and provided archetypes to use their intellects to gain wisdom. The only surviving species of archetypal rulers was the genus of ancient cosmic (Manus), who carried their family name as Vaivasvata.

Archetypal rulers stayed far from the evil powers at the sacred place. They ultimately appear during the seventh generation as Homo sapiens. Along with unmanifested astral bodies, it established a base a small distance aboveground (Prithvi). The seventh generation of Homo sapiens offers praise to the creator of the eternal flame, Agni, the provider and protector of astral bodies (Viṣṇu), which are placed in physical bodies with oblations to bring food to support them.

Agni placed the eternal flame in physical bodies to support the astral body to serve as precious gear that helps them depart from all intellectual and material wealth that during life offers food that brings pleasure to the ancient Manu serving as Homo sapiens. They bring glorious energy coming through the sun and the moon from the heavenly power (Surya). They all support the manifested bodies with holy verses and oblations to provide a peaceful sleep.

With such delighted gifts, Homo sapiens generates a brilliant inner flame that spreads enlightenment like the light of the sun. They learn like mighty strong chargers moving to their stalls while other chargers produce sounds as they bring food to put in storage. Both kinds sing hymns in their houses while Angrisa, a brilliant envoy of Agni, brings the eternal flame to regulate breathing and produce the inner warmth they crave.

As friends of Manus (Rig Veda, Book 5, Hymn VII) from Agni, they receive with praise more nourishing food than any other living creatures receive. They become sons of strength and learn to hold assemblies where all living creatures meet to rejoice. They are presented with food and sacrificial gifts. As the sovereign, Manus, they witness fire hiding in the wood. They build crests along the elevations on the ground where water-like drops of sweat are offered to Agni.

The sovereign Manus mount elevations where they find places to settle down and receive food, establish happy homes, grow crops, and shear herds. The eternal flame from Agni remains hidden in its unabated might serving the mother (Aditi), who tolerates all this until it reproduces or reincarnates what has been destroyed or subjected to physical death. With love, Agni sheds pure heat and bestows prominence and intelligence among Manus so they can serve as mortal splendours. The Manus become resistless as they gain what is given to them through the powers of Agni and its envoy (Atri).

They seek more and more as they support sages to overcome evil power (Dasyus). The heavenly power Agni urges the Manus to use their physical and spiritual strength and follow powers of eternal love and the eternal laws that in old age enkindle the ancient power (Rig Veda, Book 5, Hymn VIII). Manus serving as Homo sapiens request aid in the form of bright light with holy powers so they can serve as the most excellent nourishers of all. In their homes, with heat and flame, they serve the elderly guests, and with the eternal flame, they serve as masters of their households and distribute wealth to seek protection from floods. With praise and worship, Manus use such hidden powers to help them cook and serve baked offerings. They keep secret Agni's existence in other dwelling places such as wood and rocks.

Through the glorified fuel, Agni makes all things visible with its roaring vibrations that produce the sound that no skilled worshipper can exceed. Singing hymns shows reverence to and pleases the godly powers (Aṅgiras), which enkindle among mortal embodiments the inner, noble divine light. By creating divine light in multiform, they support the existence of every embodiment supported by the mighty food blessed by shining light and protected by the blazing flames, which exist only in the eternal fire representing Agni.

The godly power inflames the bearers of oblations and turns them into youthful eternal flames, which as a messenger, go widely and reach individual homes to appear in the eternal flame along with the mythical juice. They invoke the flame that generates noble thoughts, and they seek the joy that lights up, with the old worshipping the eternal flame that produces sacred thoughts. Such mighty thoughts are absorbed by the embodiments like Agni and are stored in plants that produce seeds and spread around all earth.

Incarnates

According to Rig Veda, Book 5, Hymn IX, Agni sends Jātavedas with the eternal flame to bring gifts with unceasing offerings along with oblations and worship to mortal embodiments to retain their worship place, where the holy ground is purified, and through priests, they offer sacrifices. This strengthens and makes individual mortal embodiments renowned. As infants, their inner body parts, give them life and skills, all well ordered to offer personal sacrifice and become the sustains of their tribes. Their bodies become hard as they grasp their offspring that are wriggling like snakes. As they consume eternal wisdom, they are overpowered by the eternal energy covering many forests, where Agni resides, hiding its power of flames in wood.

As Agni sends forth smoke before its flames to mark its place in the height of heaven, they call on the rescuer solar deity (Trta) with the ultimate powers of causation to appear before it reaches the state in a smelter that sharpens as it is blown on. To avert hate, it calls on the friendly powers of eternal love (Mitra) to subdue wickedness and help heroes bring riches and become victorious by protecting and nourishing others.

On their way (Rig Veda, Book 5, Hymn X), the Manus incarnate and bring along many other Manus that become irresistible splendours in streams, rivers, lakes, and oceans. These mighty splendours create their own paths using wisdom and mighty powers to move away from unregulated evil powers (Asuras). They follow one path used by the regulated noble powers (Adityas). Using the noble and spiritual power of eternal love (Mitras), they overpower evil that uses witchcraft to overpower the eternal laws (Varuna), which imposes limits on their existence. Using prayers and hymns, the noble powers (Adityas) make their mortal embodiments royal leaders by serving as those who regulate noble power, and they acquire higher knowledge and win great riches.

They use direct light from the sun and reflective light from the moon to illuminate their physical strength and perform selfish acts, but they avoid cultivating egos and arrogance. Using their loud praise when they are blessed, they gain access to heavenly powers serving as the resplendent eternal flame of Agni that goes forth like lightning, and they use their bodies to rattle as they seek spoils left behind from the ending of fire as ashes (Savah).

They seek eternal freedom using remnants of the spoils or ashes to serve as holy souls or earthly priests who draw imminent support while they offer ashes as gifts to subdue patrons and serve all regions of the earth (Prithvi) like messengers (Angiras) of the godhead, Agni, and they became the invokers of wealth using their strength like singers.

The messengers (Angiras) are incarnated through the watchful Agni serving as the guardian. The messengers come with manifested embodiments and noble souls with physical strength and mortal embodiments that bring prosperity among newly created avatars (Manus), who appear as a noble tribe (Bharatas) with emollient on their faces generating shine with a heavenly purity. They arrive bearing the ensign of sacrifice to serve as the household priests representing the threefold powers: creation, sustainability, and transformation.

Having Indra and several demigods on their side, as a noble tribe (Bharatas), they all gather on the sacred grass and sit in front of the wise priest, who completes the sacrifice by worshipping the godly mother as the creator with purity who has the power of sustainability and is unadorned with the power of change or transformation. They appear like the ancient sage (Vivasvān), who was born with a banner of smouldering fire and smoke reaching to the sky coming from the sacrifice made by Agni, so every mortal embodiment on earth is blessed with a body to house the immortal spirit.

The envoy (Vivasvān) appears among all others who have exceeded in acquiring wisdom bearing selected gifts and performing sweet prayers that are dear to the spirit. Vivasvan transforms the individual minds to produce noble thoughts like the envoys (Angirases), who, as Shiva, discover hidden paths by fleeing back and forth from wood to wood with the strength provided by Agni. They conquer mightily and become known as the sons of strength or manifestations of the primordial power (Shakti).

Serving as Vivasvān, they meet with evil powers (Asuras) and teach them proper prayers and worship and provide them with the eternal laws (Rig Veda, Book 5, Hymn XII). With songs specially directed to invoke the mighty powers of Agni, they offer sacrifice and mark the law by putting pure oil into the mouth of fire, which sends a stream of the eternal laws. With the eternal laws, Vivasvān overpowers witchcraft and any other form of falsehood, and thus evil powers (Asuras) learn to follow Vivasvāns and their sacred law.

Appearing as the red steer, they become knowers of new hymns that they use to worship Agni. They know all about the creator, who, as the eternal soul (Paramatma), serves as the guardian of nature (Prakriti), which controls the seasons. They know all about the splendid helpers who guard their astral and mortal bodies through their dwellings. They protect their bodies from falsehood and lies.

The evil powers become friends of Agni and become gracious and righteous by offering homage and sacrifices. They follow the eternal laws, each operating in dwellings serving as the red steer. They wander like the noble offspring (Nahuṣa), who wander from home to home, serving with righteousness. Their mortal embodiments, eager for material wealth, praise with hymns and offer worship to Agni, which touches heaven as they serve humankind (Rig Veda, Book 5, Hymn XIII).

Agni awakens the celestial, immortal powers with high solemnities. They appear as glorified immortal powers appearing as both evil (Asuras) and noble (Aditya). They carry a ladle filled with distilled emulation burning with the eternal flame and kill the darkness brought on by their evil ruler (Dasyus). Using bright light, they help mortal living beings in serving the animal kingdom along with the vegetation kingdom and thus discover the powers of the sun. They know they are all served with the powers of Agni, which enlightens sages. The eternal flame as light allows them to hear the divine callings. With hymns, they transform humankind and become devout, eloquent, righteous, and noble souls (Dvitaya).

According to Rig Veda, Book 5, Hymn XV, with Agni enthroned in oil along with ancient and glorious blessings, they offer firm support to the evil (Asuras) just as they provide to the nobles (Adityas). They abide by the holy law. This allows mortal embodiments to be born with the immortal, unborn bodies (astral) and attain a seat to serve heaven's firm sustains, which remain on earth averting woe with their hard labours. They spread forth like a mother nourishing each mortal embodiment. They preserve their strength and vigour to cover much broader streams that bring riches. They keep their refuge secret, only sharing, like Atri, their great wealth through proper teaching.

They know Agni as a great power. They praise this godly power, who is set in a foremost place. With priests, they help all able men. They request each one to convey their oblations to the patron (Bhaga). Agni brings rich power and produces roaring sounds of great strength. The mortal embodiments serving as faithful friends of Agni become their friends who bring liberal gifts to strengthen them. With strength and fame, the heroes become youthful ones who surpass the limits established by heaven and earth. Agni quickly comes to those who glorify it and bring precious wealth along with others, like princes who hold assemblies for all good who are fighting in the righteous war to win and prosper.

Agni calls on mortal embodiments to come well prepared (Rig Veda, Book 5, Hymn XVII) and ready to offer solemn rites needed to protect those who are making sacrifices to save those who are near the mightier power. With native glory holding apart the vault of heaven, they fill it with lovely hued flame but beyond mortal embodiments' thoughts. Once the mortal embodiments accompanied by song receive powerful heavenly light, they remain bound to the beams of splendour, which generates a flash that springs from heaven loaded with eternal wisdom. It appears like the seed coming to manifest as demigods to serve as the wonderworkers who drive individual embodiments to become wise ones. The wonderworkers meet with all invoked tribes, those glorified by the powers of Agni, to serve as the princes who generate sweet sounds and speech. With such powers, they protect others as they lend their assistance by serving as sons of strength.

At dawn, Agni appears as a houseguest and makes oblations to Asuras and Adityas. Injured mortal embodiments receive the delightful gift of incarnation (Dvitaya), which is received in the form of drops of the mythical juice filled with wealth and strength that helps noble worshippers gain immortal powers. With such powers, their embodiments shine with singing songs and displaying inner illumination; they are filled with lengthened life as they move from place to place unharmed. They carry noble thoughts in their bodies instead of producing them with their lips. Before the light, they spread over the grass to deck themselves with renowned immortal powers as they share their holy powers with the chiefs and heroes. They institute the rite with illustrious and lofty fame, which at the synod meets with praise presented with fifty kinds of steeds.

As one state disappears, another state is begotten from the mother's side (Rig Veda, Book 5, Hymn XIX) with a distinguished voice and is guarded with a strength that never spoils. They are pressed upon a strong embodiment (Śvaitreyas) that protects them like a fort where each embodiment (Bṛhaduktha) has gloriously increased in might. They carry the mythical juice like they wear gold chains. They come together, conquering all that is unconquered. With the quest to drink milk and longing for the food that fills the cauldron, they come in sportive fashion like beams of light. They move with the wind that fans their wasting flames.

The winner of the spoils always comes before the godly powers with praise. They do not protect mighty powers knowing they could stir up the wrath, anger, and hatred of those with evil natures. Even Agni chooses its messengers to serve as priests. With perfect strength and skill, they bring sacred food to invoke the chief with holy rites and songs. They toil and conquer using eternal wisdom to enforce the eternal laws. They rejoice like the wise ones at the feast with animals and heroes.

Manus establish themselves (Rig Veda, Book 5, Hymn XXI) by using other Manus. They kindle the powers to help others become pious like the messengers (Angiras). They worship Agni and other deities. As pleased demigods, they use the ladles with fire as a lubricant as they go straight to mighty godly powers. Serving all of one accord, they establish their own messenger who serves with sacrifice to adore the supreme power presented by the sages or prophets. They let mortal embodied souls adore divine power knowing that ultimately, that goes to Agni. The lord of fire shines as the radiant one sitting in the chambers of the law and gaining friendship through sharing food.

The sage (Atri), like the envoy (Viśvasāman), sings praise songs to invoke the eternal, inner purifying light and offers holy rites (Rig Veda, Book 5, Hymn XXII). Welcoming the embodiments of priests in their places, setting them like the messengers (Jātavedas), they get guided by the same godly powers of Agni. They offer sacrifices to gods and demigods while mortals continue to seek aid by worshipping the divine power that individuals long for. They mark this by paying attention to the victorious sages (Atris) who, as strong-jawed, keep the homestead and exalt it with song.

Agni brings victorious wealth until they conquer. In one accord (Rig Veda, Book 5, Hymn XXIII), they provide the ground with sacred grass and invite the folk to build temples where dear priests offer noble souls the choicest eternal wealth with wisdom that helps quell foes and brings light and prosperity to their homes.

As the nearest and gracious friend, Agni kindly delivers wealth to enhance mortals so they can keep far from every sinful act. They serve the brightest and most radiant gods, who bring happiness to all. They, with divine songs, bring grace (Rig Veda, Book 5, Hymn XXIV) so that the mortal powers can serve as the sons of the marques. They grant the gift of righteousness to save their friends from foes.

Agni remains true to the sons of the marques (Rig Veda, Book 5, Hymn XXV). They enkindle the ancient mighty powers and use their sweet tongues along with inner illuminated souls to bring out the glorious beams of wisdom. They graciously surpass all with their excellence and allow the sons of the marques to shine through with hymns of praise.

Agni further extends the gift of the eternal flame to refine individual thought. The mortals process them to serve the worshippers. They help to invoke the mightiest eternal flame. With deep devotion that cannot be subdued, they continue to use the divine will to bring glory to the sire. Agni further bestows the sons of the marques as the heroes of steeds that fight and conquer foes. Along with the mightiest prayers and worship songs, Agni brings the eternal flame that turns into bright light. The light continues to shine on high like the chief consort or a king. From there, they proceed with the resplendent rays of light and produce loud sounds like meteors coming out of heaven.

With splendour and pleasant tongues, they pray for the nectar (Amrita). It enhances bright rays and enkindles a feast that identifies devotees and sages (Rig Veda, Book 5, Hymn XXVI), all coming with the bright light from the sun. They see the envoys (Jātavedas), which bear sacred gifts. They serve as the most youthful who were brought down by the celestial, mighty powers. They appear as the ministers who even today offer sacrifice to all the godly powers sitting on the holy grass and serving in company with other powers of causation (Maruts, Aśvins, Mitra, and Varuṇa).

Immanence

Mortal embodiments in the material world experience the essence and encompass intrinsic immanence (Tryaruna). As a doctrine of philosophical or metaphysical theories, it applies to monotheistic, pantheistic, and panentheistic faiths. This, in the spiritual world, permeates even through the mundane material things and is often contrasted with theories of transcendence. The essence through the divine will remains outside the material world. There is a big difference between immanence and transcendence. According to Vedic knowledge, immanence is the immortal power which, as the universal soul, permeates all creation, including cosmic bodies, rocks and minerals, vegetation, animals, human beings, and any other manifested moving and unmoving bodies. The universal soul (Pramatma) and the individual spirit (Atma) are both related. The transcendent universal soul prevails outside the material world, and Atma prevails in the material world.

The manifested godlike heroes carry their physical bodies with immanence (Rig Veda, Book 5, Hymn XXVII). These godlike heroes appear as Trvrsan, as the unmanifested heavenly bull and the heavenly cow (Tryaruna). They distinguish themselves as the unmanifested universal soul (Paramatma) and embodied living spirits (Atmas). They, as earthly manifested envoys, are granted with many more than ten thousand legs. They, with their very strong powers, protect and serve the epithet of fire (Vaisnavara).

The manifested, embodied, immortal living spirits as pairs appearing as cattle and horses are granted twenty times a hundred eyes. They serve Indra as their bay steeds, all breathing through the mouth and yoked with physical strength. Appearing as most youthful mortal embodiments, these godlike heroes serve the solar race. They offer mighty songs to the living spirit (Atma), and as divine princes, they recite the divine will with essence and declare it as a sacrifice to be accepted, gain power, and keep the eternal laws. After receiving physical power, the godly power (Asvamedha) is delighted. It provides the power of a hundred oxen as a gift and is offered thrice-mingled draughts of the mythical juice. Thus granting the Asvamedha power like the solar deity (Surya), and with the union of Indra-Agni, it supports the lofty rulers of the mid-air as well as the terrestrial regions.

Agni sends its heavenly lustre to shine on earth (Rig Veda, Book 5, Hymn XXVIII). It goes eastward as the sun with praise, homage, and oblation and brings the morning light. The enkindled ruler serving as the king of the immortals offers to grow the material world and all associated and increased urges. Agni sets all their urges and claims possessions by showing their mighty strength to attain bliss. The powers of Agni thus make it easy to maintain their households with lordship and overcome the might of those who hate. The glory of Agni as adored and exalted brings strength like making the steers the brilliant splendour that with sacred rites invokes and enkindles the godly powers.

Mortal embodiments offer sacrificial rites to all the three celestial lights—the sun, the moon, and the stars (Rig Veda, Book 5, Hymn XXIX). They, through the cosmic host (Maruts), bring from the mid-air, which brings pure strength. The sapient rishis (Rsi) are adored by serving the messengers of Indra and serving the ruler of the earth. Even the cosmic host sings joyous songs to honour Indra.

While drinking the mythical juice, they get ready to grasp its thunderbolt to slay the dragon and loosen mighty flows of fresh water. The holy earthly powers (Brahmans), along with the cosmic host (Maruts) and celestial godhead (Indra), drink the mythical juice

(Soma). With such oblations, they slay the dragons and make the heavenly and earthly powers happy as they see them surrender for support like terrified beasts.

Indra helps mortal embodiments along with their cattle. Representing all the godly powers, Indra brings the juice and divine will with essence to free all living beings. With the support of the messenger (Maghavan), individual spirits, like the sons of Trvrsan, come from the heavenly body flying like stallions and decorated like dappled horses with wings (Etaśa).

With immanence, Maghavan and the cosmic host come with the thunderbolt and sing the songs of the solar deity (Trṣṭup) as they demolish ninety-nine castles. It pleases Indra to see all obstructions between earth and heaven removed. To aid his friend, Agni disguises the living spirit in three hundred buffaloes that come to drink the mythical juice from three lakes.

The animals like buffaloes and elephants provided to Indra as gifts serve the mortal embodiments once they have slaughtered the evil powers (Vṛtra). The living spirit forms evil embodiments that are provided with special flesh (Meath) that can be filled with the mythical juice. This provides them with special physical strength that is honoured and provided by Agni as a gift that is presented through messengers (Maghavan), who, with shouts of triumph, raise praise to Indra after slaughtering the evil powers (Vṛtra).

Once mortal embodiments of steeds become strong, they move swiftly to their dwelling place of the spiritual master (Uśanā), who regulates demons. They, like the sage (Kutsa) with immanence, join with Maghavan to conquer the evil power (Suṣṇa), and with the weapon, they kill or eliminate the ruler serving as the savage barbarian with many eyes but without a face serving the head of the evil powers (Dasyus).

271

Indra placed the immortal spirit (Atma) with immanence among Maghavan, which guides the army that is seeking to fight the righteous war (Rig Veda, Book 5, Hymn XXX). They create vibrations that could be used by the mighty force to search in caves and find milk-bearing animals hiding in caves or behind rocks. The Maghavan's name became renowned in far-off regions spreading among scattered foes, who, for prosperity, bring milk givers. The devotees (Dāsa) pound hidden snakes (Namuci) on their heads and make them become associates of Indra. Like meteors from heaven, they differentiate the weaker (Dasa) from the stronger (Dasyu), thus forming two armies that fight using the stronger (Dasyu). They use the weaker (Dasa) to go lowing around from every side, serving like the shepherd tribe (Rusamas). They perform good deeds. They are assigned four thousand cattle. With the most heroic wealth, they come to serve like sages (Rnancaya).

The shepherd tribe, along with milk-bearing animals in the thousands, are sent home with fair adornment and strong libations; this makes Indra joyful. Their passage ends at night, and by the morning, their passage is changed. They serve like a strong fleet of coursers that surges onward to gain four thousand head of cattle. They are all presented as the shepherd tribe; as singers, they come to serve the heated cauldron of metal (Pravargya). With a fire ceremony, the mythical juice is sacrificed along with fresh milk and poured into the heated vessel (Gharma) or Mahavira, which is used to serve the twin demigods (Aśvins).

With such ceremony, their chariots move downward, displaying their strength through the tribe of herdsmen who drive their cattle (Rig Veda, Book 5, Hymn XXXI). They hasten to serve Indra as the lord of bays by bringing out strength that arises from the quest to conquer. They all display with powers that they possess. Coming forth from the cave, they bring out the milky mothers from holes and let chariots fly out.

To increase their strength, the holy souls (Brahmans) worship Indra with exalting songs. With their might, they slaughter snakes like fish so they cannot attack the cows. The heroes sing their songs to honour Indra and the godly mother (Aditi). Without or with steeds, their chariots roll over the godless of evil powers (Dasytis). To exploit such deeds, Maghavan makes its heroes as strong as the lord of primordial power (Shakti). The primordial power that separated earth and heaven serves as the force that brings them together through creating cosmic vapours.

This noble deed of immanence (Maghavan) even today sings as the most wonderful act just as Indra slays fish to generate even stronger magic that turns rock into a weathered substance (Gossan's guiles) and that chases away the godless evil powers (Dasytis). Indra watches the gushing waters coming from the Yadu and Turvaga rivers to assail the living tribes (Kutsa). When by pulling the chariot, Indra faces the deity (Uśanā), which regulates demon power, Indra takes the living tribes to a new place to dwell away from darkness to become the noble spirit (Vatas).

Even sages come looking for the noble spirits (Vatas). They have harnessed the movement of the mind and heart that, through blood, control the movement of thoughts. Such noble spirits (Vata's) can even tame wild animals. Like the dear companion of the cosmic host, they, with prayers, increase their might. They, like the cosmic host, come under the cover of darkness to support the noble spirits. They carry them to the sun's chariot that is passing through the moon. Running backwards with the shielded power (Etasa), they turn the wheels to stay firmly at a place so the sun can provide them courage as it sets eastward.

Indra sees the noble spirits at dawn like a friend seeking a friend holding the mythical juice. The noble spirits (Vatas) are laid on groaning stone that the ancient priest (Adhvaryus) turns into an altar. The immortal powers thus make sure that mortal embodiments remain happy. With divine love, they share these embodiments in faith with divine vigour.

Accepting and serving the supreme universal soul (Paramatma) brings Indra with a thunderbolt to slay the ultimate evil dragon (Danava) that, like a great mountain with fissures, gushes waters and creates floods to set free its eternal powers serving as the spirit (Rig Veda, Book 5, Hymn XXXII). Indra turns mountains into udders flowing with the vigour that creates seasons and brings calmness to water.

When Indra extends over with aggression, it uses weapons to smite any living creature that is filled with wild and mighty evil power. They find and destroy food and anything else that can become potent; they destroy without ever being destroyed. With heavenly floods, they bring delight like a child of the mist, sending a strong pressure crouching in the darkness. They use thunderbolts, which bring lightning, to smite with wrath (Śuṣṇa) and burn with fire to destroy the evil dragon (Dānava), which has never been wounded, and it continues to feel its vital force as the godly bolt. Indra, manifested as the immortal power (Bhagavan), comes willingly to encounter those who have laid down the huge open pit that extends in length, all covered with darkness and gloom.

After listening to the threatening voices, the lord of devotees along with the chief of the converted devotees (Deva-Yakṣas), with humble words, encourage the coiled deity (Ulkāmukha) to serve the universal soul (Bhagavan) and serve libations to honour Indra, which lifts the darkness created by the evil dragon (Dānava), which no one can combat. The huge, restless, coiled deity (Ulkāmukha) impels others to drink the mythical fluid and to smite the footless, evil monsters such as serpents and their power. By encompassing all forms of demise, it bows down like the coiled deity (Ulkāmukha), which Indra supports. It is like a lover imparting all its vigour to support the embodied living spirit (Śatakratu) that honours Indra as well as the godlike powers (Bhagavan) that regulate the ground and terrestrial bodies.

Coming as the lord of heroes, Bhagavan is heard and worshipped by all embodied spirits who manifest to represent the five races that grasp the true powers of worshipping in the evening and morning. They recognize the universal souls as the ultimate source of nature that, through seasons, urges manifested mortal embodiments to perform similar enriching actions. As singers with knowledge, the devotees (Brahmans) cultivate faith and respect and honour the powers of Indra.

With great praise, the demigods with powers ranging from the feeble to mighty decide which band of embodied souls they will show favour to and share the spoils with. With attentive hymns and by fastening their girths, they come along with messengers (Maghavans) driving through with the divine will to subdue bay coursers and remain unharnessed from those who hate the noble souls. Indra wields thunder to draw the bay coursers under their reins and allow the powers of the messengers (Maghavans) to go aggressively into the fields to actively seek milk-bearing animals.

In its abode, Sūrya provides rays of light and has horses serve as devotees (Dasa) of Indra and other godly powers who are fighting along with embodied souls to kill evil powers, in the ocean such as marine creatures (Ahi) and on the ground the evil powers (Vritra). The devotees of Indra receive mighty gifts as the inner power or conscience that sets all this in motion, including the evil powers (Asura's) to invoke beauteous war.

Invoking the individual dormant spirit brings mighty inner power that turns from dormant to evil powers (Asura's), which seek noble powers (Aditya's) and appear with much-desired strength to perform immortal acts and bring mighty wealth. They appear as generous givers (Bhagas) who, as the godly power, protect the noble soul, heroes, and rhymesters who produce and sing hymns that solve any dispute.

As their embodiments drink the mythical juice, they become friends and are filled with inner illumination that passes through their skin. With transformed manifested embodiments such as the gold-rich chief (Purukutsa), they give birth to ten offspring (Trasadasyu), all brightened with the divine will to serve as a dynasty (Gairiksita) that conveys and bestows sacrificial rewards to make manifested bodies strong and powerful as the twin demigods or the cosmic host. Those who produce and sing thousands of musical notes are bestowed with abundant adornment to produce special tones (Cyavatana) that bring stallions appearing with bright and active companion godly powers (Laksmana), who appear with the magnitude of riches (Dhvanya) and join the holy sages (Samvarana).

Without much investing in the heavenly powers, the dynasty (Gairiksita) serves like foes of the guardians, who perform lesser wondrous deeds and offer gifts with zeal to antagonists (Rig Veda, Book 5, Hymn XXXIV). As the receiver of many glorified offerings, the antagonists come in prayer with their bellies filled with the mythical juice and full of wisdom and appear like Usana. They control minds from a single focus point and serve with a weapon that can slay the monstrous beast.

The mighty messengers (Maghavan) receive Soma in sunshine or the rain and serve as sages; they serve friendly embodied souls and provide progeny so they can advance. Once they acquire eternal wisdom and godly power, they no longer flee; instead, they serve as fathers, mothers, or brothers to the mortal embodiments that are subject to death. Knowing they have the powers to seek gifts from the gods, they remove the shackles of materialistic attachment, sin, and other memories. They appear as avengers (Pali) as part of nature (Prakriti), and through nature, they seek no more than five to ten times to reappear as manifested souls to make foes (Gairiksita) with aids like other mortals who, despite their prosperity and fame do not seek Soma.

By using their spiritual powers, they conquer the evil forces and travel in their chariots, constantly pushing those who are not willing to be liberated as devotees (Dāsa) but prosper along with their own will. The Āryaman gather goods that are taken away or stolen by parsimonious people and give them to those who offer gifts. Not even in wide strongholds are they provoked to anger; they stand firm surpassing any mighty powers. When two wealthy men among their followers fight for beauteous cows and stir up all things, the messengers (Maghavan) mark them. They make one a close ally and send him to the house of Satri, where he acquires piety. They send the other to the house of the heroes, and he becomes liberal (Agnivesi) and resides near water that provides him plenty to build a powerful and bright dominion.

Embodied

To further support the heroes, Indra brings its most effective mystical power to help conquer the invincible spoils (Rig Veda, Book 5, Hymn XXXV), and they quickly come together to establish the five embodied tribes, all based on acquired excellence and the mightiest mortal, primordial, and physical powers; they are all born with spiritual power. They prosper with invisible strength, the valour of the universal soul (Paramatma) that becomes visible once it is manifested with mortal embodiments providing dwellings for Atma. With this structure, mortal embodiments comprehend the powers of causation. The divine will with essence gives birth to living things that are ultimately regulated through the manifested planetary system located far away.

Unlike the celestial region, all the planetary bodies ride independently in the cosmic region. Like warriors in chariots, they assail their foes.

Indra covers all the surface of the manifested terrestrial ground (Prithvi). Indra invites embodied souls (Śatakratu) to come into battle to settle the ultimate dispute to protect the manifested individual minds and hearts (Manas). Such manifested bodies are regulated by the divine will with the essence that circulates among the foremost planetary bodies. They keep them apart from every fray using invincible powers to protect their intelligence. With the powers of higher knowledge and eternal wisdom, they become the mightiest ones through meditating, and they obtain excellent eminence at the break of day.

The mightiest ones receive eternal wisdom (Rig Veda, Book 5, Hymn XXXVI), and they rightly know when and to whom to give riches of eternal wisdom. Knowing that with the milked mythical juice (Soma), they can rise to mountain ridges like coursers, they invoke inner strength and make the fear of destitution drive away like meteors. With their hearts rolling like wheels, they create internal seismic activity and radiation.

They, like singers, produce vibrations to praise Indra and mount on a carriage driven with immanence by the messenger (Maghavan). With its left hand, Maghavan gives riches, and with its right hand, it provides heavenly strength so they can travel like strong bay horses (Aśvins) as demigods. They, with bravery, go to battle with mighty, strong-willed, thundering arms to win the righteous, moral fight to support humanity.

The noblest souls pay respect to the demigods serving as the cosmic host (Maruts). They bow as twin, youthful, manifested bodies (Srutaratha) which appear as twin dark red horses representing three hundred heads of cattle; they all serve the mortal embodiments. Indra manages the hierarchy of the universal soul, which regulates the manifested universal soul (Paramatma) and serves as the highest power to bring creative intelligence represented by a batch of deities (Bhrigu, Atri, Angirasa Vashista, Pulastya, Pulalaha, and Kratu).

The enlightened youthful princes (Srutaratha) as the swift ones (Rig Veda, Book 5, Hymn XXXVII) with eternal flame come covered with holy oil and offer suitable worship; they appear as a beam of light that creates many dawns. As a third person, they come with the fire to extract faith along with singing worship songs and drinking the mythical juice. Like priests, they go down with oblation. Indra appears with its loud thunder, making a thousand revolutions as a spinning wheel and generating faith among all. It brings faith to mortals commingled with milk and juice. They drive away enemies and guard embodied souls. With a cherished name and as supporters of peace, they win the battle by mastering the heavenly powers of Sūrya and Agni.

The holy sages form a fair dominion of friends among mortal souls who bring wealth to share among all. According to Rig Veda, Book 5, Hymn XXXIII, the source of the darter of the stone, along with the divine will, uses magnetic and gravitational forces to guard everything between heaven and earth. With their heroic strength, Indra as the evil slayer (Vṛtra), overpowers evil forces operating against embodied mortal souls. They provide aid to hundreds of heroes serving Indra.

The wondrous ones find treasures that fill their hands (Rig Veda, Book 5, Hymn XXXIX). They are considered by their worth and wishes to prevail on earth as they bring boundless divine collections from the heavenly region. They, like the stone darter, win compassion and gain spiritual strength and become singers who produce many promising songs. Once they attain fame, they are honoured by the most liberal, wealthy king, and they praise Indra, which raises sages to become noble sages (Atris) of high beauty.

Noble sages produce the mythical fluid, which they use to call on embodied spirits (Atma) to serve like immortal spirits (Rig Veda, Book 5, Hymn XL). They call on Indra to kill the strong evil power of Vṛtra with its thunder-arm and to provide aid by appearing in various forms. The power of gods (Viśvedevas) calls on thunder as the mighty force to produce juice as water mixed with Soma. They acquire powers and become the potent ruler who fights as the evil power slayer (Vrtra). They yoke with bay horses and gladden them with noon libations. They transform the descendants into evil powers (Asuras) that create black magic (Svarbhanu) to obstruct the bright light coming from the sun. They generate cosmic obstructions such as eclipses that can be observed by all creatures. Not knowing such obstructions are standing in time, they are nothing more than black magic that spreads beneath the sky to smite light.

The noble souls (Atri) represent the first of the seven sages (Saptarishi), who first understand only after four sacred prayers the powers of the heavenly body (Sūrya), which removes the concealment of the gloom that functions as the sun and does not let any oppressor, trepidation, or anger overpower or swallow the noble heavenly powers (Sūrya).

The first noble soul (Atri) serves as the son of Brahman. They send comets representing Mitra and Varuna and bless through offering praise and adoration like the ferocious fire as Agni and calm and peaceful Indra manifest as embodied souls. In heaven, with the established eye of Sūrya, it brings direct light from the sun and reflective light from the moon, and through those lights, it gains control of magic (Svarbhanus) and makes sure it is vanishing at least for a given time created with darkness.

The pious servants (Mitra-Varuṇa) bring gifts from earth to heaven and set holy order that preserves the seat (Rig Veda, Book 5, Hymn XLI) with the powers acquired through winning support from Mitra, Varuṇa, Aryaman, and Āyu along with the loving devotion coming from Indra. They bring the cosmic body (Ṛbhukṣan) along with the cosmic host (Maruts). The heavenly power (Rudras) with bounteous wind power generates vibrations that create specific hymns delivered through the Aśvins serving as flying horses; they capture Asuras, the evil power that prevails in the heavenly regions. The ruler of the heavenly region, Dyaus, has been fed oblations through the priests (Kaṇva, Vata, and Tṛty), who come with the fleet of steeds regulated by the patrons Pū5an and Bhaga.

They bring upon their horses, riches, and treasure that, like the priest (Auśija), they use for their courses as well as to help the cosmic host (Maruts) and the heavenly body (Rudras), who generate ferocious wind that, through the powers of godly singers, transforms ferocious wind into the air (Vāyu) and with the earthly singers creates praise songs the devout use to invoke the mind of prudent, noble souls. Their minds acquire spiritual powers to honour with songs and distinguish the mighty, heavenly, feminine retention power that separates the awareness of morning from the unawareness of night. The unawareness and awareness bring to the mortals as sacrifices those who eulogize through nourishing heroes (Vastospati, Tva5tar, and Dhi5aṇā).

Such transformed heroes bring gifts that transform seedlings into plants and trees and, within the animal kingdom, promote offspring to serve nature (Vasus) and the son of cosmic vapours (Aptya). As friends of embodied souls, they exalt and strengthen themselves by staying near them always.

With the power of Aptya, praised heroes (Trta) become embryos (Vastospati, Tva5tar, and Dhi5aṇā), who like water, serve as the offspring of the earthly heroes. They sing pure songs to honour Agni, and with their mighty neighs, they loudly come like flying balls with flaming hair to destroy the forests and kill evil powers. Rudras speaks highly of the patron (Bhaga) as they bring with might and fill with richness the ground, plants, and water; they preserve woods, tresses, and trees in the mountains.

The swift wanderer with mighty Bhaga as the lord of refreshments listens to and produces rhythmic vibrations with which heavenly clouds come out of the cleaved mountain and flow onward in the sky. As they move down toward the ground, they create bright castles knowing the mighty patron's ways. They receive mead, which makes them fly like strong birds (seraphs) descending to attain mortal powers. Bhaga strives not to reach the terrestrial region. With its swift blow, like a celestial warhead or missile, even today, it is summoned with feasts they bring along with vibrations and dawn that produce prosperity among its conquered streams through increasing the flow of water.

Each one duly offers as a means of relief a loud sound of sacrifice (Varūtrī) that ejaculates sperm from the great mother (Rasā), which supports princes who are striving to produce liberal ones. With the support of the Maruts, they receive a swift course in far-renowned invocation. Thus, through such worship as a favour, the mortal wins to increase herds of cattle and wholesome food needed to feed mortal embodiments even though old age and before they are consumed by death, the goddess of darkness, Nirrti.

With deep devotion (Rig Veda, Book 5, Hymn XLII), Varuṇa, Mitra, Aditi, Surya, and Bhaga, with blessing and oblations, fight the evil powers (Asura). They open the path into the dwelling of the evil power so they can hear their lineage and relationship with the celestial mother (Aditi) and welcome them as dear, heart-gladdening sons.

The godly powers of Varuṇa and Mitra, with songs of love, invoke the prevailing dormant spirit by providing the mythical juice mixed with specially prepared food that enhances individual intellects, and they help serve the sagest of the sages who are ready to bring splendid treasures offering sacrificial oil from the heavenly body (Surya). Five priests with willing minds vouchsafe the patron Bhaga; they serve the lord of bays by offering them godly prayers and loving-kindness, and they give pious patrons prosperity by bringing them milk-bearing animals.

Genetic Linkage

Genetic lineage (Gotra) broadly refers to the astral body that descends in an unbroken line; it is commonly referred to as the male ancestor among the Brahmins. With specific lineage, it means family kin like that one from the same herd in an enclosure. With this, it establishes the progeny, and through Gotra, one traces descent from the unbroken Septarishi Gotra. This includes noble souls that have prevailed on earth (Gautama, Bharadvāja, Viśvāmitra, Jamadagni, Vashishtha, Kaśhyapa, and Shandilya). The progeny of these seven sages are called Apatya, and further offspring are called Gotrâvayava. The offspring of the first five sages are called Pancha-Rishaye, and the offspring of the other three sages are Tri-a-rishaye.

The holy deities (Vāja, Ṛbhukṣan, and Purandhi) come to protect mortal embodiments and help them attain noble powers by performing noble deeds. The celestial host accepts the messengers (Maghavans) and later provides them with other manifested bodies with the spiritual powers to appear like ancient mythical figures (Bṛhaspatis). They serve mortal embodiments depending on the given era. First, they invoke as chiefs with eternal flame among those malevolent souls (Asuras) who praise and sing hymns to receive protection. They serve as counsel by bringing and distributing riches, and with blessings, they give out abundant wealth with raiment and bliss and provide them with fleets of horses and cattle.

Coming from the sun with godly powers, they drive down with heat and light, and with praise, malevolent souls (Asuras) bow to every unquestionable force. They are helped with a mighty balm to overpower their terrible king of hell, who rides a pale horse (Bealeth).

With eighty-five legions of demons all under the command of the chief, they produce and hear all kinds of music full of demonology and the best-known grimoires that are adored by the evil powers (Asura). With salutations, Rudra sends as house friends the cunning artist Ribhus to go along with Vibhvan as the wife while Rudra carves out powers that enhance streams.

Bringing honour as the fair ones, the divine goddesses (Sarasvatī, Brhaddiva, and Rākā) with special hymns protect the enhanced streams that bring eternal love. With such powers, the singers invoke the godly rain (Idaspati), which comes roaring with thunder to produce water-bearing clouds that move at the speed of light from heaven to earth. Appearing as the unwearied ones, the young sons of Rudra join the troops and help them attain riches. The demigods help them through the mid-air region by winning earthly riches and feeding plants that produce fruit.

They listen without ill will and elect to follow every demigod ruling Mother Earth. They learn to dwell freely in undisturbed bliss. They appear with Aśvins with newfound ancient powers and bestow happiness, health, and guidance to immortal souls.

The devotee milks cows to provide the sweet mythical fluid to singers (Rig Veda, Book 5, Hymn XLIII). Serving like the seven mighty ones (Saptarishis), they produce reverence along with fair praise that brings enjoyment, and they acquire exhaustless strength to serve as Mother Earth and Father Heaven. With sweet speech, they appear along with heavenly priests (Blrhaspatis) to protect the sages (Adhvaryus) serving as the earthly priests.

The sweet libations of the mythical juice bring beautiful bright light that joins the wind (Vāyu) to produce breezes. They control the incoming and outgoing breezes in manifested embodiments that, through divine will, transform the breeze into breath. Those who receive breath are blessed with the mythical juice. The breath fixes the spinal cord, and with the mythical juice, it serves the backbone like watering a stalk. This allows wisdom to spread through the body, creating branches that transfer the eternal wisdom along with the food to generate the bright eternal flame like the one that dwells among plants in the mountains.

The pressed juice brings eternal love (Mitra) to induce the mighty powers that accompany the higher level of gratification needed to be invoked. With such invocation, it turns like a cart being pulled by two well-trained bay horses and traverses divine paths established by Agni. The embodiment traverses like the celestial lady (Aramati), exalting with gifts and paying homage to comprehend the powers of divine will regulating the dynamic universe, fully following and practising the holy law. Like a son in his father's lap, they experience the warmth of hymns that holds intact the fatty membrane of the physical body.

The heavenly priests (B1rhaspatis) invite the Aśvins to come with sweet, pleasant songs to set a ceremonial meal. They place bolt and nave, and they set a binding pole to bring it all together. As the joy giver with speech, it declares with adoration that the solar deity (Pūṣan) is represented as one of the noble souls (Adityas) that bring air (Vayu) to set the victorious breathing process. This process helps consume food and helps milk-producing animals; it also brings unions or marriages between males and females. It further helps in attaining self-realization and protection from bandits and wild beasts.

The breathing process is also used to protect living beings through guiding individual spirits or as the psych pump that reaches individual spirits such as archangels, deities, or those who are responsible for escorting the souls of the newly deceased mortal embodiments from earth to the afterlife site. Their role is not to judge the deceased but simply to appear at funerals and help guide them to a safe passage like helping the animal kingdom—horses, deer, dogs, ravens, crows, owls, sparrows, and cuckoos.

The role of the manifested solar deity is to guide the astral bodies and the cosmic host with their bounty to inspire. They bring out the united godly power (Jatavedas) to come from high heaven and, with sacrifice, bring Sarasvatī. From its auspicious lofty mountain, they offer sacrifices along with songs and praise to disperse divine powers, which they can hear. Such effectual invocation helps those who have their backs filled with the darkness of prior memories, all seated in the splendid inner dwelling of the astral body. With a red and golden hue, as the sustainer, Vishnu comes from heaven as the bounteous one ready to serve with a celestial body that invokes the astral body with all favours.

The dwellers with divine dames standing like unwearied plants or triple-horned steers serve to bestow life after death. Eloquent tuneful priests who live to seek the mother's bright and loftiest station come ready to receive the mortal manifested living body offered with gifts and homage that deck the most auspicious unborn child (astral body) in a physical embodiment.

Agni provides the great, mighty, vital power in the form of the life force paired with the old devotional powers and joins with every demigod. They swiftly listen with no ill will to Indra, representing Mother Earth; this allows the thoughts from the demigods to dwell in the body and let the free spirits be blessed with new mortal embodiments. The manifested bodies are served by the Aśvins, who bestow health and receive happy guidance by bringing riches and felicity to heroes.

As in old times (Rig Veda, Book 5, Hymn XLIV), it is a custom to draw forth the ancient genetic lineage (Gotra) to seek specific divine powers through singing specific hymns sitting in a specific place of worship or sitting on holy grass. Gotras establish a specific kingdom to rule mortals. Based on Gotra, mortal noble souls are selected based on the powers of the individual states of their inner illumination.

The ruler uses powers to conquer and prevail over all kingdoms, including the vegetal, animal, and human kingdoms. With inner brilliance, they serve unobstructed from heaven's regions, and with its sheen, they are bestowed with enlightenment to serve as guardians who cannot be deceived by illusions (Maya) created through the holy law to motivate individual mortals through the creation of want, greed, drive, ego, and superego to perform their obligatory responsibilities.

Serving as good guardians, through unveiling eternal truth, they learn the powers of illusion (Maya), and through victory over such powers, they serve as holy souls or earthly priests. They glide along on the sacred grass like a mighty child who helps the youth of the kingdoms grow. Using their reins as guardians, they guide all creation using their assumed names. They go deep within and hide with inner spirits and move together as an embryo.

The good guardians appear as pregnant females who, with vigour, snatch branches to transform plants into trees, and with mythical powers, they shine through eternal truth and uphold the divine will. Beholding it increases their consort through making a selfless sacrifice, and they become effectual splendour that transforms solid surfaces or land into the ground that yields ample food and enough water to create floods and extend widely.

With invincible power now stored among heroes, they manifest as the sons of unwedded holy sages. With a divine will serving as the spouse, they establish themselves in the manifested world's battlegrounds. They serve only their loving spirits, which help by serving as self-granting excellence to move against their foes, thus transforming their physical embodiments into a home by providing spiritual power that shelters them with the eternal flame generating heat to ward off evil powers from every side. The good guardians as sages sing hymns and become enlightened souls (Rsis). They go farther toward the one, the loftier moving light, with winning skill that sets a boon in individual hearts and allows things to pass without disturbing tranquillity.

The chief and best of the Rsis abides in deep water without failing libations, wherein it is prolonged with the praising heart that does not tremble or fear as it establishes links with hymns as sources of divine vibrations. It further connects with purity and eternal truth by worshipping the mystical powers of Ksatra, Manasa, Sadhri, and Evavada.

With sweet songs of avatar, they become the Avatsara representing the divine will. They strive to win the mightiest strength to fly like hawks. With their mighty force and the Soma from Visvavara, they stretch their might by travelling with the wind (Vayu), and with Yajata, they acquire eternal truth, and thus overpower illusions and delusions created by Maya. By drinking Soma, they know when the right time is to halt drinking it and join the holy powers (Sadaprna, Tarya, Srutavit, and Bahuvrkta). They slay their foes and help gain their wishes to serve both worlds as they adore their hosts with well-advancing steeds.

As worshippers, they come under the defence of the defender (Sutambhara) that produces holy thoughts and uplifts like cows bringing milk to serve those who deal with their sacred love and produce hymns. At all times, they wake and watch with Sāma verses.

Invisible bodies are heaven's daughters that serve as the counterpart to mortal bodies. These invisible bodies are composed of the highest form of air, representing the fifth element, ether. The invisible body prevails in the manifested physical body as it regulates the subtle faculties such as the mind and heart during semiconscious states such as sleep. Through their mystic powers, they establish a link with the nervous system of the physical body and thus become responsible for the generation of passion, emotion, and desire. They transform vibrations into oscillations, and through hymns and prayers, they invoke the spirit and generate experiences through clairvoyance or auras.

The holy earthly priests serving as messengers or poets comprehend the heavenly region and relate with the heavenly manifested bodies like the power of illumination (Surya) and the power of vibrations (Rudras), which approach earth by bringing the morning light and the life force. They spread wide to fill the mountain with the light as the rising sun (Rig Veda, Book 5, Hymn XLV). This establishes open portals through which the godly powers allow light and air as splendours and bring milk to cows and vigour to other animals.

They spread like flowing water and establish streams filled with waves that reach even barren areas, including deserts. They establish firm pillars that hold the burden of splendours, such as the mountains between the heavenly region on the top and the earthly region at the bottom. As the heavenly daughters with their ancient birth come through the mighty waters, they support and become part of all the divine splendours.

With constant sacrifices offered by the worshippers, Indra and Agni come as skilled sages to offer sacrifice to the mighty powers and worship the demigods and the cosmic host. They bring noble thoughts to serve holy souls throwing open stalls and meeting the mother cow. They carry out as friends and keep a distance from those who hate noble souls or cast misfortune. As wandering merchants, they come as the heavenly power (Manus), bringing the heavenly liquid to conquer the male (Visisipra) and the female (Sarama) by running through and plodding on hands for ten months. Singing the right praises brings godly power (Aṅgiras), which because of all their labour, gives birth to the dawning mighty goddess (Aṅgirases). Singing like cattle, they spring forth and bring from the loftiest place the female (Saramā) to meet with and establish its kind by an order that establishes the ancestral pathway.

Born out of a heavenly body (Surya) as the seven heavenly sisters, after a long journey, they visit the wide fields and rapidly swoop down as birds to reach where young sages generate brilliant Soma. They then move along with the herds of cattle where the heavenly body (Sūrya) mounts upon the shining ocean and comes with the tawny horses (Aśvins) that yoke with wisdom and draw down like a ship in the obedient flood, where water moves through the water, and it descends to lie on with hymns the light winning Navagvas. After completing their ten months in secrecy, with hymns and support from the demigods, they pass over to a safer place that is beyond affliction.

Like horses bound to a pole (Rig Veda, Book 5, Hymn XLVI), they become known to the godly powers (Agni, Indra, Varu,)a, and Mitra), who carry them and give them help. They immediately know the cosmic host who guides them with the supreme powers of causation (Vi5h,)u, Nāsatyas, and Rudras) who with heavenly powers (Pū5an, Sarasvatī, and Bhaga) serve as the matriarchs. They accept dual powers (Indra-Agni, Mitra-Varu,)a, and Aditi-Vish5u), and for help, they call on Pū5an, Brahma,)aspati, Bhaga, Samsa, Savitar, and Vāta, who injure none and grant the mythical juice to bring joy and the power to remember the eternal wisdom regulated by the celestial powers (Ṛbhus).

The cosmic host sets their dwelling in the sky with Aśvins, Tva5tar, and Vibhvan to visit as the holy one (Bṛhaspati and Pū5an) sitting on the sacred grass. Varu,)a, Mitra, and Aryaman build shelters in the mountains from where they offer the noble souls full support and keep them safe from harm while they travel the rivers.

The powers of Bhaga as the dispenser brings from afar the pervading mother (Aditi) like godly spouses to listen to their calls and, with their own free will, aid the offspring, who win the spoils and grant protection through gracious goddesses who prevail on earth. They serve as dames, wives of gods, and they enjoy serving as manifested bodies (Rat), including Aśvini, Agnāyī, Indrā,)ī, Rodasī, and Varu,)ānī.

The matriarchs (Rig Veda, Book 5, Hymn XLVII) call on their father, the heavenly body (Surya), and invite him to the home of the mother (Aditi), an earthly body where they hastily perform their duties to bring the astral bodies even before they reach the life force (Prana), and they serve as matriarchs even before coming to earth.

Serving as the heavenly daughters, they travel spacious paths supported by heavenly immortal powers. As steers, they cover the ground, and as marine animals, they travel the oceans along with the red bird with strong wings covering the sky. As the ten heavenly daughters, the astral bodies are given dwellings like the one provided to the primaeval father serving the esoteric region.

With an established path, the astral plane, they serve as cosmic bodies in the planetary sphere between the limits of heaven and earth. The ten goddesses travel and pass swiftly around to invigorate and set individual boundaries where wondrous astral bodies, all possessing mystic knowledge, create a place to stay among the streams flowing all around where water stands still.

With the help of Aditi, they weave their physical embodiments like garments that separate the Aśvins as male and female who support each other and remain closely united. They perform lengthened prayers and perform acts of worship to rejoice by impregnating the spouses before they move on their paths to heaven.

With praise, the twins (male and female) meet the lord of the eternal laws (Varuṇa) and the lord of eternal love (Mitra), thus obtaining strength and health. They with Agni establish on the ground a firm link that, through the eternal flame, moves them to a blessed space where with all the heavenly glory, they rest in the astral plane and build a lofty habitation.

With beloved spiritual energy prevailing on the ground, they meditate (Rig Veda, Book 5, Hymn XLVIII) using mythical power (Soma) residing in water, and they spread to an immeasurable level. Within the middle region, they appear among clouds and advance uniformly over all the region. Then they spread out to give back the strength to heroes, who lengthen life, and then they travel in reverse as pious coursers passing by the cosmos after they have travelled like the broadest bolt travelling along with cosmic pressing-stones (meteors).

They, with the bright day, hurl together with a hundred wanders who have their own abodes and serve as the astute ones. They drive afar and bring again the joy and the beauty of their own kind. They behold a rapid rush as if they were on an axe's edge of time and space. As mortal bodies, they fight for spiritual wealth like their dwelling filled with food regulated by four-faced, nobly clad Varuna.

They are urged to be pious, and they stir themselves among other unknown powers of the goddess (Savitar). They serve Bhaga, which brings them boons. Even to this day, Savitar and Bhaga meet (Rig Veda, Book 5, Hymn XLIX) among all mortal embodiments as heroes; they seek friendship with the demigods. Knowing fully well the time of arrival of the evil powers (Asuras), they help all with worship, hymns, and praise. They send along blessings brought by Bhaga and Aditi.

As wonderworkers supporting the heavenly supreme powers of causation (Indra, Vishnu, Varuna, Mitra, and Agni), they, with auspicious work, build a shelter that can be approached by godly powers such as Savitar serving the rivers and helping them meet with the priest, who is offering sacrifice to invite the lords with wealth.

With rich possessions, they willingly serve all the devotees worshipping the powers of nature (Vasus). Making sure no one gets hurt, Varuna and Mitra come along with songs and hymns, serving as guardian angels who ward off danger and guide them on a path with ample room for all.

CHAPTER 8
COGNITIVE DOMINION

Every mortal embodiment cultivates a friendship with the highest, six-winged, manifested guardian angels that come with celestial or heavenly powers that appear to fly around singing, "Holy, Holy, Holy!" With triple invocations as the guardian angel, as an angelic being, belonging to the highest order of the ninefold celestial hierarchy, it is associated with light, ardour, and purity. They come as celestial or heavenly seraphs to protect astral bodies designated to return to earth. They are honoured by heroes as males and females, and they are welcomed as guests who remove evil powers. They keep them safe from foes and have them blocked with the moral embodiments on the path to nobility. The seraphs even set fire and swiftly run in to save victims. As heroes, they can come home with their friendly spirits and continue to run like a constant stream.

Guiding Gods

According to Rig Veda, Book 5, Hymn L, every mortal embodiment is elected to develop a friendship with the guiding God; each one solicits wealth and seeks to be renowned and prosper, joining with the guiding God. They wait for them to speak, provide wealth, and even wait to be served with honour as divine gods and goddesses. They remove and keep them far from foes. They block all their paths from reaching devotees. They set themselves on fire and then swiftly run into the victims' dwelling in the ditch. This is how they win and provide the heroes with homes. Friendly to the manifested mortals, they establish constant flowing streams of water. They themselves serve as the godly power that brings riches to bless others with wealth.

According to Rig Veda, Book 5, Hymn LI, with the assistance coming from Agni and the mythical juice, they follow the righteous ways and abide by the truth. They follow the law, like Agni, and they come with singers to drink the mythical juice. They come with grace as archangels and join the earthly powers served by Indra. They appear in the sky with wind power (Vāyu). The mythical juice produced in the embodiment fills their internal jars. They, as the spotless pair (Aśvins), come along with the seraphs to accept the blend of milk and water flowing in the rivers.

As seraphs, they become subordinate to the supreme powers of causation (Agni, Atri, Varuṇa, Mitra, and Vishnu). They enjoy such juice and refer to situations where the physical mortal body,

through the invisible powers, connects with the subtle astral body and thus with the immortal spirit (Atma). As self-luminous embodiments, they receive liberation through inner illumination (Rig Veda, Book 5, Hymn LII). Freeing the immortal spirit allows them to connect with the universal soul (Paramatma) and serve all the differentiated parts of the universe. This concept is notably known as the attainment of enlightenment (Bodhi, Kensho, Satori, Moksha, Kevala, and Jnana Ushta). Among Western faiths, it refers to attaining radiance, kenosis, metanoia, revelation, salvation, and conversion. In spiritual mysticism, it is referred to as the ultimate awakening, the supreme noble powers (Adityas) in its state self-luminous.

Such bodies prevailing in regions among living beings become responsible for the manifestation of complex embodiments were residing individual spirits (Atma) are awakened and are supported by the heavenly powers. Here, external illumination with a special gift brings direct light from the sun, and internal illumination comes as reflective light from the moon. The fully awakened experience the presence of the living spirit (Atma). Residing in mortal embodiments, this allows bodies to be ultimately regulated by the heavenly power, Surya, which provides and supports embodiments with fame and glory.

Through manifested and unmanifested demigods in the form of the twin horses (Aśvins), it appears with the rapid coursers that fly like stallions. They support the cosmic host (Maruts) and maintain close kinship with the impetuous heavenly body (Rudras), serving as wind (Vayu); all others serve as the children of the father (Rudras) and mother (Prsni). Through the pantheon of Surya, it provides self-luminous light that transforms all into the noble supreme power (Adityas). They are supported by the milk-bearing animals that provide additional strength while they serve, travelling fast like steeds in the terrestrial region and learning to prevail in shallow rivers (Yamuna).

Totally pure, shining with vital power, the noble supreme powers prevail in the mortal body accompanied by the immortal living spirit fully decorated with luminous power. They provide radiance and appear like any cosmic body wearing ornaments with shining swords, breastplates, and other armour.

Such bodies appear as a group riding on clouds with chariots and bowing swiftly as they deliver heavenly treasure. They arrive, moving with the ferocious wind as self-luminous beings coming from Rudra ready to serve heroes. They accomplish all this by setting free storm clouds. They bring the supreme powers of causation, which are responsible for the original creation of heaven and earth. They cause floods by overflowing streams that first cover the dry land, including deserts. The water runs on every side and creates glittering creeks in the mid-air region (Rig Veda, Book 5, Hymn LIII). They hasten their journey until they get to their resting place, where the water brought by the heavenly body (Rudras) fills the four largest rivers covering the mid-region— the Rasa, Anitabha, Kubha, and Sindhu. The amount of water is so large that even the deity of water (Sarasvati) cannot obstruct such activities. After Rudras receive eulogies, they follow with favourable hymns. This keeps bringing and gathering brilliant youthful forces. Hiding among the clouds, they are accompanied by more rain that is needed in the areas.

As in the past, the self-luminous bodies call on the mighty cosmic host. They energize their army fleet by fleet, troop by troop, band by band, and even company by company to bring back the noble ancestry. With its prevailing zoom, the cosmic host provides an ample supply to safeguard the bounty. They send in the form of seeds of the noble ancestry and bring all blessed to embryos that keep being reborn.

To regulate the powers of breath (Prana), they establish dawn and dusk. From the mid-region, they keep bringing down rain that establishes a level of tranquillity. With the heroes of heaven and blessings from Rudras, they come down to disperse eternal wisdom through activating mythical souls to come as a group of demigods. They, serving as Rsi, offer blessed rites like liberal patrons and protect their mortal bodies.

Further, Rudras uses its native splendour (Vayu) to shape wind into a breeze and creates breath (Prana) to support mortal bodies. Like mountains, it brings renowned strength that can sustain heat and face the challenge of attaining heavenly heights. Life force harnesses like steeds and cultivates far-wandering powers that learn to produce roaring sounds. As the life force passes through, it brings along stone casters as the heroes of heaven bringing light—the comets, asteroids, and meteors.

The heroes of heaven travel under thundering clouds and generate lightning that travels under the clouds, sweeps the flooding waters, and generates thunder. Even when they are overthrown and go down below, they set off violent sounds accompanied by heavy rain that brings hailstorms that devastate nature.

With the support of the heavenly body (Rudras) and the life force (Prana), they even ride farther through night and day, shaking up the realms of air into the sky. They arrive at the broad fields where they ride all along hills like ships. They receive support from the heavenly body (Rudras) as they pass through, overextending their way far from the heavenly body (Surya).

They pass through the imperishable rain. Along with the cosmic host, they provide subdued powers that help excel with their life force as they go downhill. They meet groups of manifested demigods, roots of sages (Rsi), with their ability to move and travel like the free-flowing power that rises and protrudes in the essence of excellence. The free-flowing power helps the life force move and, with vibrations, turns into waves. They go through passing like breezes among the trees striking and shaking evil powers buried in manifested plantations. They come out of the tree as worms and fall on the ground.

The imperishable power (Prana) with the free-flowing powers moves in the embodiments of sages they never confront—never staining, overcoming, dotting, or decaying. It removes distress and always gives embodiments treasures and resources that are never wasted. They always give equally, whether as the receiving or giving party, as a ruler, or as a physical or spiritual power.

As cosmic hosts (Rig Veda, Book 5, Hymn LIV), the free-flowing powers with their native bright splendour full of vibrations cover the mountains. With their great strength, like sages (Rsi), they bring out their renowned ability to face the heat coming from heaven. As manifested bodies, they build their inner strength to serve like strong bands of steeds that establish their home to return to after wandering for a long time.

To push away the enemies, they seek support from the solar deity (Trita) to produce roaring sounds with lightning. All accompanied by the flooding waters, they as manifested bodies sweep around the thunder and lightning; like meteors, they turn around and overthrow anything that comes their way.

With the cosmic hosts, the terrestrial hosts (Rsi), they travel night and day, running with mighty winds and passing through the sky. Continuously shaking everything as they drive along over broad fields, they move without harming the underlying regions; they continue to be regulated by the heavenly body (Surya). With heroic strength and majestic powers, the heavenly body (Surya), through the sun, provides them support and appears with the solar rays that extend over a long way.

Appearing like subdued deer, they bring imperishable rain to bow to the bright, self-luminous, visible bodies. Within the interstellar dominion, where matter and radiation coexist, they form galaxies and star systems where matter includes ions, gas in atomic and molecular form, and the dust that forms cosmic rays. The interstellar space is filled and blends smoothly into the surrounding galaxies.

In the form of electromagnetic radiation, the interstellar radiation field is established. From the interstellar medium, it composes multiple phases, whether the matter is ionic, atomic, or molecular and based on the temperature as well as the density of the matter. The interstellar medium is composed primarily of hydrogen, followed by helium and trace amounts of carbon, oxygen, and nitrogen. The thermal pressures of these phases are in rough equilibrium. Magnetic fields and turbulent motions provide pressure typically and dynamically more than thermal pressure.

Primordial Energy

The supreme primordial energy responsible for the separation of dormant and dynamic universes comes to work to establish a new home base for the new creation that encompasses creation, preservation, and destruction. This supreme primordial energy, the goddess (Shakti), is worshipped and considered the most powerful among all manifested powers of divinities, deities, and demigods. Shakti is depicted with its immortal weapons: the wheel (Chakra), the thunderbolt (Vajra), and the mace (Gada). As a goddess, Shakti is respected as the most powerful covering all in one and one in all, which is situated in the centre of the manifested mortal embodiments' pituitary glands.

From there, the godhead regulates the three most destructive powers (Ida, Pingala, and Suhasmana) in the universe that transforms dark matter into cosmic energy or transforms cosmic energy into dark matter. It is proven to destroy infinite time (Kaala) hence ending all creation to come along with Shakti as immense energy. It is so intense that it can burn the universe into ashes without any other weapon that can match its powers, including nuclear power.

The goddess with breasts adorned with iron and gold manifests with gleaming lances along with the life force and performs actions by striking forth (Rig Veda, Book 5, Hymn LV) and rushing onward after gaining powers with each victory. They transform in the space from far away to use the sky to measure their onward movement and use their mighty strength to create mighty manifested forms that, with the life force, gain even greater heroic majesty like the ancient primordial power to bring primordial, glorious illuminations, which spread light coming from the heavenly body (Surya) serving like the noble sage (Rsi).

It keeps moving onward, receiving mightiness provided as reflective light coming from the moon and direct light coming from the adored sun. Jointly, all represent Surya. They keep producing shining rays that aid the noble powers, sages (Rsi), to attain immortality and serve as the wonderworkers who lift moisture from the ocean and transform it into cosmic vapours.

Knowing the heavenly body (Rudras) well, they use cosmic vapours to bring down rain that, like a steed, keeps moving to its target. They appear like spotted deer who put on coverings to chase or disperse enemies. The heroic majesty (Rsi) neither turns its back to the solid mountains nor moves away from the flowing rivers. The heroic majesty produces vibrations that can even go up and scope around heaven, acquire ancient mythical power, and bring it to the recent time. These vibrations, with their ancestral powers, are transmitted through the elements of nature (Vasus) to create sounds that connect creations with their creator. They set the three-party communication system of the trinity among supreme powers of causation to regulate and support manifested bodies.

Once manifestations become fully aware of such immortal powers, they are no longer subject to fear of being slain; they learn to be gracious and even look to build many sorts of shelters, including constellations. They extend their friendship with the trinity to help other powers attain greater fortune accompanied by lauded affiliations. Using water casks allows the trinity with impetuousness to spring forth and flow among teams of heroes. They harness pleasant water to inundate the earth. Just like in heaven, water uses the air to travel from the mid-air region to terrestrial planets and cover them with water.

The rising sun brings delight and turns coursers into heroes of the sky, fast-flying animals, and birds with lances on their shoulders and gold chains and gems around their ankles glowing with lightning on their breasts. They move on with flashing flame in their hands and inlay their visors with gold. They eagerly stir and shake the vault of heaven to create splendours beyond comprehension. They no longer become fatigued even when they are speeding on their way to reach the end of their path rapidly.

With their mighty deeds, they flash forth by sending the pious ones to appear with a far-resounding shout knowing all about the riches with a full life; they dwell in thousands by giving wealth that never vanishes. Even after distributing to others such wealth, the lives of the heroes of the sky extend by helping sages who are skilled in chanting by helping them become cherished ancestors, Bharata, who serve with the strength that they bestow on noble souls to become listeners. By giving and sharing acquired wisdom, they quickly fulfil other needs and become the true, noble kings serving the host (Maruts) of the cosmic region.

In the illuminated dynamic universe representing the heavenly region, they are supported by the Surya, which had started to ascend by transferring more matter into energy (Rig Veda, Book 5, Hymn LVI) and creating a vacuum. This allows the supreme powers of causation to form a consortium and carve out additional space to expand as a base to build interstellar dominion, thus expanding farther the differentiated dynamic universe out of the undifferentiated dormant universe.

The supreme powers of causation never come close to the outermost space where the manifested heavenly body (Rudra's) as the crusader serves all manifestations. Using its ancient fleet of ferocious godhead power (Agni) and from which it creates primordial energy (Shiv-Shakti), it regulates the interstellar dominion created as part of the differentiated universe. This brings the interstellar dominion close to the ultimate luminous stratum just below heaven, where manifested heavenly bodies (Rudras) bring the Aśvins and regulate the dynamic universe.

They travel as the messenger between heaven and earth. The heavenly body (Rudras) further expands its fleet of ferocious offspring serving as Maruts to more than sixty that as the host of the cosmic region travel between the cosmic and the terrestrial regions. Both demigods (Aśvins and Maruts) jointly lead the spiritual force manifested or unmanifested, appearing among all as a life force (Prana), which serves the expanded interstellar dominion reaching from outer space to the terrestrial region.

They bring bounteous gifts as they come out rushing like impetuous bears with mighty strength, like triumph protecting all the unmanifested life force (Prana). They even overthrow the evil powers (Asura) like bulls or oxen that are difficult to yoke. With newly acquired powers, they create loud vibrations by creating unequalled earthquakes accompanied by volcanic activity that throws fire stones into the air accompanied by heavenly fire (Agni), generating bright-red flames with burning fireballs like hot lava that builds strength like a carriage being pulled with loud neighs by the fleet-footed tawny steeds. This all appears with vigour producing a bright red colour like lava coming from molten rock.

Indra and Rudra join and serve in one accord as they appear in the golden carriage and bring prosperity to all who recite hymns and offer spiritual rites (Rig Veda, Book 5, Hymn LVII). They, with heavenly water as a gift spring along with weapons of all forms—spears, quivers, arrows, and bows—carried on a carriage pulled by flying stallions. After providing water, they, as planetary bodies, come down from the hills of heaven with victory and shake down wealth to worshippers, especially those who, out of terror, have bowed to meet the cosmic demigods (Maruts) as young sons of the mother (Pṛśni) sent to serve the earth or underworld.

Cosmic hosts let out bright blasts as they meet the spiritual heroes who, out of fear, run like spotted deer. Indra-Rudra wrapped in their rain robes covering their noble aspects, and their lovely forms appear to turn the spotless steeds into red-hued, tawny horses (Aśvins) with strong and mighty powers ready to spread wide on the ground with rich adornment as in heaven.

Singers with immortal fame and munificent bright aspects yield to become like the spiritual heroes who endure with noble births through winning the sky adorned with gold on their breasts. Born with spears on both shoulders and strength in their arms, they hold their thoughts and keep hidden their weapons in their carriage. The spiritual heroes appear glorious like the children of Rudra serving as the young sons like the cosmic host (Maruts) with majesty moulded in their bodies. They vouchsafe and provide splendid bounty in the form of cattle and steeds; they receive the highest distinction and enjoy a godlike nature. Skilled in immortal laws and with gracious and rich treasures, they hear eternal truth and grow up as youthful sages who dwell in lofty mountains.

They acquire through their heritage gracious richness (Rig Veda, Book 5, Hymn LVIII) filled with immortal treasure as eternal truth. Spiritual heroes can hear and comprehend the power of the divine will through their mighty co-host while riding on their rapid horses. They plan on their glorifying impetuous journey to establish new dwellings with their radiant personality. They travel with their mighty glittering bands with arms bound with bracelets through the interplanetary zone and appear like lofty mountains with the unmeasured greatness of outer space.

They arrive with bountiful powers, and they approach any object that gives the bliss to serve as the water bearer; those who have been duly kindled with eternal flame by Agni have already induced sunlight with falling rain. Like the host of the cosmic region (Maruts), they rise on the ground above the underworld to become active rulers accompanied by the holy ones serving as sages. They especially serve among those who have been designated as warriors to fight righteous wars supported as brave fighters.

These spiritual heroes spring forth with added strength and glory and become ready to serve as the spokes of a wheel. Affirmed in their own intention to the highest and mightiest, the young cosmic host

(Maruts), sons of the mother (Prsni), cling together and hasten with strong-wrought fellies like spotted coursers that spread with water to accommodate needs. They continue to move water sent down from father Dyaus to distribute like shattering wood and send water into the mouths of volcanic craters. They appear like the thundering red steer, as volcanos covering the wide-open ground that is ready to welcome the coming of emissary water from heaven. As an offering and sacrifice for prosperity, the steeds sing and bathe as they hasten to the firmament.

Spiritual heroes with manifested bodies like comets spread abroad (Rig Veda, Book 5, Hymn LIX), run through clouds, and create terror and earthquakes. They reel onward like quivering ships on their way, letting the water be pushed away; they become visible and appear from afar with full support pressed between their mighty missiles. As newly formed manifested bodies (Rig Veda, Book 5, Hymn LXI), these spiritual heroes continue to regulate in the outer heavenly space and serve the heavenly Rudras that observe and call on Agni to produce the ferocious heat and fire needed to support their mortal forms.

The spiritual heroes seek spoils, offerings, oblations, and praise songs. Like Rudra and Agni, they continue to provide necessary support and direct manifested bodies' moves by turning them in the right direction.

Spiritual heroes in their unmanifested forms continue to appear in outer space as mounted and spotted bodies appearing as galaxies. They swiftly move like deer pulling wood carriages, and they bow in terror but continue to climb over tall mountains; some reach the height of heaven. This frightens the ground even more as they make outer space tremble and shake.

The manifested spiritual heroes armed with lances as manifested cosmic hosts rush along with their bodies, which appear to be comets

(Marutaganas). They appear in the sky like children from wealthy houses riding in their carriages; they are commonly identified with the glory and worshipped as the lordly ones in outer space. They are identified as the planets Saturn and Jupiter. They set new standards for all splendours. They establish their style, which they move. None is the eldest or youngest; they serve as brothers and learn to attain happy fortune as they are honoured as the king or the ruler.

They receive the mythical juice from their ancestors, which they pour along as they travel from the lowest point on the ground in the terrestrial region to the mid-air region. With a fair dwelling, they receive support from the lords of all, including Rudra and Agni, each offering sacrificial food.

As they pass from the heights of the mid-air region, they become the shakers of all. They rejoice in serving as slayers of the foe and passing along freshly pressed Soma to all the worshippers. They appear gleaming as planetary bodies. Appearing as Marutaganas, they travel together as the planets Saturn and Jupiter, form a troop, and rejoice in the mythical juice they produce and purify. They form a banner with their ancient hereditary, the lineage going back and beyond current life, and they proceed farther to overpower the other regions with the lordliest of all (Vaisnavara). They even singly come forth like the ancient cosmic host (Maruts) and reach into the most remote regions like the underworld or other terrestrial regions.

While passing through with fast-blowing solar winds, they find it difficult to hold onto their reins. The knowledge provided by Rudra is used to guide them. Sitting back with their thighs stretched apart like a woman ready to deliver a baby, they use their whips laid on their flanks. They arrive like the bridegroom to a lovely spouse. They go forward along with ferocious Agni in the same manner, providing warmth and intimacy as spouses provide each other, which is fully demonstrated among thousands of cattle and hundreds of sheep, steeds, and other animals. They teach them to stay warm by generating bodily heat and providing meals to their offspring.

New Marutaganas embrace other members to demonstrate that warmth can be gained through embodiments by generating the kind of love like a female that is even better than what God offers. They demonstrate that motherly warmness can help weak or worn embodiments. Eternal love from the heart sets the mind to follow a path of devotion, the same path that the two red steeds as demigods (Aśvins) follow to fame that can be far extended and bestowed among others as a liberal gift. The same gift is born in a hundred cows, all rapidly producing the mythical milky fluid (Soma), and they give others delight to attain the highest glories.

Like the mythical juice, such divine splendour allows them to spread over the worlds as the purest golden gleams that allow spiritual heroes to band together and come from heaven to appear as manifested embodiments moving to gain victory checked by none. No one can know the truth of these one-time shakers who take delight in being born spotless and are always committed to the sacred law, which they use to guide them. They remain lovers of holy hymns that they can hear from any mortal soul that cries for help.

Serving as destructors, like comets with exceedingly bright light, they bring down treasures for worship and create craving among all manifested living things. This serves as the spiritual force as the destroyers of the foe. They first appear at night as the goddess (Urmya), which, in a deep sleep, endures them with hymns of praise and songs to welcome the living spirit (Atma). This brings the spirit to come from far away and pass over to the goddess (Darbhya), who regulates the great elements of nature (Vasus). The living spirit (Atma) is carried by Indra, serving as the lord of the herds (Rathaviti). By drinking the mythical juice, Indra makes the invisible immortal spirits serve astral bodies that support individual living spirits in the manifested mortal embodiments to climb the spiritual mountains.

Covenant

The creator prevails beyond the universe, but the divine mandate continues to function according to the laws established at the time of creation, serving both illuminated heaven and underworld earth. These laws operate without any need for divine intervention. The divine will, with essence, provides the commandment as established by Agni. These commandments as covenants define the order of the eternal laws. The high the eternal laws established by (Varul)a) through the divine will with essence (Devavani) regulate the mortal bodied, including flying horses, with a firm order. These covenants even regulate the heavenly body (Surya), which operates through the sun, moon, and stars. They travel through the regions to monitor and make sure covenants are being implemented. Even today, they monitor ten hundred thousand mortal bodies as one chief. With glory, it is represented through the act of marvellous ancient deities (Mitra-Varul)a). These deities jointly provide special acts of greatness that, through movement, transform cosmic vapours into water.

With further motion, they create floods that generate vibrations to support the two supreme powers of causation, Agni and Indra—fire and water—that firmly stabilize the ground (Prithvi) to produce sounds that retain knowledge as hymns. It prevails within the limits of the eternal wisdom encompassing the powers of causation that regulate the created dynamic universe—the earthly and the heavenly and the esoteric mid-air regions. This unveils the genesis of the dynamic universe created from the undifferentiated or dormant universe. In the dynamic universe, living things are supported by the powers of running water flowing as streams and travelling to oceans. The water, like vapour, creates moisture that even seeps into the ground to feed life in the underworld.

Well-harnessed cosmic vapours even travel like heavenly horses drawn with reins by the heavenly body (Surya). These heavenly horses, like clouds, travel to provide sacred lubricants as the mythical juice that makes sure streams flow and bring lustre to wider regions like ground filled with sacred grass.

The power (Mitra-Varul)a) is provided from a firm throne to sit on amid the oblations coming from the hands of nature, which shed no blood in guarding the pious. Mitra-Varul)a together provide the eternal laws and love to build the dominion with a thousand pillars that provide a solid base adorned with gold and built with strong iron columns upholding heaven and bring divine will with essence (Devavani), like heavenly horses' whips, on a mounted, gold-hued car with the sunrise and sunset. The sun and moon are like bountiful guardians offering an impenetrable shelter.

As the guardian of order, Mitra-Varul)a ascend from the sublime heaven along with rain and appear with sweet streams coming down from heaven to serve the earth. According to Rig Veda, Book 5, Hymn LXIII, as guardians, they look at the light coming from the heavenly body as a holy synod to rule and serve with rain bringing immortality as the godsent gift.

From heaven to the earth, the divine link is established with the universal soul (Paramatma) that brings divine will, the essence with Devavani, which serves the imperial kings (Mitra-Varul)a). It supports the strong heroes and serves the active ones by extending from the earthly region to the heavenly region and serving as the lords of earth and heaven. The thunder waits on them, bringing many tinted clouds all filled with rain. They overpower the magical forces as evil powers hiding in clouds and holding the rain hostage.

They, as spiritual heroes (Marutagana), establish themselves as demigods that come to support Mitra-Varu,)a. They, as spiritual heroes, come accompanied by rain and thunder. In clouds, they roam through regions and create varied hues and dew that bring the mythical juice to the imperial kingdom. Through refreshing their voices, Mitra-Varu,)a sends forth mythical power clothed in the clouds. They produce mighty voices with rain that enforce unique abilities along with the essence and divine will (Devavani). Serving as spotless, manifested wise ones (Adityas), they overpower evil (Asura) magical power with red mythical power. While guarding the ordinance, Mitra-Varu,)a come with refulgent light especially provided at night by the moon.

Mitra-Varu,)a as a foe slayer (Rig Veda, Book 5, Hymn LXIV), with hymns and prayers, invoke their powers to encompass all. They, with the round of dominion light, stretch arms to seek the favouring love in all places. This brings friendliness among many souls as they step on to the path of Varu,)a-Mitra. Gaining protection from their dear friends, they praise to win eternal wisdom. The resentment stirs among wealthy chiefs as the fair splendours (Varu,)a-Mitra) gather high supremacy among wealthy chiefs. Along with their friends, they thrive, vouchsafe their winnings, and strengthen their power to bring prosperity and wealth.

In the morning, Mitra-Varu,)a, along with the holy ones, come from the godly dominion. They bring eternal wisdom to manifest among the holy white cows that shine and support heroes offering blessed animals that run with the speed of cheetahs to bring the mythical juice.

Filled with wisdom, the Marutagana serve as spiritual heroes and learn to communicate with praise songs. They widely spread among humanity (Rig Veda, Book 5, Hymn LXV), providing even the holy ones with glorious fame. Serving as the kings of noble might, lords of the brave come to be strengthened with the eternal laws. They approach together with a prayer to provide aid to good steeds that stand beside sages and provide physical and spiritual strength. They come out of misery to join with the offspring of Mitra. They provide a protective dwelling like those who are fighting at the forefront. Those who worship with grace receive extended shelter from the offspring of Varuna. They get a direction wherever their embodiments become unmanaged. They are provided with guarded care without neglecting the wealthy chiefs to whom they serve their milk with respect as their guardians.

The spiritual heroes (Varuna-Mitra) overpower the foe. They establish holy places such as worship halls, where they follow the law to win back the unbroken command (Rig Veda, Book 5, Hymn LXVI). With the essence of divine will (Devavani), they are unable to set the high laws (Varuna). They seek full perfection to lighten the beautiful world with eternal love. This allows the mortal embodiments to travel far with light and accept praise hymns (Ratahavya) as eulogies. With acumen marked with mighty purity, they show their mortal embodiments filled with wisdom and the divine will with essence (Devavani). On earth, like noble sages (Rṣis), they prevail as those who are prepared to gain from the ample overflow of eternal love (Mitra). They, with their wandering eyes, watch the worshippers and help them reach the spacious dominion that rules and protects all mortal creations.

According to Rig Veda, Book 5, Hymn LXVII, the trinity of Varu,)a, Aryaman, and Mitra manifest as noble powers (Ādityas) and set themselves apart to obtain the supreme powers of causation. While sitting in a golden dwelling place as the high holy, they serve as the supporters of mortal living things. They serve like Indra as the foe slayers and bring blessedness and wealth to all. the trinity of Varu,)a, Mitra, and Aryaman follow proper ways to make mortal embodiments serve true to the law. Among every race, they serve as good leaders (Devavani), upholding the essence and holy divine will that brings bounteous joy through gifts, and they protect them from distress.

The mighty good leaders (Devavani) sing to the union of Varu,) a-Mitra (Rig Veda, Book 5, Hymn LXVIII), inspiring songs that spring forth in full law and come to serve as sovereign kings who are fully glorified among the deities. They explore the great riches of the terrestrial regions by bringing the divine powers among them like celestial wealth. They carefully tend to the law and divine will with essence and thus attain vigorous might be devoid of guile. Like Varu,)a-Mitra, they bring rain accompanied by the strength that brings heavenly gifts.

They comprehend the three spheres of light and learn to serve faithfully as the divine splendour (Devavani). According to Rig Veda, Book 5, Hymn LXIX, they serve the dominion, which is guarded with the ordinance of the essence and divine will that last forever. Varu,)a yields refreshment to bring Mitra among the floods that pour sweetness among love and friendship. All standing as the trinity of the supreme powers of causation (Varuna, Mitra, and Aryaman), with splendid brightness, serve with amiable moisture covering the three worlds. Jointly, they call on morning light serving the mother goddess (Aditi). At noon, they call on the father (sun) during the day, and during the evening, they call on the reflective light (moon). As the divine power (Aditya), they provide safety, wealth, and progeny. They work together to uphold each of the three spheres of brightness while the immortal gods (Varu,)a-Mitra) never impair their everlasting edicts.

The benign and divine powers, Varu,)a-Mitra, extend goodwill, which through the heavenly body (Rudras) comes to sustain and guard them by providing skills to survive. They show them how to subdue the evil powers (Dasyus). They make sure this evil power never enjoys a feast belonging to the spiritual heroes (Marutagana) or their offspring serving as the progeny of Varu,)a-Mitra.

According to Rig Veda, Book 5, Hymn LXXI, they slay the foes and come with godly offerings to all sages. They sacrifice to serve the sovereign rulers and provide them with the mythical juice. With the perceived degree of merit of the source—orthodox or heterodox— they cultivate unconditional faith and trust. Based on the direct communication with the supreme powers of causation, they cultivate from the orthodox source (Astika). Based on indirect communication with the supreme powers of causation, they cultivate faith and trust from the heterodox or unorthodox source (Nāstika).

Sitting on the sacred grass (Rig Veda, Book 5, Hymn LXII), the union of Varu,)a-Mitra share the mythical juice passed directly to the astral bodies through the orthodox (Astika); the physical and spiritual knowledge comes to dwell among the mortal embodiments like the ancestral souls that are born from the seven sages (Septarishi) serving as the holy sage (Atri) in the mid-air region. The demigods like the Aśvins come from far and near (Rig Veda, Book 5, Hymn LXXIII) and perform their wondrous acts to provide those seeking to learn about the loving, mighty powers.

The physical and spiritual knowledge comes to dwell among the mortal embodiments like the heterodox or unorthodox knowledge (Nāstika). The heterodox knowledge establishes through direction a relationship with others while roaming. They create neighbouring tribes to build their mighty dominions.

The Aśvins' deeds are done with birth or entered otherwise through a spotless kinship bond extolled through faith (Visvas) mounted with rolling light coming from the heavenly body (Sūrya), which appears through birds of red hue such as the sun. A community of heroes with friendly minds and mouths stir up the spotless eternal flame (Agni) to manifest and advance with the powers of demigods (Nāsatyas). They move swiftly and extract prominence with their great deeds and serve the community as chiefs or the sage (Atri) with dutiful reverence. They use the inner eternal flame from Agni as the ferocious powers that come to serve along with the solar wind (Rudras) with the sweetness that makes flowing waters blessed.

The chiefs of the sage (Atri) travel over the oceans with the ordinance and law and bring gifts of self-righteousness that are carried as well-dressed food filled with the sweetness of truth. Like the Aśvins, they bestow felicity and offer a sacrifice that can be heard as the most gracious sacrifice. They perform prayers that please and magnify their embodiments, and in a mighty fashion, they bring the high reverence through the divine will with essence (Devavani), which is directly shared through spoken words.

The holy sages are spotless flames blessed with devotion from the demigods (Nāsatyas) and are invited to serve like sages (Risi), which bring purity to the region. Serving as strengtheners, they are captured as lions and snakes, knowing their skin is nothing more than a robe. They, as youth, come back again to serve with mortal embodiments and long for the essence of the divine will (Devavani). Especially those who are rich among themselves with eternal wealth use their mortal embodiments like demigods (Aśvins), which, in newly created vehicles and with excellence, move with speed to pass through many regions while going through the process of reincarnation. With laudation, as the twin (Aśvins), lovers of eternal wisdom, they even learn to fly like winged steeds and appear as falcons filled with wisdom and loving hearts. Any time their mortal embodiments receive the divine calling, they sacrifice and perform to enhance themselves and be designated as higher mortal embodiments.

To fulfil their obligations, they appear blessed in the form of mighty mortal embodiments (Rig Veda, Book 5, Hymn LXXV). They even represent themselves as the ancient demigods (Aśvins), which are reincarnated with eternal souls. They are raised from birth with praise and divine songs and brought up as sages (Ṛṣi) who serve as lovers of sweetness (Mitra).

They bring eternal love to pass on to all selfish tribes and show them the wonderful golden path to follow that turns selfish tribes into gracious givers. As a pair of demigods (Aśvins) serving as male and female and supported by Rudra, they follow the path to attain eternal wisdom. They rejoice like the Aśvins filled with inner divine will with essence (Devavani) that produces good laud and wonderful meals. They serve with the noble support of the immortal spirit (Atma) that cleaves to the embodiments like a great beast.

They attain inner awakening by hearing the divine calling, which is sent for through the prevailing body as the life force (Prana) with wings like spiritual eagles that come down swiftly to overpower the evil snake (Cyavana). Dappled with wings, they yoke like flying steeds and bring bliss and noble thoughts that can be heard by other twins (Aśvins), male and female.

While drinking the mythical juice (Nāsatyas), the twin demigods, filled with motivational power, long for piety and freedom from guile. They turn away from their home and move on to reach their new destination. Serving as the lords of splendour seeking divine grace, they stand along with their offering as a sacrifice.

They appear at dawn, joined with the eternal flame placed in the direct light coming from the sun. The immortal twin souls appear among mortal embodiments, ready to harness and serve as the strong male and the kind female and jointly serve as the wonderworkers. They, with the morning sun as immortal twin souls along with pious voices, turn and ascend to the higher region to provide all with libations. The wonderworkers serve those who are scorned and in trouble with loud sounds provided by their most frequent guests in the morning and the evening. They come to help at milking time in the early morning, at noon, and when the sun sets. They bring auspicious favour that sets the new breeze to bring forth heavenly waters from mountains. They bring health and bestow guidance to attain happiness.

They come with the first worship in the early morning, letting the twins drink water with Soma before any stingy or ungenerous person gets the water (Rig Veda, Book 5, Hymn LXXVII). The twins claim their sacrifice at daybreak when the sages yield eulogies to dawn and instigate others to eulogize in the evening before it is forbidden before night.

Besides wonderworkers, others crave and worship highly undisclosed wisdom that is gold tainted. Wonderworkers provide food to the embodiments while travelling over all obstructions. Along with the solar deity accompanied by demigods (Nāsatyas), they appear with the eternal flame while they perform holy works by distributing sweet food. To their offspring, they pass along such flames to ascend and obtain favour that bestows health, provides guidance, and brings riches to heroes.

Supreme Knowledge

The wonderworkers with mortal embodiments (Rig Veda, Book 5, Hymn LXXVIII) along with the solar deity accompany the wonderworkers (Nāsatyas). They receive full support as they fly like two swans or a pair of deer. The ancient demigods (Aśvins) appear with the wonderworkers who seek wisdom. As two wild cattle, they accept sacrifice and give it as gifts to become like the sage (Atri).

They descend and move like a howling woman producing sounds that go back to the cavity and bring fresh, auspicious flocks of birds such as falcons that reside under the tree to bring forth children. These wonderworkers (Aśvins) listen to calls from Saptavadhri that they are free from bonds like a frightened prophet who weeps and wails.

With magic powers, the wonderworkers, like unborn babes, provide the traumatized wind coming from every side like a distressed tree in a pool stirring lotus flowers. In ten months, as babes descend like wood from the traumatized wind, they appear to awaken life in the deep waters of the sea. After birth, lying on their mothers' sides, they learn to come forth unharmed and alive and live with their mothers.

The supreme knowledge (Prajana) is attained through intuitive insight and following a perfected way of seeing nature in totality, as a body created to represent Mother Nature (Rig Veda, Book 5,

Hymn LXXIX). The heavenly morning light awakens the sons of eternal truth (Satyasravas) with ample opulence, and then a daughter of heaven (Sunitha) born as a mortal embodiment supported by wind ((Vayu) is supported by the divine will (Devavani).

With their treasure, they are identified as bright males and bounteous females. They serve as divine chargers such as domesticated animals with much wealth to offer as they band together. They perform and please to win material and nonmaterial wealth. They, with pleasure, give rich gifts that, like the immortal powers, never drift away.

They bring resplendent fame to wealthy patrons and princes. They, like the daughter of the sky together with sunbeams, bring highborn and delightful subsistence. In the form of herds of animals, they shine forth to perform their tasks, making sure that the sun's fervent heat does not steal their energy. The morning light bestows radiance on those singers who sing praises to the highborn.

The goddess of dawn as the singers are welcome at dawn with hymns and praises (Rig Veda, Book 5, Hymn LXXX) as they bring the sunlight, the eternal sublime, with true order. With red-tinted light, they guide those walking and rouse their embodiments, thus making their pathways easy to travel.

Dawn gives splendour by injuring purple oxygen and ozone. It brings perpetual riches through opening paths to happiness. The goddess shines with praise and blessings as the giver of gleams. They as double splendour changing with the tints display her body with the coming of the sun moving from the east and travelling perfectly on the path of order and reaching unknown quarters.

Bathing in conscience with appendages that remain bright and standing erect, they drive away from the malignity and darkness among the children of heaven. With lustre like the daughter of the sky, they come through as pure women who bend their foreheads like maids revealing the godsent in the form of worship to those who bring forth the daylight again and again.

Well skilled in hymns (Rig Veda, Book 5, Hymns LXXXI), the lofty priests harness the living with spirit (Atma) with their holy thoughts as if they were the daughters of the sky who were assigned priestly tasks. They know their work, and they welcome the goddess (Savitar) with lofty praise. After dawn, they, as the daughters of the sky, appear as shining sapient ones. They look at and arrange every form of quadruped and biped that has been brought forth by the goddess.

Deities follow them with their might as they measure the terrestrial regions. With great power, the goddess (Savitar) covers all three spheres, and they encompass the night like the lord of eternal love (Mitra) and look through the eternal laws (Varuna). They comprehend all generations and their heritage going forth to the solar deity (Pūṣan), who has long dominion over this world.

Even the patron (Śyāvāśva) praises the goddess (Savitar). With treasure, all enjoy the best by generating conquering gifts that gladden the patron (Bhaga) and offer Savitar supremacy as the most glorious and beloved of all. Savitar's worshippers send Bhaga wondrous riches to implore and keep till today. Savitar keeps sending prosperity with progeny to drive away evil dreams, sorrows, and calamities and keeps only what is good and sinless.

In the sight of Mother Aditi, the Savitar brings lovely things whose decrees are true (Rig Veda, Book 5, Hymns LXXXII). Ever-vigilant Savitar proceeds with the twins to create day and night and, with noble thoughts, gives glory to all living creatures. With songs and noble thoughts brought forth by Savitar, in a state of unmanifested consciousness, the immortal, invisible powers (Brahma) transform and manifest as embodiments with pure spirit (Atma).

Appearing as a living being, Brahman receives respective names and forms conditioned by its divergent embodiments. The same entity with an astral body under different conditions becomes diversified and appears as multifarious creatures.

Coming as truth-seekers, they come to comprehend thoughts differently. They develop manifested embodiments on different intellectual planes ranging from average awareness to super consciousness to a state of being with conscience acquired through self-regulation. With invoked super consciences, they can monitor, evaluate, and modify the extrinsic and intrinsic emotional reactions. Through complex emotional processes, they even modulate their state or behaviour in a given situation.

Based on subjective experiences (feelings), cognitive responses (thoughts), emotional and physiological responses (hormonal heart rate), and emotional behaviour responses (bodily expressions), they learn to regulate their emotions. Through self-regulation, they can even process their tendency to a single point focus, pay attention to a task, cultivate the ability to suppress inappropriate behaviour and perform highly significant functions.

Those living beings who are continually exposed to a wide variety of potentially arousing stimuli and inappropriate and extreme unchecked emotional have reactions that impede their functioning in society. Therefore, such living beings find it difficult almost all the time to engage in emotional self-regulation. By using the powers of transcendental wisdom (Prajana) or gaining supreme knowledge through intuitive insight, one can come see a perfect way of Mother Nature created to represent divine truth and see the reality.

Through singing divine songs (Rig Veda, Book 5, Hymn LXXXIV) and welcoming with adoration and praise, one calls on the mighty powers that, like the roaring bull, swiftly send their bounty to smite trees apart, slay the hidden demons, create fear, and plant seeds that germinate the ultimate fear of the end of life—death. They, in the form of self-regulation, appear as the eternal force (Parjanya), as

Mother Nature with thundering force and strength. They appear like the messengers who come riding on the rain, springing forward and slamming the manifested solid or semi-manifested bodies that are wicked. Even the guiltless are whipped. Mother Nature (Parjanya) fills the sky with rain clouds and lightning that help seedlings shoot up. In the dominion of Mother Nature (Parjanya), light quickens the earth with moisture and thus brings abundant food for all living creatures. As Mother Nature (Parjanya) bids the earth to bow before cattle commanded to fly over all the terror and let the plants yield all colours with great protection, they send rain for all living creatures. The cosmic host descends, accompanied by torrents, to allow the thunder to pour the waters down to provide the stallions' flood serving like the heavenly father. With roaring thunder, while flying around with its water-laden chariot, it deposits germs of life by opening its skin to draw water.

Moving downward farther, it fills hollows to a level that lifts mighty vessels in the oceans and lakes and pours down water to liberate the eternal force. Mother Nature (Parjanya) covers all the regions between the sky and the ground. It creates corpulent streams that rush forward to saturate the region allowing cows to supply abundant milk. (Rig Veda, Book 5, Hymn LXXXV). With its thunder and roar, Mother Nature smites the sinners and exalts them from terrestrial planets. With pouring-down rain, it even creates floods to bring water to transform desert places into fertile areas for the herbs to grow and provides enjoyment for all, winning praise from living beings.

Above the regions, neighing steeds generate a distinctive dust cloud that is filled with the primordial, ancient, physical power (Shakti). While descending, they carry water and lightning to transform barren surfaces into fertile ground that provides a home for the life force (Prana). The universal spirit as the sovereign power germinates to create a kingdom of vegetation, including plants and trees.

To support the sovereign power, the universal soul enhances and resides in manifested mortal embodiments as the living sprit. As the immortal power, it resides within to serve as provided by Mother Nature (Parjanya), the eternal force, which through the fire (Agni) provides the eternal flame that resides in the plants appearing in the terrestrial region.

The differentiated part of the universe swiftly gains a larger part of the undifferentiated universe and separates matter and energy by creating bull roars that are filled with lightning and thunder and pass through all the three regions forming the dynamic universe. The eternal universal soul (Paramatma) smites dark clouds that are beholding the cosmic deity, the goddess of water (Apas), and the eternal power (Parjanya) as Mother Nature. They destroy the blockage by slaying demons, thus allowing water to flow freely. Like a carriage driver whipping his horses, the eternal power (Parjanya) springs forth, making rain as it moves forward and far off. With resounding noise, they fill the sky with bursting rain clouds accompanied by ferocious winds (Rudras) and produce lightning.

Releasing eternal power (Parjanya) as part of Mother Nature, with moisture, it quickens the ground, where plants shoot up in the dominion with streaming light and bid onto the ground hoofed cattle that bow low with birds flying in terror.

From the eternal power (Parjanya), they send down the rain of heaven that yields great protection to the plants, which assume all colours and provide food for the stallion descending in torrents. As the thunder roars, the water from heaven pours down, depositing germs of life. They are later carried around in shells by the air, and after they soak into the ground, they open their shells to draw down farther and onward, allowing the hollows and the heights to become all levelled.

In mighty vessels like lakes, they pour down water to create streams that rush forward to saturate the ground. Both the ground and the sky, with resoluteness, provide water to cows and other milk-bearing animals to provide abundant milk for all creation.

They protect the planet with their thunder and roaring; the eternal power (Parjanya) even smites sinners and exalts any threat that may come from outer space. Through their eternal power, the rain and floods make herbs grow for those who travel and, with praise, win from other living creatures.

Once the living things comprehend the eternal powers (Parjanya) and as seekers acquire eternal wisdom, they unveil the hidden eternal truth and know all about the powers operating behind all creation. They then unveil the answers to mind-boggling questions such as, "What precedes light? What brings milk into the udder? What generates the nectar? What makes things quickly manifest? What makes bulls roar? What makes germs create plants and infants? Who provides growth to plants? What makes all creatures move? Who operates the threefold refuges? What provides the threefold light and threefold supports (Trpta) to cultivate friendship?"

Ultimately (Rig Veda, book 5, Hymn LXXXVI), all manifested spirits end up following the mighty deity (vishnu), one of the imperishable powers that regulate and illuminate the underworld in the terrestrial region. They, as an impetuous band of new young heroes, come reciting hymns about the cosmic host adorned with charms. They come rushing with joy and, with ever-roaring vigour incorporated among their manifested bodies, appear as the offspring of the mighty deity (vishnu). The cosmic host (maruts) presents eternal wisdom that can easily be comprehended Rig Veda, book 5, Hymn LXXXVII),. While prevailing as noble mortal embodiments, they are blessed to cultivate gifts of greatness as their true strength. They acquire the ability to remain intact like mountains, and they sing psalms that can be heard in the lofty heaven. By themselves, they become strong with brightly shining souls. They remain firm in their position until there is no mightier one. Then they are called on and urged to move along with water and fire, generating lightning with roaring sounds. After striding out of heaven, their spacious dwelling place, the mightier ones come down from the heights, appearing yoked with strong horses ready to make a new home in the terrestrial region.

They appear like flashing lights, like a strong speeding rainier, and make everything tremble and serve as the messengers of joy-giving with tremendous roars. Unbounded and with their greatness, mighty power, and bright vigour, they appear to aid in the time of trouble. Instead of being invisible, they become visible helpers glowing like fires and generating inner eternal light to save others from shame. Instead of demigods like the cosmic host (maruts), they appear as the messengers of the heavenly body (rudras) and serve as mighty warriors with splendid brilliancy as archangels. They serve individual dwelling places and bring courage to the terrestrial region. Serving as a single-minded and imperishable power, they are supported by the mighty power of vishnu. They hear and recall from soul mates or friends of the spirit. They keep enmity far from their deeds and deliberately make sacrifices to free friends from demons. With blessings and help, they follow the high laws and the divine will.

With this, the imperial ruler (Varul)a) declares that they have completed their mission. Standing in the firmament, they could measure the earth right under the sun. None has ever let or hindered this, the most-wise God's mighty deed of magic whereby with the flood, the lucid rivers fill not one sea wherein they pour their waters if humanity sinned against the noble souls who love and have never wronged a brother, friend, comrade, neighbour, or a stranger. The imperial ruler (Varul)a) removes those who trespass. Varul)a punishes gamesters who do wrong unwittingly or knowingly.

CONCLUSION

The first five chapters of the Rig Veda establish the genesis of the dynamic universe filled with esoteric energy and esoteric matter that prevails in balance, keeping a body rotating in space. They are balanced through regulating vibrations that generate action among the manifested bodies constituting the dynamic universe. These bodies were all created when primordial energy invoked through vibrations generated a ferocious fire that transformed dormant matter into dynamic energy, thus creating the upper stratum, the heavenly region filled with illumination generated by transforming all matter into interstellar energy. The middle region was transformed to establish the esoteric region, where transformation still continues and leaves behind dormant matter forming the lower, earthly stratum representing the underworld all encompassed by the terrestrial region.

Within the mid-air region, esoteric environments creating new splendours continue to manifest and are placed between the highest heavenly region and the lowest earthly region. Right below the heavenly region is the celestial region, which extends from east to west and is moving up and creating the transitory vacuum within which stellar splendours are formed, consisting of heavenly illuminator bodies filling the vacuum with planetary bodies, thus creating a cosmic region filled with invisible and visible interstellar bodies that extend beyond the esoteric region and reach the terrestrial region, forming the planetary solar system. Giving birth, the terrestrial bodies—Mercury, Venus, Mars, Earth, and Pluto, along with other secondary bodies—represent the underworld creations that are not subject to illumination.

The primordial energy in a tranquil state comprises physical, spiritual, mystical, natural and many other forms. With the formation of the dynamic universe, the primordial energies are released, thus freeing many supreme powers of causation. These powers of causation transform from unmanifested to manifested bodies that keep expanding through existence and nonexistence and vice versa. To regulate manifested stellar bodies, the supreme powers of causation established an ultimate power that prevails throughout the universe and serves as the ultimate soul or universal soul, which regulates all manifested imperishable and perishable bodies, the moving and not moving, through the process of existence and nonexistence.

To regulate existence, the primordial energy established the invisible, immortal, universal soul to reside in mortal embodiments as the individual living spirit that regulates the actions and activities of each individual creation. The action and activities that contribute to the enhancement of mortal embodiments generate noble powers and allow them to prevail among the top seven luminous spheres. The activities and actions resulting in the defamation of creation are called evil powers, which prevail in the seven-bottomed underworld.

The luminous noble powers and the underworld evil powers are regulated by the same supreme powers of causation, and they manifest with individual immortal spirits as masculine and feminine to establish progeny. They provide the opportunity to live and grow, further enhance individually, and build a society.

To entice and have each perform actions and activities, the supreme powers of causation established a material world in the terrestrial region right above the surface (Prithvi), where embodiments establish their dwellings and grow their families by performing obligatory responsibilities (Karma) that are subject to a cycle of life and death. They follow the process of encirclement in which the universal soul creates imperishable or perishable phenomena appearing with visible and invisible mythical or optical phenomena or hallucinations.

ACKNOWLEDGEMENTS

I am extremely thankful to my wife, Chris Malhotra, who has been my partner for the past forty-eight years. Over the past ten years, she, with great patience, allowed me to focus on writing this book. To enhance my quest to know all about absolute truth, she made a major sacrifice and took over most of the household activities. In addition, she read my writing and provided valuable guidance. It is through her Jewish faith that I was able to learn a lot more in conducting my research and spending time visiting Jewish spiritual and historic places.

I am very lucky to have Swami Shiv Sewa Nand Ji as my inspiration. He is a teacher residing in Tapovan, Sadhupul, Solan, India. This book has been produced with his blessings and by honouring me as Atamnanda, the happy soul. It gives me great pleasure to be associated with such a noble individual. Through his blessing, I build a school in Sadhupul. I am fully committed to supporting this educational institution that teaches spiritual wisdom along with normal education.

I am so happy to have received a blessing in a dream from my deceased mother. On September 16, 2018, my daughter, Jodie, delivered her first child, Madelyn Ann McBride. During my visit with this new soul, in my deep sleep, my mother unveiled to me the ancestry relating to her, my daughter, and my granddaughter. She reminded me that she had left this world a few days after the birth of my daughter but had been with me in spirit. Through the birth of my granddaughter, she is back on earth in person. This granddaughter has the same spirit that resides in my daughter and at one time resided in my mother. This spirit, through my mother's offspring, is here to serve all creations and make this world a better place for all.

I have also received a lot of moral support from my son, Robert, who, with keen interest, continuously supported my efforts devoted to this mission.

SOURCE BOOK
RIG VEDA

The Rig Veda is the earliest literary record of the Indo-Aryan civilization; it encompasses earlier revelations that define eternal truth and reveals maxims that have stood the test of time in terms of eternal wisdom and absolute truth.

The revelations in the Rig Veda are based on vibrations that, through oscillations, express sounds that are captured and recorded as hymns and speeches that are used to formulate languages such as Sanskrit. It is through this process that the relationship between the creator and creation—spiritual involution—is unveiled.

The hymns, incantations, and rituals acquired in ancient India are very similar to those incorporated in the Book of the Dead, the Enuma Elish, the I Ching, and the Avesta, plus many other holy scriptures, some of which have been lost. As with most ancient extensive texts, these scriptures serve as invaluable tools in the study of comparative etymology utilized in learning about physical evolution and spiritual involution.

The Vedas are well recognized by British scholars, including Max-Muller, Bloomfield, McDonnell, Whitney, and Wilson, as well as by many other scholars from Germany, Holland, and France. During the nineteenth century, scholars around the world uncovered the exciting field of eternal truth in the Sanskrit document (Devanagari), which was later translated into Greek, Latin, Persian, and English.

As they became widely accessible, the translations shed new light on the Vedas. The interpretation of the Vedas by scholars created new developments to unveil the divine message, which was recorded by their predecessors, the Aryan civilization. By encoding the hymns, it defines the morality in their society. They understood that through invocation, the supreme powers of causation could be persuaded to descend from the heavenly region to help mortal embodiments understand spiritual evolution and involution. They sat on the sacred straw floor and ate and drank while they worshipped to receive the blessing of a long and happy life.

While studying such holy scriptures, individual worshippers even experience a form of vigour or a kind of intoxication very similar to that caused by adrenaline. In medical terms, it is defined as carisoprodol, and it is described as the mythical juice (Soma). Worshippers in their altered states experienced wondrous visions and strange sensations that made them behave as if they had acquired mystic powers.

During the Puranic period (200 BCE–500 CE), esoteric wisdom was received by noble souls (Aryans) through worshipping the trinity of the male god (Brahma, Vishnu, and Shiva), which is accompanied by the female goddess's trinity. Jointly, through primordial energy (Shakti), they serve both the gods and goddesses, sitting as prolific parents who protect and support creation, preservation, and resurrection. They invoke powers through prayers (Puja) and undivided devotion (Bhakti) offered with personal sacrifice.

The noble souls (Aryans) introduced concepts to differentiate the immortal, universal soul (Paramatma), which resides outside manifested embodiments of the individual spirit (Atma). The Aryans believed the universal soul and spirit were regulated by the primordial energy (Shakti). This concept was adopted by many other cultures.

The Vedic holy scriptures contain four large volumes of hymns and are full of mythological stories that have been used to establish historic evolutionary records and encourage philosophical discussion; they serve as source material for sermons and teachings.

The Rig Veda is the oldest scripture, and it contains ancient legal texts in Sanskrit (Manusmrti). There are six orthodox schools of Vedic knowledge, which classify the holy scriptures as either direct or indirect. The direct includes scriptures based on revelations. The indirect includes interpretations or reflections on the revelations. All knowledge is based on the synthesis of the vibrations and is composed in the form of hymns and mantras expressed in local languages such as Sanskrit. In Hindu mythology, the direct revelations are defined in four holy scriptures. The Rig Veda contains hymns that spiritual scholars use to unveil revelations regarding the creation of the universe.

The second scripture, the Sama Veda, contains hymns that spiritual scholars used to establish practices to affirm the lineage between creator and creation.

The third scripture, the Yajur Veda, contains hymns that spiritual scholars used to acquire wisdom to establish the true relationship between the universal soul and the immortal spirit, which is also known as the union.

The fourth scripture, the Atharva Veda, contains hymns used to fulfil individual needs to survive and live happily by conforming to the laws established by the powers of causation.

These four Vedas are believed to have been compiled over a span of years, beginning around the second millennium BCE and ending sometime in the Late Bronze Age.

The Vedic knowledge reached its peak during the Buddhist period when such wisdom began moving away from the oral tradition and was transmitted into texts using birch bark or palm leaves preserved with precision through elaborate mnemonic techniques. These techniques rarely surpassed an age of a few hundred years. To ensure such texts were transmitted from generation to generation, ancient cultures established schools of philosophy, some of which cited scriptural authority or orthodox philosophy. Others who did not accept the authoritative stance referred to them as heterodox or unorthodox.

ABOUT THE AUTHOR

Ramesh Malhotra is a successful business entrepreneur, philanthropist, and author. He owns and directs the activities of more than seven businesses in the fields of trading, manufacturing, import and distribution, real estate, innovative technologies, and brand marketing. He balances his natural business acumen with his personal search for spiritual enlightenment. Ramesh explains the Spirituality Circle as "the three aspects of life, including service, support, and sacrifice, and they directly relate to Karma, Dharma, and Dakshna as defined in the Vedas or Buddhism as the true path to sanctity, Moksha or Nirvana. By fulfilling personal obligatory responsibilities (Karma), one attains tranquillity, and by fulfilling social and cultural responsibilities (Dharma), one attains inner peace. Finally, by fulfilling altruistic responsibilities (Dakshna), one attains freedom of the individual soul. This all leads to eternity, the goal of each living being."

Ramesh Malhotra was born in Lahore, Undivided India, in November 1943, on the day of celebration of Guru Nanak's birthday. After India's partition in 1947, the author's family moved to a small town, Solan, in the Himalayas, where he received his education. Later, his family moved to the newly built town of Chandigarh. He completed a master's degree in geology at Punjab University and worked as a geologist for the state government in Shimla, Himachal Pradesh.

In 1967, the author left India to work toward a postgraduate degree in mining and prospecting from Mont. Hochschule Leoben in Austria. In 1968, he came to the United States for postgraduate studies. After receiving an MS in earth and space science from Stony Brook University in New York and an MSBA from Michigan Tech, he joined Columbia University to pursue a doctorate in mineral economics.

In 1971, he joined the Illinois State Geological Survey as a mineral economist. In 1974, he entered the business world and worked for Freeman United Coal as assistant vice president. In 1981, he joined NERCO Coal; after six years as the president of NERCO, he left the corporate life to start his own business. In 1987, the author established Coal Network in Mason, Ohio.

Over the past several years as an entrepreneur and an angel investor, he has been actively involved in seeding new business ventures and acquiring and expanding existing businesses to create new jobs and help others realize their dreams.

His passion for exploring and acquiring higher spiritual knowledge started during the early 1990s. He has travelled in India and other parts of the world and visited spiritual centres to learn and experience spirituality. He has used spiritual knowledge as an integral part of his personal as well as his business life.

This is the author's first attempt to present his thoughts on the Rig Veda in the form of a book, and he is fully committed to acquiring higher knowledge and helping others in seeking such knowledge.

In 2011, he initiated funding for an elementary school near where he received his early education. At this school in the Himalayas near Sadhupul, Solan, the fundamentals of higher knowledge are being taught and practised. The author will dedicate the proceeds from the sale of his books to support this institute.

The author has been a patron of the arts and has been supporting budding artists. He sponsors other art-related ventures, including MOSA, the Museum of Spiritual Art, the ONENESS Harmony centre, the MOSA Academy of Art, and the Healing Heart Yoga and Dance Studio.

Printed in the United States
by Baker & Taylor Publisher Services